GEORGE

WALLACE

From Segregation to Salvation

He showed the courage of asking for forgiveness.

By **George Wallace Jr.**

For information regarding permission, please write to:
info@barringerpublishing.com
Barringer Publishing, Naples, Florida
www.barringerpublishing.com

Cover, graphics, and layout by Linda S. Duider
Cape Coral, Florida

ISBN: 978-1-954396-51-7
Library of Congress Cataloging-in-Publication Data
George Wallace: From Segregation to Salvation / George C. Wallace Jr.

Printed in the United States of America

From Segregation to Redemption

George Wallace (standing in door at left in a suit) refuses to allow two Black students to register at the University of Alabama in 1963. Minutes later, Governor Wallace stepped aside and the students were allowed to enter.

Civil rights leaders meet with Governor Wallace in his Montgomery, Alabama, office on the 20th anniversary of the 1965 march from Selma to Montgomery.

In loving memory of my son, Corey Wallace
(1984 – 2009)

Dedicated to our children:
Courtney, Leslie, Corey, and Robby
with my Love and Devotion

By: George Wallace Jr.

This is a study of one of the most controversial, misunderstood, and in many cases misrepresented men in American political history. His life's journey was Shakespearean in a modern-day drama that was the life of George Wallace. His life included power, success, pain, sorrow, suffering, conflict, enlightenment, redemption, reconciliation, love, and forgiveness. This book will take the reader inside, to learn about the real man from his family's perspective. The intimate stories never before told, with rare family photographs of personal, as well as more public moments in the life of the Wallace family, will take the reader inside the inner sanctuary of history being made, and to many will remind you of the George Wallace you knew and to many others reveal a man you never knew.

My mother and father at a tea at the Alabama Governor's Mansion.

Contents

Foreword

Rebecca Parish Beasley
Editor and Publisher
The Clayton Record

Governor George Corley Wallace, Alabama's only four term governor, ranks at the top as one of the most recognized governors past and present, in the nation. Yet, he is probably the most misunderstood.

The inner soul of a man, whom I knew as a father to my close childhood friends, and a husband to one of the sweetest, dearest ladies I have ever known, lived and breathed the world of politics. It was often said by those who knew him best that he loved the campaign during which he could meet people and speak with his charismatic charm much more than he loved actually serving in office.

Why was he so misunderstood by those who knew him only as a public figure? The media packaged George Wallace from the outside looking in as they broadcast throughout the nation the way they perceived life at the time in Alabama. George Wallace has been said to be one of the best politicians the state has ever produced and he stood for the things that were politically popular at the time. He wanted to be elected.

He gained media attention nationwide when he staged an event such as standing in the door at the University of Alabama to block a student attending the institution. My mother, Bertie Gammell Parish, who was editor and publisher of his hometown newspaper, *The Clayton Record*, told him at the time, "George, we all know that you are just doing this to get attention of the media, you know that you do not intend to block anyone from attending college." He did this throughout his career as a public servant as purely a political statement.

In this book, his son, George Corley Wallace Jr., portrays the father he knew, the friend those of us in Clayton and Barbour County knew, and the public figure that many Alabamians knew. As I reflect on the life of Governor Wallace, I think about the man who would give us a nickel to buy a cone of ice cream, the man who genuinely cared about all the people no matter what their ethnic background may have been or their status in life, and the man who worked to provide better opportunities for the people of Alabama.

After reading this book, I sincerely hope the memories of misconceptions about Alabama's most distinguished governor will fade and the man whom the home folks knew best will forever be his legacy. He will no doubt go down in Alabama's history as one of the most dedicated men who lived for the betterment of his state and its people. It is up to us to learn and to know him for the real man that he was. I thank his son and my dear friend through the years for sharing his intimate life within the Wallace household with the public.

Preface

In reflecting on my journey of being the namesake of one of the most controversial political figures of the 20th century, and understanding how dramatic and traumatic the experiences were, and how they affected my immediate family, I have always believed our experiences were unlike those of any other family in our nation's history. What we endured, we endured under the watchful eye of the public. These writings will reveal for the first time, from a family perspective, the real George Wallace, not the myth that has grown up around the legend.

The stories you will read take a close look at our family and what it was like inside our home while there was a storm raging just outside. We had become the focal point of threats and found ourselves in the middle of the Civil Rights controversy by virtue of being the family of George C. Wallace. He had become the very embodiment of resistance to the social changes on the horizon, and the controversy that caused manifested itself in many ways for my family.

He understood, because of his "Segregation Forever" speech and his, "Stand in the Schoolhouse Door," that the issue of race while bringing him to power, would prove to be the burden he would have to bear until eventually, through his suffering, his own sense of our common humanity was revealed to all. The bargain he had made on the issue of segregation gave to him the power he had always sought, but this "Faustian" bargain also brought him many regrets.

At the moment my father hit the pavement after being shot, and as blood flowed from his body, a bond was formed between him and the Civil Rights workers who had shed their own blood. Their sense of struggle and pain was now shared, and his sensitivity and empathy for those he had been accused of harming, either by words he had spoken or actions he had taken, was deepened and strengthened.

I have sought to capture the man, George Wallace, and the talents that made him such a folk hero to those who loved him, and those who came to love him. His political talents were unrivaled, and an examination of how he used those talents makes it clear why he was successful as a politician. At the same time, these talents are what took him away from Mother and our family, and caused tension between my mother and father that brought them to the brink of divorce.

The 1958 and 1962 races for governor and the dynamics present in those races are examined. His 1962 race for governor, at which time he had become the hard-liner on the issue of segregation, was successful and he was to shortly thereafter say on a cold January day: *Today I have stood where once Jefferson Davis stood and took an oath to my people. It is very appropriate then, that from this Cradle of the Confederacy, this very heart of the great Anglo-Saxon Southland that today we sound the drum for freedom as our generations of forebears have done, time and time again through history. Let us rise to the call of freedom loving blood that is in us and send our answer to the tyranny that clanks its chains upon the South. In the name of the greatest people who have ever trod this earth, I draw the line in the dust and toss the gauntlet before the feet of tyranny and I say, "Segregation Today, Segregation Tomorrow, Segregation Forever."*

This decision was based upon pure political pragmatism driven by a burning ambition to be elected Governor of Alabama. He became the embodiment of fighting federal encroachment on States' Rights which had been a Southern tradition based upon Constitutional principles for many years, and he also became the symbol of resistance to integration as well.

My mother's love affair with the people of Alabama was genuine, endearing . . . and enduring. She had been a simple country girl, a tomboy of sorts working in a dime store, when she met a dark and mysterious young man, by the name of George Wallace. Their respective personalities and demeanor complimented each other and appealed to the folks. They were a great team, but she in her own right became a confident public servant, with an ease about herself and gentle spirit that lifted the spirits of her people. Her death at forty-one, after waging such a courageous battle with cancer, was the inspiration for the Lurleen B. Wallace Comprehensive Cancer Institute, at the University of Alabama in Birmingham.

My father being labeled the "Grandfather" of the modern conservative movement in our country, even prior to Ronald Reagan was a source of great pride to him. He was simply taking the value system which had been instilled in him by the people from whence he came, and the people of the country responded to it. In many ways, his national popularity became a certain vindication of sorts given the perception of Southerners perpetuated by many in the national media, a perception that remains even today.

A look at my father's life teaches us many things. For all of his actions as a man and politician, he would have to make choices and live with the consequences of those choices. His ambitions propelled him to great heights and those same ambitions took him to the depths of despair. Ultimately, it was his faith that he held so dear that gave him the strength to carry on. When he was faced with the harsh reality of being confined to a wheelchair and in constant pain for the rest of his life, he would have to make a choice. When he was faced with the thought of Arthur Bremer, the man who sought to take his life, he would have to make a choice. He felt that in many ways he was broken physically, so in order to survive he must not let himself be broken mentally, emotionally or spiritually. He made the choice to forgive, and through prayer and a devout faith he found peace.

Over the years, I invariably have been asked the question: What was it like growing up the son of George Wallace? The person asking the question could never know how deep their question reached inside me. While I answer the question in terms they can understand about events they have in mind, they would never know how the father and son relationship was affected by the father's political ambition and what that gave and took from the son. Our natures were different in that he was outgoing and had to have people around him winning their approval, and I sought a more solitary existence from an early age hoping to win his approval. While I was reaching out to him, he was reaching out to the people of Alabama and the nation, and it would be years for us to reach each other.

The Shakespearean drama that was played out in the public life of my father was also played out in his private life as well. As we all grew and matured, we each in our own way came to grips with the magnitude of the life and times in which we lived as the family of a national icon. We loved him and he loved us, and our journey was a journey that brought us from estrangement and alienation to understanding and affection. This is my story.

I am hopeful these writings will reveal the father I knew, the mother I knew, and introduce you to our family and many of our friends. In addition, I hope the photographs will allow the reader a sense of the times in which we lived and our lives today.

BOB DYLAN TALKS OF GEORGE WALLACE

There are two separate windows with the faintest of light that beckon me. From one window flows music and melodies and from the other, thoughts and reflections both speaking of a life lived and lessons learned. They both beckon me to tell the story in their own unique and special way.

We are, if we are anything, at least two things. We are what we are, and we are what others would have us to be. When I consider the nature of the environment in which I grew up, and then reflect on what I believe my nature to be, I am struck by how the contrasts manifested themselves personally and politically for me.

An interesting example of the two worlds in which I lived contains itself in Bob Dylan's music. In listening to Dylan's words, and realizing he was talking about my father in, "The Times They Are A-Changin'," was an interesting experience for me. What made it even more interesting is that I played that song for my father one night as he sat on the side of my bed. He would often come in my room and ask about school and things, and then ask me to play something on the guitar, as he would lean his head back and smoke his cigar. He especially enjoyed Hank Williams songs, and I often would play those while my mother and father waltzed to, "I'm so Lonesome I Could Cry." This one night, he was by himself and he asked me to play. I had just learned Bob Dylan's "The Times They Are A-Changin'," and I started to play it for him. As a fourteen-year-old, I was singing to him lines such as, "Come senators, and congressmen please heed the call, don't stand in the doorway, don't block up the hall, for he that gets hurt will be who has stalled, there's a battle outside and it's ragin'." I remember him turning to me with a startled look in his eyes. And after hearing only the Hank Williams's songs about loving and losing when he came into my room, he was now hearing a song from his fourteen-year-old son about social conscience and social change, change that found him as a major player in the midst of this cultural transformation of which he was considered to be the very embodiment of opposition. What was he thinking when I got to the part of the song that said, "Don't stand in the doorway, don't block up the hall," and he realized the lyrics were talking about him? He got a faraway look in his eyes and perhaps he was thinking of positions he had taken to be elected governor. Perhaps he was thinking of the bargain he had made in order to be elected governor concerning the issue of segregation. Was he thinking about how as a circuit judge and Son of Alabama he had worked to enhance the quality of life for all people, Black and white? Was he thinking about his public pledge in the 1958 race for governor when he said, "If I can't treat a Black man fair, I don't deserve to be your governor?" Was he thinking about how he was perceived by so many across the nation as one who had hate in his heart and was a racist? This was a hurt he would have to live with and endure until the day he died. I thought I saw the look of regret in his eyes and while I saw it for only an instant, he knew I had seen it. Was he thinking about where life's journey had taken him, and how the song being sung to him by his son brought that home to him? It was an interesting moment hearing the premier protest song of the 1960s that referred to him as the bad guy, sung to him by his son. It was sung to him by a son not intending to point out that his father was the villain, but sung only because it was a song from his son's generation. As I reflect on it now, the rest of Dylan's lyrics in the verse I sang to my father say, "For he that gets hurt, will be he who has stalled, there's a battle outside and it's ragin'." My father would eventually be hurt because of the controversy he had caused when he did stall. He understood the arc of history and where the winds were blowing, but how could he have known his path was taking him into a headwind that would change his life so drastically.

My father and I were both thrust into the midst of one of the most dramatic and traumatic times in our nation's history. At that point in my life, I withdrew to my room in the Alabama Governor's Mansion with my guitars, albums, and music. I listened to lyrics very carefully and thought about them most of the time. We all remember where we were when certain events happen in our lives, and I was so attuned to music and the words of the songs; I can remember where I was when I heard a certain song. I recall being driven by a state trooper to the Woodley Country Club in Montgomery to play golf, and hearing Simon and Garfunkel's, "Sounds of Silence." I spent a considerable amount of time playing music at the Governor's Mansion until all hours of the night, listening for the sounds of silence.

It was my sanctuary from what our family was going through personally as my father and family became the target of threats, demonstrations and finally in a Laurel, Maryland, shopping center parking lot, my father became the ultimate target in an assassination attempt that changed his life. The bullets seeking to take his life possibly gave to him more than they took. The changes in his personal life and the struggles he endured actually gave him strength, insight and led him to a place in time, to a place in heart and mind that was his own road to Damascus.

George Wallace Jr.

"Affliction is the good man's shining time."

— EDWARD YOUNG, ENGLISH POET

Acknowledgements

Photographs courtesy of:

Alabama Archives and History
Benita Pinson Roberts
David Azbell
David Morris
Devin Maddox
Lori Sullivan
Mason Fischer
Michael Griffin
Paul Robertson
Raymond Griffin
Roy Smith
Shannon Odonahue
Sherry Leaks
Tommy Giles
Wallace Family Archives

A special thank you to Jeff Schlesinger for Believing . . .

Redemption

Brothers in Christ, "Amen."

In gracious and spiritual words, Joseph Lowery, a leader in the original march and now the president of the Southern Christian Leadership Conference, thanked the former separatist "for coming out of your sickness to meet us. You are a different George Wallace today. We both serve a God who can make the desert bloom. We ask God's blessing on you."

This scene at St. Jude's—he is the patron saint of hopeless causes—invites an obvious and skeptical question: Was Wallace, the one-time arch segregationist sincere?

The evidence suggests genuineness. In 1979, at the Dexter Avenue Baptist Church in Montgomery—where Martin Luther King Jr. pastored in the 1950s—Wallace made an unpublicized and unannounced Sunday evening visit to the congregation. As recounted by Stephen Lesher in his 1994 book, *George Wallace: American Populist,* the former governor was pushed up the aisle and spoke: "I have learned what suffering means. In a way that was impossible {before the shooting}, I think I can understand something of the pain Black people have come to endure. I know I contributed to that pain, and I can only ask your forgiveness."

With grateful appreciation to my wife, Elizabeth,
without whose love, inspiration, and belief this book
would not have been possible.

*The man you never really knew by the man who
knew him best. The author with his father.*

CHAPTER ONE

Why Was My Father a Populist?

IMPACT OF THE DEPRESSION YEARS

It is interesting to note that many people who have risen to great heights tend to possess certain eccentric tendencies. I have always believed my father fit that category. He was an extremely complex man who was driven by burning ambitions and the single mindedness and stamina he exhibited in pursuing those ambitions was fascinating to observe. Part of this had to do with the experiences in his early life when as a sixteen-year-old and the oldest of four children his father died at age forty. This left my father and his very independent mother, Mozelle, to face the harsh realities of the post-Depression South, and simply try to survive. The rules by which they lived were: life is hard, make every day count, and fight for what you believe. Living in Clio, Alabama, my grandmother taught piano, took in sewing, and did a number of things to help the family during a difficult time in the rural South.

My father, being a child of the Depression, saw suffering firsthand. He saw economic suffering and also saw physical suffering when he made the rounds with his grandfather who was a prominent doctor making house calls across rural Barbour County. Coupled with the poverty he saw all around him, he also saw the double tragedy of a family suffering from severe health problems such as cancer or any number of health issues. In many cases, the family had no way to pay Dr. Wallace so they would offer a meal, sweet potatoes or perhaps a chicken. The sadness of watching his grandfather boil morphine in a spoon to give a shot to comfort a dying cancer patient had a profound impact on my father. These conditions coupled with the conversations he heard from his father and grandfather so affected my father as a little boy that he would do things to try and help. When he would go to the grocery store with his mother, he would ask her to buy something made in Alabama because that would help Alabama. To be that attuned as a six and seven-year-old is extraordinary. Seeing all the things he saw as well as experiencing the dire poverty around him, shaped and molded his desire to help the Southern people by enhancing their quality of life. As time passed, it came to him that the best way to do this was through education.

My father's mindset was shaped by this life experience and coupled with his burning desire to be successful in politics and his distracted nature caused by his ambitions was the father we knew. I have always thought that these experiences taught my father that anything is possible with determination and hard work. My father lived with this and while his family was not in dire poverty, they were hard pressed to get by because of my grandfather's death at age forty. My father grew up fast and became extremely serious-minded and driven. This experience molded and shaped him in a way that manifested itself in his public policy positions over the years. He never forgot and he never would forget the suffering he saw Alabamians endure. This ignited a fire within him that burned brilliantly until the day he died. That was the fire that burned for, "The Little Man." That was George Wallace's clarion call and he responded. He would also speak of the poverty he had seen and been around as a youngster growing up in Barbour County, Alabama, during the Great Depression. These stories were my baptism into the political world, and to me it was as clear as anything I had ever considered and reflected upon, even given my young age, that to help these people was more than anything else what public service truly meant. That should be the spirit and essence in offering yourself to serve. In pursuing this path with such a passion and dedication, it causes in many instances a conflict with certain interests that wield considerable influence in government at all levels. It has always been that way and will always be that way, because even as the faces change over the years, the traditional political alliances generally remain the same.

When I consider what I heard my father talking about from the time I was a small child, in terms of helping the average citizen, and making certain that the least among us are not forgotten, I am struck by how similar that message was with the message of the Civil Rights movement. The Civil Rights message was about educational, economic, cultural equality, and justice. It embraced empowerment and enhancing the quality of life for people. My father's populist message was about championing the cause of the average person, the elderly, and the frail. It is ironic to me that his early position on the issue of segregation should cast him in the role of holding insensitivity toward those he had always sought to help as much as anyone—Alabama's Black citizens. While his heart was leading him that way, he was accused by many of allowing raw political ambition to cloud his heart. He made that bargain and the ramifications of the bargain he made not only changed the national political landscape but changed him as a man.

I found myself deeply affected by my early exposure to his rhetoric and it was accentuated by a story I read while in the fourth grade. In Alabama, for many years, the fourth grade was the time for a child's introduction to Alabama history. I recall reading a story about a rural family in Alabama during the Great Depression who were desperately poor. They had a very young son who for all his young years had been sickly and frail, a condition made

3

even worse by the poverty in which they lived. The lack of good nutrition was the major contributing factor to the poor health of the boy. This caused great pain for his parents because of their inability to provide the nutrition he so needed. As they were riding down a dusty Alabama dirt road, they came upon a man selling apples and the boy's father stopped to buy his son one apple because that was all he could afford. The seller of the apples was so moved by the extreme poverty of the family and the frailty of the child that he gave the father a full basket of apples without accepting any payment. The father's Southern pride led him to protest that he couldn't possibly accept the basket, but the vendor explained that he wanted him to have the basket, and to please accept it for his family. As the father reluctantly took the apples, he expressed his heartfelt appreciation knowing inside how the fruit would help his son. For a while, the little boy actually improved as the nutrition from the apples helped strengthen his frail body. But after they were gone there were no more apples. The little boy eventually died in his father's arms, the victim of circumstances he did not create as was the plight of so many in the great Southland, during that difficult time in our history. A flickering young light had gone out; another heart-breaking story of a people who were suffering in so many ways. I have read that story over and over again through the years about the death of this young child, and I seem to correlate it with some of the stories my father would tell during his campaign speeches, as he spoke of the past suffering of the people of Alabama.

In thinking about how he was molded and shaped, I am reminded of his heartfelt words from his fourth inaugural address in January of 1983 when he said:

Alabama is blessed with an abundance of resources known to few others. Her mines and minerals, her rivers, streams and harbors; her forests, factories and farms; her cities and villages; and most of all, her people . . . eager, willing and capable, industrious and determined to create a better way of life for themselves, their families and neighbors. This spirit cannot be extinguished or defeated. We will overcome our problems . . .

We recognize and applaud the monuments to corporate profit that tower in glass and steel above our cities. We recognize and applaud the desires of those of great individual wealth to build among us monuments to high culture and entertainment. We recognize and applaud the great temples of worship and Christian education that religious denominations seek to build and assert upon our landscape to glorify Almighty God.

But for God's sake, let us also hear the sighs of the hungry and the cold among us. Let us do among the least of these, and God will reward us with His blessings in His way in His time . . . Any nation that forgets its poor will lose its soul.

WE HAD TO SHOW THEM, COACH

I recall a story he told me about an experience he had while a member of the Clio High School football team. Clio was scheduled to play the Troy High School football team the coming Friday night, and the Troy players were bigger and stronger and their team had more backup players than a small rural town like Clio had on their entire team. My father wondered what could be done to make certain the Clio young men played as hard as they could against such formidable odds. A letter appeared addressed to the Clio High School football team that appeared to have been sent from the Troy football team. The contents of the letter spoke of how the Clio players were, "Country boys" and that "the Troy team was going to whip you in your own hometown this Friday night." That letter got the Clio team ready to play like nothing else could have. Clio played the Troy team to a hard fought seven to nothing score with Troy winning. Now while Clio had not won, they played a game that was talked about for years in South Alabama. The spirit and determination of the Clio football team, led by my father as

5

the quarterback, has become legendary. After the game my father's coach took my father aside and said, "George C., you wrote that letter didn't you." His young 110-pound quarterback and captain of the team, looked his coach square in the eye and replied, "Coach, I wanted the boys to play their best game; we had to show them, Coach." There was an understanding he instinctively had about what motivated people even then, and that would become one of his most valuable insights during his political career. Years later, he would return home to Alabama from some of his early presidential forays and tell the crowds who gathered to welcome him home, the same thing he told his coach years before, "My friends, we had to show them." He along with the South was still fighting the battle over Southern pride.

HIS COLLEGE DAYS, THE UNIVERSITY OF ALABAMA

I have often thought about how his leadership abilities began to grow and strengthen while he was a student at the University of Alabama. In thinking about the fact that he was from a very rural area of Southeast Alabama, he now would learn valuable lessons about human nature and fine tune those famous Wallace instincts.

He was on his own as he had been earlier when his father drove him to Montgomery to be a page in the Alabama Legislature. This earlier story is fascinating as it reveals his early political acumen, and his total determination to work and, through sheer will, win. At that time in 1935, when he was fifteen years old, a page had to be elected by the full senate on the first workday. Most of the young men counted on their senate sponsor to carry the day for them, but not my father. He secured a copy from the senate clerk of where the senators were spending the night, and he went to visit every one of them. He talked with 27 of the 35 senators and received commitments from 23 and possible votes from 2. As the rules were written, the candidate would have to receive a full majority which was 18 votes. He knew there would be some absent from the chamber during the vote, so he thought if 20 to 25 senators voted he would win.

He went to the gallery to watch and as he kept his count and thought about how they voted and what they had told him, he kept a mental photograph in his mind as he would do the rest of his life. He won! He was ecstatic and later said it was one of the "Proudest moments of my life." What is truly interesting is that after the vote he approached every senator in a respectful way to thank those who voted for him, and to ask those who did not keep their word, why they didn't. All of this was a valuable lesson for him and just a short time later, he would be applying those same political skills at the University of Alabama.

When he arrived at the University of Alabama he had a few dollars in his pocket, and a burning desire to obtain his undergraduate and law degrees. He worked several jobs and studied when he could. He could not have joined a fraternity if he had so desired, because there was no money for that. He waited tables and washed the football team's uniforms for extra money. He worked on an NYA {National Youth Administration} job and with all of this, found time to be the captain of the University of Alabama Boxing Team. As such, he was a member of the A Club which was one of the most prestigious and admired clubs on campus.

One of my father's friends from those days was Henry Leslie, who with his Pike County roots, became a close, personal friend of my father's at the university. Henry Leslie went on to achieve great success in the banking industry and was always a close confidante of my father's. Before his recent death, Henry talked with great warmth of those days and has related some interesting experiences he and my father had at the university, together.

My father was the President of the Spirit Committee, and part of his duties in serving in that capacity was to fire the students up at the pep rally the day before a big Saturday football game. Henry told the story of how at one of the pep rallies the students became unruly and were attempting to shout down President Foster because the students had decided they wanted some kind of holiday from the administration. No one seemed to know what to do so my father walked across the stage to Henry who was the leader of the Alabama band and asked him to play the "Alma Mater." When they started playing, and because of the solemn and sacred nature of that song, the students all stood silently, and following the song, sat down, and were better behaved. My father's quick thinking of how to control a crowd was present even then, given his acute understanding of human nature.

The location where the pep rally was held is intriguing when you consider that it was Foster Auditorium where he would make his famous, "Stand in the Schoolhouse Door," years later. The irony of this is that his desire to control the emotions of people as a student and as Governor of Alabama, at Foster Auditorium is something I wondered if he thought about when he made his historic "Stand in the Schoolhouse Door."

Henry Leslie relates an amusing story of how he managed my father's campaign for Cotillion Club President and having lost that election my father would kid Henry that, "The only election I lost was the one you managed." They remained close personal friends until my father died. When I served two terms as Alabama's State Treasurer, I developed my own personal and professional relationship with Henry and his family, especially his son, Arthur, who has written some fascinating novels and is a close friend.

Henry tells me that when my father arrived at the university, he started making friends immediately. And as a member of the College of Arts and Sciences with his personality and winning ways, he started immediately running for freshman class president. He became so popular that he was elected before the fraternity machine knew what had happened. This preemptive strike would be one of his most popular political tactics during his later political career.

He was described by those who knew him during those years as very intense and possessing wisdom beyond his years of how to relate to people. This would serve him very well in the future that was awaiting him.

My father had some social life at the university even with all the other responsibilities he had. It is interesting to note that there were occasions when my father and Frank M. Johnson socialized together and became friends. How could they have known that years later they would become the bitterest of political enemies? Frank M. Johnson became Federal Judge Johnson and was the symbol my father used in his attacks on the Federal Judiciary. Their relationship had gone from one where they had been friends in college, to a relationship that was never mended. It is interesting to note that in my father's later years he sought to make amends with people he felt he had wronged and he attempted to reach Judge Johnson to seek his forgiveness. They never spoke, and Judge Johnson told Bill Moyers in an interview on PBS that, "If George Wallace wants forgiveness, he will have to get it from God; he will not get it from me."

There were others he socialized with and it has been said that he was popular with the ladies. My father, while in college, had a certain Gregory Peck or Cary Grant look, and it has been said when he would walk down sorority row, the girls would lean out their windows to see him. He was popular and well-liked. One of his college running buddies, Glen Curlee, told me years ago, "George Jr., your daddy got dates with girls I couldn't get conversation with." There is a story about a young lady, from a wealthy family, who fell totally in love with my father. She always wanted him to ride around with her in her expensive red convertible, but he refused because he did not want to be seen in such an expensive car. His populist roots were speaking to him, and even as a very young man he was thinking about appearances and how it would look to the people.

It seems this young lady had so completely fallen for my father that in a fit of anger she drove across the state line into Mississippi and married another young man. As she and her new husband were returning to Alabama, she realized the mistake she had made and upon arriving in Tuscaloosa went to the boarding house where my father lived and he helped her get an annulment.

As he was experiencing his college days, there was a young girl by the name of Lurleen Burns growing up just a few miles from him, and he would meet her upon his graduation from law school, while driving a dump truck preparing to enter World War II.

MY FATHER'S BOXING DAYS

Earlier, when he was in high school, my father went with a crew to sell magazine subscriptions in Michigan and Wisconsin. Ironically these two states would play a pivotal role in his life many years later. He won the Michigan Democratic Presidential primary in 1972 by winning every county. And Wisconsin was the state from which Arthur Bremer, the man who attempted to take my father's life, called home, but more on that later. It was an interesting time for him because he traveled for the first time in his life, out of Alabama. The leader of the crew was Elton Stephens who was from Clio and a few years older than my father. Elton Stephens went on to found EBSCO Industries and built one of the largest printing corporations in the country. He and my father remained friends throughout their lives.

10

As the team would go from door to door making their magazine pitch, my father had an interesting time. One lady told him he had such beautiful teeth that she would buy a subscription. Another lady told him if he caught her chicken, she would buy a subscription. Upon his catching the chicken after running around for several minutes, the lady changed her mind and decided she did not want a subscription. My father tells how he was tempted to let the chicken go but did not and gave her the chicken and was on his way.

During this trip, my father would search out the barber shops, and while getting a trim, ask if there were any boxers in town, and if there were he would like to have a boxing match with them. He told the men sitting around the barber shop that it did not matter how much they weighed, he would fight anybody. My father probably weighed at the most 110 pounds and was in many respects still a boy. In his clothes, he looked almost frail, but underneath was a fine-tuned body and a fierce competitive fighting spirit. A spirit that served him well the rest of his life.

The barber shop being the best place in town to get the word out worked, and he had some boxing matches in some back alleys with men gathered around making bets. He was so small that the spectators waged their bets for his opponents in many cases because they were so much larger than my father. Of course, what they did not know was that he had been a Golden Gloves champion in Alabama and had learned how to fight much larger men. He understood the "Sweet Science," and was written up as one of the best counterpunchers in the Southeast when he captained the University of Alabama Boxing team. All of these things were unknown to the unsuspecting spectators and he had to hope no one would ever find out, or he could be in real trouble. As the word would travel around town that the challenge had been made, the locals solicited one of their toughest young men to accept the

11

challenge and the fight would occur usually in a back alley. The scene must have looked like something from a movie, but this was real, and had all the drama and danger that personified my father's life to come. As a teenager growing up in Clio, he had set up a boxing ring in the back yard. All the boys boxed and my father learned how to fight sometimes much larger opponents in that arena. Later, as the Captain of the University of Alabama Boxing Team, he sparred with the heavyweights and it was said that he had an uncanny ability to bob and weave and keep his opponent guessing. Here again, another trait that manifested itself during his political career as he became the ultimate sage due to his astute sense of timing.

The men would gather around as the two combatants readied themselves for the match, money in hand, placing their bets and thinking there was no way this small youngster could best the town's toughest men. My father had one of his companions on the magazine team with him to make certain they could make a safe exit. There was always the possibility that, because my father was such a fine boxer that he perhaps was a professional who had come to take advantage of them. Had the spectators suspected that and acted upon it, it would have been run for your life. Thankfully, that never happened, and my father made some extra spending money albeit with a few bruises to show for it.

He told me a story once of an experience he had at the University of Alabama, when at a party another student much larger than my father approached him and attempted to push his face into his drink. It appeared this young man had become jealous because his girlfriend had talked about how handsome George Wallace was. So, impetuous youth caused the young man to make a bad mistake. My father immediately tackled him and drove him across the room where they fell through a plate glass window. At that point my father hit him so many times and so fast that the young man was out within seconds. My father told me later that for him, when he fought a bigger man, he always tried to take him to the ground, and overcome him with his speed. That was not the end of the story as a few weeks later, this young man and two of his friends confronted my father in a café at which time my father grabbed a knife and jumped up on the table, and with knife in hand was able to hold the high ground until the police arrived. My father never heard from those young men again.

My father was an extremely gifted athlete from all the stories I was told over the years by his brothers, sister, and friends. He was very interested in the sport of boxing although he excelled in all sports. At the University of Alabama, he was captain of the boxing team and had won Alabama Golden Gloves tournament twice. He had been written up by a sportswriter from Tennessee as, "The hardest hitting little man in the South." The following Paul Harvey commentary from a few years ago speaks of how he fought for the weak even as a young man.

THE BOY WAS GEORGE WALLACE
By Paul Harvey

He was too small to be a fighter, but he was a fighter. The boy weighed a scant 95 pounds. The YMCA sponsors to the Golden Gloves Tournament said there were no other entrants in the paperweight or flyweight divisions.

If he insisted on fighting, he would have to fight featherweights, 127 pounds. He'd have to fight boys 30 pounds heavier. He insisted. Frail as he appeared, the lad had a wallop in both hands and natural boxing skill.

13

He fought large contestants in his hometown and was crowned its champion. He fought his way three and four fights a night, through the preliminaries, semi-finals and into the state finals.

Physical culturist, Bruce McFadden was co-sponsoring the state championships. Former champion, Bennie Leonard, was to referee the big night, for you see this happened in 1935.

The slight youth—his name was George—was "edgy" the night before the main event. His coach J.P. Hanks invited the lad to go for a walk to discuss strategy. They'd walked about a block from the YMCA when they encountered a street fight. Coach Hanks grabbed young George by the arm and tried to turn him away from the row.

But George jerked his arm free and stepped into the middle of the altercation. He ordered the two hoodlums to leave the Negro boy alone. Both the hoodlums were much larger than George and the larger of the two threw a punch without warning. In an instant, George was flat on his back on the sidewalk. In another instant, he was on his feet dazed but fighting mad. He waded into the two toughs. The first curled over from a pile driver punch to the stomach and an uppercut to the jaw. The second was staggered with a volley of blows to the middle finished with a broken nose.

Coach Hanks remembers there was no need for him to help; no time for it. Diminutive George had knocked two heavyweight toughs unconscious within less than a minute.

"Your hands!" coach Hanks screamed. But, it was too late.

The boy's knuckles were split and bleeding, his wrists were swelling. And the next day was the championship fight for which he had planned and dreamed and trained since his earliest recollection. He refused to see a doctor; he knew he would be disqualified. By fight night, George's hands were twice their normal size, so painful there was blood on his lips when the coach finished lacing his gloves. He insisted on fighting, coach Hanks remembers. "He could barely defend himself, nothing more. He lost that night, but I keep remembering how and why he'd won the night before."

As I confirmed these details with Coach Hanks and with newspaper accounts of the incident, I kept wondering how many persons now giving lip service to brotherly love . . . I kept wondering how many of them, then or now without fanfare or photographers, would pay such a personal price to rescue a Negro boy he never knew . . . as did that boy that night in Montgomery, Alabama, in 1935. That boy, George Wallace, who grew up to be Governor of Alabama.

I believe this commentary pierces the veil relative to the kind of man my father was. How many among us would be as moved as he was at the injustice of the moment, and the inhumanity to man he witnessed to take such action. That and so many other examples of kindness and consideration toward others I witnessed over the years, spoke of the man I knew.

Coach Paul "Bear" Bryant told of how he watched my father box one time and that he was a "Crowd Pleaser." When asked what that meant he said, "George would knock his opponent down and then help him up, and the crowd loved it."

WORLD WAR II—B-29 BOMBER ENGINEER, SERGEANT WALLACE

As President John Kennedy said many years ago, "The first job for my generation was to fight a war." He and my father were of the same generation and their life's work as very young men left an indelible impression. My father was an engineer on a B-29 Bomber, flying night missions over Japan. As a member of the Army Air Corps, as it was called at the time, his dream was to be a fighter pilot. I recall him telling me how he and his classmates at the University of Alabama law school admired the Air Force planes they saw and hoped that they could one day be pilots. After my father joined the Army Air Corps, his dream to become a fighter pilot was interrupted by a serious life-threatening bout with spinal meningitis. He contracted the condition and was unconscious for two days and close to death. It took time for him to recuperate and begin to gain some of the weight he had lost. Given that he was slight of build, the weight loss for him was even more dangerous. Even given this brush with death, he still was determined to fly. He made the application to be a member of a B-29 bomber crew, and he became a flight engineer, which was one of the most important members of the crew. The engineer was seated behind the pilots and monitored a large panel, where among other things he controlled fuel mixtures, and gave the pilots valuable information on how to adjust the fuel to get them back to the island of Tinian in the Philippines, which was their home base. There was an incident where the pilot told Sergeant Wallace that he believed they would have to ditch the airplane. My father gave his assessment of the situation to the pilot, and assured him they could make it back, which they did.

In thinking about flying night missions over Japan, my father talked about how the airplane was your enemy, as was the dark, the ocean, kamikaze pilots, and flak. He spoke of visiting with young men from other bomber crews during the time they awaited their next mission, and then following the mission learning that the entire crew had been lost, and all these young men were his friends.

Members of my father's bombing crew said that when they were trying to relax on the beach awaiting their next mission orders, someone would turn and ask, "Where is George C.?" The response was that he was in the airplane, reviewing the procedures of the pilots in case they were wounded and he would need to fly the plane back to base. This experience for all these young men, as their first job in life, was to defeat Fascism and make the world safe for democracy. What a debt we owe them. They truly are as Tom Brokaw called them, "The Greatest Generation."

Wars affect all who fight in them regardless of what country for which they fight. It is a simple human condition that having as your mission to bring destruction, and thus forced to live with a mentality of kill or be killed, is life altering. There are many names for the type of stress that occurs during and after the war experience. Post traumatic stress disorder and other names have been given, but whatever the name, it not only affects you, but others around you as well. Given that my father's life ambition of being Governor of Alabama was already etched in his heart and mind, and with a young wife and a baby daughter, my sister Bobbie, he had much for which to live. He along with other members of his B-29 crew were discharged at the conclusion of the war receiving a 10% disability for mental anxiety and stress. This condition manifested itself for him in various ways during his early years of marriage upon his return from the war. He was edgy most of the time and could not be still. He was a bundle of energy and he tended to have a quick temper. He, by nature, was an anxious man in very much of a hurry, who had great ambitions and could visualize himself accomplishing all his goals. The experience of war had penetrated his very being, and he knew from a tender age how precious life is. Thus, the need to hit the ground running literally and figuratively stirred deep within him.

So, his life's journey continued, having faced suffering and military combat by the age of twenty-three. Given that this was the case with those of his generation and that they were bound by these shared experiences, the manner and courage in which they responded to the Great Depression and World War II saved our nation. They knew that life can be hard and unfair and there were principles and values for which they must fight. So, this "Greatest Generation," went about their business, understanding that sacrifices would have to be made, and, in knowing this, secured the hope for a strong and peaceful future. Thank God for them!

HIS DAYS AS THE FIGHTING LITTLE JUDGE

As a boy, I had great admiration for my father and as most young boys feel about their fathers, he was my hero. I can recall sitting in the court room in the Barbour County courthouse in Clayton when he was presiding as circuit judge and feeling very proud of him.

I can also recall walking around downtown Clayton and how he seemed to know everyone's name and all of their family members. It has been said that George Wallace knew everybody in Barbour County, even the "chicken thieves." He worked hard at knowing everyone and information about their families, and his reputation for helping the folks was legendary. I recall a story about his time serving as a circuit judge when after ruling on a particular case he had adjourned court for lunch. As he was walking across the street past the Confederate monument to Sam Seal's Café, he was approached by a man who was upset with his recent ruling. It appears the man intended to physically assault my father because of the ruling, and as he approached my father, he took a swing at him. At that point, my father's boxing instincts took over as he ducked the punch and came back with an upper cut that knocked the man down and out.

There were a couple of interesting confrontations he had while serving as a freshman in the Alabama legislature that speak to his impulsive nature in his younger days. One such incident was precipitated by a political operative in Montgomery at the time who owed my father some money. After my father's repeated attempts in diplomatic but strong terms did no good, he devised another plan of action. One night while in Montgomery during the legislative session, and after a meal with many of the movers and shakers, my father asked the man who owed him the money if he would step outside so they could talk privately. Once outside my father asked him for the money and the response he received was one of total disdain and laughter about the matter. In the wink of any eye my father threw an uppercut that immediately knocked him down and had him dazed. My father then took the man's wallet and retrieved what was rightfully his, then placed the wallet back in the man's coat. My father had a wife and a baby and given that money was so hard to come by his desperate actions spoke of trying to survive.

There was another encounter he had late one night when he was driving back to Clayton from a legislative session. He pulled into an old service station run by an elderly man who lived out back, and while getting a coke and some crackers he noticed a man and his wife arguing. As the argument became more heated, my father attempted to intervene in talking to them and appealing to their reason, but to no avail. The man continued to yell at his wife and then began to hit her hard several times. At this point my father stepped in between them and said, "You either stop, or you're going to have to fight me." At this point, the man hit my father and knocked him down and when he got up the fight really ensued. During the fight, my father broke his right arm and actually had to fight with his left arm, which he used to knock the man down several times. Ultimately, my father was able to get the police there and have them sort it all out.

The name "The Fighting Little Judge" I believe came from the fact that he had been a fighter literally in the ring, and all through his young life due to the circumstances in which he had been raised. Couple that with the fact that he took those same skills mentally into the arena of public policy along with his other talents, and it is easy to see how a legendary historical political figure is born.

As the years passed, the issues that he addressed, he addressed in a way that Southerners had been longing for, and I believe he was surprised at how he was able to fulfill their longings. They wanted a fighter, and as I have said, someone to make them proud. He had been a fighter all his life, and I wonder if he knew the almost mythical spell that he would cast over so many due to his nature as a fighter. Whether he knew it or not, it was to be, and would take him on his public and private odyssey.

CHAPTER TWO

Some of the Men Around Him

BILLY WATSON

I remember walking downtown with my father and going by Billy Watson's dry goods store. Billy Watson always had an ample supply of baseball caps, and he would let me have one free when it was about time for a new one. Billy Watson, of course, was my father's chief political mentor and father figure. Considerably older than my father, Billy Watson had experienced a lifetime of observing Alabama politics and this was something which my father would absorb and learn. Billy Watson had quite a reputation around Alabama as an astute political operator, who understood the political landscape in Alabama as well as anyone. My father and Billy Watson were very fond of each other and enjoyed a wonderful relationship filled with substance and affection. They had a great sense of humor between them and had a lot of fun with each other.

One story that comes to mind occurred when my father and Billy were returning from a speaking engagement around 1960 when my father was preparing to run for governor again in 1962. In returning from the speaking engagement, my father was driving and as he so often did was speeding. Billy to the chagrin of my father had brought along a little flask and was having a nip on the way home. That made my father nervous enough although he understood Billy was going to have his evening libation. Anyway, here they were on the way home and an Alabama state trooper pulls in behind my father and turns his blue light on. As my father was telling Billy to put his flask away, it was obvious Billy's intake had already made him a bit more talkative than normal. As the trooper came up to the window, my father was telling Billy to be quiet, but Billy would not be quiet. The trooper recognized my father and said, "Judge Wallace, I didn't realize it was you." At which time my father, as he always told us to do, told the trooper how sorry he was to be speeding and he would certainly slow down. At this time, Billy leaned across into my father's lap smelling of alcohol, and started telling the trooper how he should put Judge Wallace in jail because his driving was endangering the public safety.

I can remember being in downtown Clayton as a young boy and walking around the town. A small Southern town in the 1950s was a scene out of Harper Lee's, *To Kill a Mockingbird*. I would often be walking by Billy's store while wandering around town, and he would stop me to talk. When the weather permitted, Billy would sit outside his store and I remember sitting beside him and talking. He seemed to be interested in how I was doing in school and as he talked with me, he was patient, kind and warm. There are many stories about the famous Billy Watson and his keen political acumen, but the man I knew was a grandfatherly figure on the streets of Clayton. I realized years later that he considered me as part of his family because of his deep affection for my father. He thought of himself as a father figure to my father, so I had become like a grandson to him.

Let me share a couple of stories that will give you a flavor of their relationship. Keep in mind that Billy was considered by all, including my father, as the one who helped nurture my father's political skills. Billy helped my father early on when he was just getting started. My father met Billy when my father was a very young man, and Billy asked his close friend, Governor Chauncey Sparks, also from Barbour County, to help in finding my father a job following his return from WWII. This was the time in his life when he had a wife, a small child, a law degree, and dreams for the future. With Billy's assistance in talking with Governor Sparks, my father got a job in the Attorney General's office, and shortly thereafter ran for the Alabama legislature and was elected.

Over the years, many in the media were fond of calling the close friends and associates of my father, "Cronies." It was interesting that other people had friends, but if you were a friend of George Wallace, especially when he became governor, you were called a Crony. Using this definition, Billy Watson was "King of the Cronies." Billy was an original. He liked to drink, tell stories, fly in the face of convention, look at pretty women, and generally give my father moments of great amusement mixed with my father's concern about Billy's antics when he would say, "Watson you're going to get me in trouble." At this, Billy would reply, "George you're like a broken record, I'm leaving." And Billy would walk out the door. It has been said that no one could faze Billy Watson, not even George Wallace. Billy was fond of telling the story of how my father asked him to represent him at a Nursing Home Association meeting once. He said, "Wallace sends me to see the old ladies in the Nursing Homes and he goes to see the young ladies at the Nurses Convention."

Billy Watson had a down home Southern country humor that helped give life to his relationship with George Wallace. Billy and my father were riding around one day in Clayton and Billy said he needed to stop by to see his father-in-law for a few minutes. Billy's father-in-law was in his '90s. Before they got there, Billy warned him, "He'll tell you the same stale joke over and over, because he forgets he's already told it. Don't bother about laughing, because he can't hear you. So just open your mouth and pretend you're laughing; he won't know the difference." When they left, my father said they must have looked crazy, sitting there on the porch for the whole world to see, laughing up a storm and not a sound coming from their mouths.

I think it important to recognize that Billy Watson was from a generation that had a clear and vivid recollection of how the South had been treated during the years following the "War Between the States." I have always believed that there were three people who helped instill the fierce love of the South into my father. His father, grandfather, and Billy Watson helped light the fire inside him that burned brightly for the South and would until the day he died. I can recall as a young boy in Clayton playing games with my friends and there would always be a debate as to who would be the "Yankees" as we played out our mock battles. This sentiment manifested itself over the years when a Southern college football team would play a team from the North. To defeat them was to extract in some small measure retribution from "Those Yankees." This feeling ran deep within the South and now Billy Watson would continue to instill in my father what his father and grandfather had instilled in him years before in Clio, Alabama. This psychological inheritance was part of a Southerner's upbringing, and it would play itself out in years to come in historic ways for my father and our country.

OSCAR HARPER

One of my father's favorite friends was Oscar Harper. They traveled all over the country together and had a special friendship that was well-known among the pundits of Alabama politics. There are many stories about them that show my mother and father's sense of humor as it relates to Oscar.

I recall Oscar talking about a trip that he and Billy Watson took with my father when he was running in three presidential

24

primaries in 1964. When my father spoke at Harvard during this period, Oscar relates a story that concerned the demonstrators and the level of hostility that was being directed at my father. A rumor had surfaced that my father's car would be bombed, and he was very concerned about this because the car he was using belonged to Governor Peabody of Massachusetts. He certainly did not want to have Governor Peabody's car returned after it had been bombed. After he spoke, a young man got up to ask my father a question and my father said, "I'll answer your question, but first answer one for me. Are you a he or a she? If you are a he then you need to find yourself a good barber." While all my father's friends and supporters thought this was really funny, some of the crowd did not. Oscar tells how the Secret Service rushed my father out of the auditorium through some underground passage, and how that left Oscar and Billy and the rest of the Alabama boys standing there all by themselves. Oscar and Billy made their way to the front door and found they couldn't get out because there were a couple of hundred people standing there singing, "We Shall Overcome." Everyone was wondering what to do, all but Billy Watson. Billy grabbed Oscar by the arm and pulled him outside, and Oscar asked him, "What do I do?" Billy at that point said, "Sing fool, sing." They sang so well they made the front page of the Boston Globe the next day.

ALABAMA STATE TROOPERS

He had many friends with relationships at all levels: From casual and professional to those who believed they were his best friend. I remember one night in the early '70s, this being after he had been injured, a state trooper coming up to his bedroom at the Governor's Mansion to help him with something. I happened to be there at the time visiting with him, and when the state trooper finished helping my father he turned to my father and said,

"George, if you need me, I'll be here immediately; please take care and know I am right downstairs." I thought at the time that it was strange for the state trooper to be referring to him as George rather than governor. I asked my father about it and he told me, "You have to understand son that he has great affection for you and me, and that is his way of expressing his friendship." I had a special relationship with all the Alabama State Trooper security team, and we shared many special moments.

RECOLLECTIONS OF MICKEY GRIFFIN

There was a young man who worked for the Wallace Campaign named Mickey Griffin. I have known Mickey since the late sixties and we became good friends during the times we campaigned across the nation. Mickey is married to Colley Rhodes of the Rhodes family, a family that has been close to my family for many years. I grew up with Colley's two brothers, Frank and Slade.

Mickey was very young at the time he became one of the leaders of the Wallace presidential campaign. He was a mere twenty-three-year-old man who had the savvy and the intelligence to move among the party elite and he demonstrated wisdom and vision far beyond his years. Mickey possessed the essential people skills that are so necessary at the level at which he found himself. He knew how to deflect much of the built-in bias toward George Wallace at that level, and was able to, in the final analysis, make friends and play a major role in establishing valuable contacts the Wallace campaign needed.

Mickey tells some interesting stories of his relationship with my father from the time he was a very young man.

Mickey reminisces:

The day I met George Wallace, I was a fifteen-year-old senate page in the Alabama State Capitol, and it was in 1963, the first year of his first term. It was a late summer afternoon, and I was leaving the Capitol at the north end through the huge brass doors, when bam, out of room 100 bounded the governor. He immediately grabbed my hand and said, 'Hello young man, what's your name? I'm George Wallace.'

I stuttered and stammered for a minute or so and somehow the subject of my grandmother, Ida Lee Dozier, came up. He immediately said, "Oh yes, I know Mrs. Dozier; she was in the attorney general's office when I worked there after the war. I know her well." She later confirmed to me he came to work the first day in his uniform because he didn't have a suit. Anyway, Governor Wallace said, 'How about flying up to Anniston with me tonight? I have a speech; I'll take care of it with Ida Lee and get you home safely.' I begged off the trip with some lame excuse but mostly I was stunned and intimidated by the invitation. I wish I had gone that afternoon. I never forgot how genuinely interested he was in meeting me and how warm and friendly he was to just a kid. I really felt important when the governor of the state shook my hand and said, 'Hi, I'm George Wallace.' Little did I know how that chance encounter would affect me in the years to come.

THE SUMMER OF 1968

The Wallace campaign needed volunteers and workers to handle petition drives to gain state ballot positions as a third-party candidate for the presidential election in 1968. I joined up as a petition worker, campaign merchandise salesman (we sold bumper stickers, hats, pins, etc.), baggage handler, and general flunky. I loved it! I got to ride on the same plane with Governor Wallace and the top staff and traveling crew. We nicknamed the old 4-engine plane "The Sow" and it was great for a kid like me! The governor was always up and down the aisles, laughing, cutting up and visiting. He always wanted to know if I was okay or needed anything. He had a genuine interest in me and the others on the plane.

Part of my responsibility was loading and unloading the bulletproof podium the governor spoke from behind at all the rallies. My friends, Charlie Patterson, Charles Dotson, and I had to set it up and take it *down. It was in three pieces and weighed a ton! We hauled and dealt with that thing all over the United States. Many years later, I saw it on display in a Presidential Campaign Exhibit at the Smithsonian Institute. We were making history in 1968!*

My first trip with the campaign was a two-week Southern tour, Atlanta, Jackson, Miami, and Pensacola. The campaign would hold massive rallies with thousands of people attending. We had a country band and Mona and Lisa. Governor Wallace would later marry Lisa Taylor. They would get the crowd up into a frenzy singing, "Are You from Dixie." I can hear it now! Then the governor would come on and give his classic speech about those "Briefcase toting bureaucrats, who can't park a bicycle straight." He would talk about those pseudo intellectuals and social engineers and academic visionaries and the crowd would go crazy! I knew the speech by heart after a few nights and I was always amazed at the governor's ability to mesmerize and control such large crowds.

In contrast, today's politicians go to where the people tend to congregate so they can have a crowd. They wouldn't dare rent an auditorium seating thousands of people and ask the people to come to them. The national politicians took note and there was no denying the crowds Governor Wallace drew that summer.

THE 1970 GOVERNOR'S RACE

This is one for all time! I don't think there has ever been a statewide in Alabama, or any other state, that was as intense, bitter, and acrimonious. People still talk about it today and hard feelings still remain. Relationships, families, businesses, and organizations were forced to choose sides, and nobody could avoid making a declaration and answering the question, "Who are you for?"

It all started with the death of Governor Lurleen Wallace from cancer in 1968. She was the beloved wife of Governor Wallace who (after legislation blocked a bill allowing him to seek a second term) ran for governor in 1966 and won in a landslide victory. Everyone felt she was a stand-in for Governor Wallace, but she in fact endeared herself to the people of Alabama and proved to be an effective governor in her own right.

Albert Brewer, a Wallace floor leader, was handpicked as the Lt. Governor candidate in 1966. He was a loyal and effective part of the Wallace administration and looked upon as an 'Up and comer,' in statewide politics.

Halfway through her term, Governor Lurleen was diagnosed with cancer and eventually lost her battle on May 7, 1968. As the focus turned to the 1970 governor's race, speculation was rampant regarding the potential candidates and especially whether Governor Wallace would seek a second term. Lt. Governor Brewer had assumed the governorship upon the death of Governor Lurleen, and immediately began reconstructing the cabinet and setting a divergent policy from the former Wallace administration. Depending on who you talked to, Governor Wallace declared that he would not run against Brewer or Brewer agreed not to run against Governor Wallace. Whatever the actual events were, the lines were drawn between the two men.

The primary race was hotly contested and many strange events and rumors abounded. One event was amazing; the interjection of outside money to defeat Governor Wallace. It seems President Nixon's re-election committee saw a great opportunity to eliminate Governor Wallace as a "Spoiler" candidate in 1972. Nixon feared the Wallace vote might be the difference between his winning and losing and sent $400,000 to Brewer's campaign. It had its intended effect, Governor Wallace trailed Brewer by 30,000 votes and a run-off between the two ensued. This is where things got really nasty, as all sorts of wild rumors and dirty tricks cropped up as both sides pulled out every stop to gain the upper hand. Brewer's campaign staff was photographing the farm of Governor Wallace's brother, Gerald, from a helicopter and it was forced to land in Gerald's backyard. The event caused much embarrassment to the Brewer campaign which had previously taken the high road by denouncing dirty tricks as generated *by the Wallace camp and trying to insist the campaign was a victim of Wallace evil henchmen.*

The biggest issue came from the 'Black bloc vote.' There was no question Brewer received the overwhelming majority of Black votes in the primary. Governor Wallace made this "The issue," in the runoff. He claimed Brewer had made backroom deals with Black leaders and sold-out key cabinet positions and platform issues to the Black groups. The Wallace campaign published Brewer's vote totals from the primary in predominantly Black precincts and the effect was profound. Also, the rumor mill was working overtime with scurrilous attacks upon members of both families. It went on and on!

I was in college during the 1970 race. The University of Alabama campus was buzzing with the campaign excitement and activity. Every fraternity and sorority house was split down the middle over the election. Both campaigns furiously registered new voters on campus and everywhere else where students were gathered.

As the run-off approached, every effort was directed to, "Get out the vote." The Wallace campaign used its strong statewide county organization to deliver voters to the polls from nursing homes, churches, and clubs anywhere voters were. If you needed transportation, the Wallace campaign delivered you to the polls.

Wallace's efforts paid off; he won the election by 39,000 votes. He erased the 30,000 deficit and won by 39,000, a 69,000-vote swing. It was an unbelievable political accomplishment! During the run-off campaign, Governor Wallace drove himself relentlessly, speaking from sunup to sundown. He outworked Brewer who relied mostly on television ads, and who was ineffective on the stump.

As the dust of the bitter campaign settled, Governor Wallace was inaugurated again in January 1971, but the rancor of that campaign never dissipated. It was smooth sailing now for Governor Wallace to focus on the national election in 1972.

THE 1972 PRESIDENTIAL CAMPAIGN

In 1971, I was working in Washington, DC for Alabama Senator Jim Allen and going to college when I heard Governor Wallace was going to run for president in 1972. I applied with the campaign manager, Tom Turnipseed, and he hired me for $750 a month and gave me the title of Ballot Position Advisor. I immediately started working on third party [sic] ballot position strategy. In the fall of 1971, I was told to forget the third-party effort because the governor was going to run in next spring's Democratic primaries. A lawyer named John DeCarlo from Birmingham was brought into the campaign to help with this massive task. We didn't know anything but started gathering information and soon had a handle on the types and dates of primaries. We worked long and hard and it was very exciting. I was 23 years old and around the governor all the time and had a key role in the campaign.

DeCarlo and I flew by the seat of our pants regarding planning. We had two desks we pushed together so we could face each other each morning. For instance, one day a Michigan supporter sent a letter with an article from the Detroit Press titled, "Guess Who's not coming to Dinner." The Michigan Democratic Party invited every presidential candidate, except Wallace, to the Jefferson-Jackson Dinner in Detroit. DeCarlo said, "This isn't right, we need to do something." I said, "Let's have our own rally the same date and time." We called the governor with the idea and he picked up on the opportunity instantly and off we went! The result of the Democratic Party's snub was a huge PR coup for Wallace. The Jefferson-Jackson Dinner in Detroit had a crowd of about 1200 party big shots and we held a rally at Cobo Hall where several thousand people attended, and we had to empty the hall and let another crowd in for a second rally. The event made national news! The National Democrats fell into our hands over and over with snubs like that and Governor Wallace always made them pay. For a couple of years (1972-1974) I worked as an administrative assistant [sic] to Governor Wallace. This was a time between national

31

campaigns and I handled everything from soup to nuts for Governor Wallace in the State Capitol. I witnessed first-hand, the effect Wallace had on the working people of the state. I remember seeing a farmer come to the office and politely say he wanted to talk to the governor about some matter, and then sat himself down in the anteroom to wait. Sure enough, Governor Wallace came out to meet him, and carried him back to his office between bewildered out-of-state bystanders and talked with him for 20 or more minutes. The farmer came out and told Miss Kate, "He had wanted to tell George about something in his county and would be back if he needed to talk with him again." That's the way it was. A big city out-of-towner with an entourage would be kept waiting until an Alabama voter saw 'George.'

It's hard to put into words the effect George Wallace had on people, but this funny story might put things in more perspective. In 1982, George Wallace was running for governor again, against the hard charging Mayor of Montgomery, Emory Folmar. I had a large group of my friends in the infield at the Talladega 500 for the spring race. The track was built by Bill France, President of NASCAR and a great friend of Governor Wallace. A couple of my buddies were big Folmar supporters even working in his campaign. They had whipped themselves up into believing Mayor Folmar was going to beat Wallace and beat him good. I said to them, 'Well, let's do a little informal polling right here in the infield.' About that time, a racing fan staggered by and said to us 'You fellas got a cigarette or a beer?' We fulfilled his request and I said, 'Captain, how do you feel about Emory Folmar?' He stared at me intently, mused a few moments, sipped his beer, and said to me 'Henry Fonda?' I then said, 'What do you think about Governor Wallace?' He immediately said, 'Why, George is going to kick his ass!' I rested my case to the Folmar boys and George went on to win decisively in the largest landslide for a gubernatorial victory in Alabama history.

WALLACE AND THE BLACK VOTE

When George Wallace ran for governor the last time in 1982, he received a huge Black vote in the state. Many people in national politics around the country could not believe it. They were wringing their hands and seeking complicated answers to the baffling question. To me it was simple, Governor Wallace went to the Dexter Avenue Baptist Church, Dr. Martin Luther King Jr's. church many years before, and said that he had been mistaken about race, that he was sorry, and asked them to forgive him. They did and he won his fourth term as governor easily.

1972 CAMPAIGN

One major issue facing any candidate running for their party's nomination is allocation of resources and time. The 1972 Campaign was a January to June window and each candidate had to decide where and when to campaign. Some candidates spent inordinate time in a particular state, like Governor Wallace in Florida. We banked everything in Florida, hoping a big win would catapult Governor Wallace onto the national scene. States like California required delegates to file early in the campaign but the primary was in mid-June, an eternity in campaign time. Humphrey, Muskie, and the others spent enormous amounts of time crisscrossing the nation while we threw everything we had into Florida with some excursions in Maryland, Michigan and a few other favorable states.

With the lopsided win in Florida, Governor Wallace spread panic through the National Democratic Party. Florida was not perceived as a "Deep South" state and with northern transplants and major urban areas it was more of a "Bellwether" state, essentially a national composite in one state. Also, the other Democratic candidates were less than impressive, with a propensity for committing political suicide. Mayor John Lindsay of New York ran out of steam after Florida, Muskie cried when a reporter said something about his wife, Humphrey was tied more and more to LBJ, and the liberal and anti-war crowd were joining forces behind Senator George McGovern, the new "Peace" candidate who was making inroads and threatening to divide the party again like in 1968. The rest of the field folded after Florida due to lack of money and momentum.

Delegates are allocated through primaries and caucuses. Primaries get all the attention from the media and candidates, but the caucus system was used by many states sometimes in concert with a non-binding primary or 'Beauty contest.' Senator McGovern's campaign with the use of ground forces composed of anti-war protesters, liberal activists, and students was stacking local precinct caucuses and adding valuable delegates while under the national radar screen.

The anti-establishment fever of the McGovern campaign with the "Wallace threat," was creating conflict and concern within the National Democratic Party and Congress as a whole. The 1972 Campaign was shaping up to be a donnybrook with the distinct possibility that no candidate would have the majority of delegates necessary for nomination and a wide-open convention battle was a real possibility. Many people were speculating that under these conditions, Governor Wallace could force his way onto the Democratic ticket as vice-president. The campaign season was getting very interesting, and we were right in the thick of it all!

Then came May 15, 1972: While campaigning at a Laurel, Maryland, shopping center rally, Governor Wallace was shot by Arthur Bremer while shaking hands with supporters. I was at my desk in Montgomery when the phone rang with the news. I could hear the screaming of the crowd in the background as the facts were reported. I was numb, I never really thought about Governor Wallace's safety. He had the Alabama Highway Patrol Security Team with him. They all had been with the governor for years and were real pros. I was stunned! Was he going to die? What were we to do? Where did we go from here? But quickly, Campaign Director Charlie Snider told us he was alive, and although seriously wounded, it appeared he was going to live. What a relief!

I started the process of suspending operations around the country and bringing our operatives back to Montgomery. During this period, Charlie Snider told me to pack up and head to Miami to coordinate our convention arrangements. I called on the DNC office at the Fontainebleau Hotel and introduced myself as Governor Wallace's convention manager. They were perplexed to see a young man of 23 who for the most part, burst their bubble about what a Wallace supporter looked like, no overalls or brogan shoes. I remember how put off all the DNC staff were initially and they seemed to stare at me constantly.

While Governor Wallace was recovering in Maryland, it became apparent that he would be paralyzed permanently. I thought the campaign would be over and I needed to look for another job. However, Campaign Director, Charlie Snider told me the governor wanted to continue with the campaign and wanted to attend the convention and even speak to the delegates. I couldn't believe it! He wanted to make a nationally televised speech less than 60 days after being shot five times and paralyzed from the waist down.

'When the campaign sent me to Miami as Convention Manager, it was my first taste of big-time party politics. The Democratic Chairman was Larry O'Brien, an old Kennedy man who was no friend of ours. He said he wasn't going to give Governor Wallace any hotel rooms and the governor said, 'OK, we will sleep on the beach.'

The party treasurer, Bob Strauss, an LBJ and John Connelly friend, took me under his wing and saw to it we received rooms, credentials, and everything we needed.

I remember that one time on a tour of the Convention Center with a group of party big shots and press, including David Brinkley, I was asked if we had much following among the delegates and party faithful. One of the construction workers had put a Wallace sticker on the ceiling vent and I responded, 'No, probably not' but pointing to the ceiling said, 'But the working man will be for him.' O'Brien was chapped to say the least and the bumper sticker was gone the next day.

I returned on my next trip to Miami and was thrown into the intrigue of Democratic politics and started making a lot of friends and contacts among the hierarchy of the party, state, and national politicians as well as members of the news media, sports, and movie celebrities and party activists. My secret weapon during this time was my wife, Colley. We were childhood sweethearts, married a year earlier in June 1971, and she was with me in Miami. Everyone loved Colley! Her bubbly, friendly personality completely disarmed anyone with a preconceived bias against Governor Wallace, and she genuinely made people like her. Later, the new chairman of the DNC, Robert Strauss, who was responsible for my selection to the powerful Executive Committee, would always say, 'Governor Wallace really sent Colley Griffin as his representative in Washington—her husband is just an 'ole redneck.' During this period, I was in contact daily with representatives of all the other candidates; past, present and future. There was a lot of intrigue and the mainstream establishment candidates were joining forces to stop McGovern; it was ABM—Anybody but McGovern! This crowd courted us like mad and they all wanted the Wallace influence and vote to help bring the party back to the center. Of course, that plan failed at the convention, McGovern had the votes, was nominated, and went on to get trounced in the November general election by President Nixon, winning only Massachusetts and Washington, DC.

I remember McGovern making gaff after humiliating gaff during the campaign. He nominated Thomas Eagleton of Missouri as his vice-presidential running mate. Soon, it was brought out that Senator Eagleton had some past mental issues. McGovern said he was behind Eagleton 1000%, and the next week he dumped him. Senator McGovern also said he would crawl on his hands and knees to Hanoi to stop the war. Such comments finished off an already doomed campaign and the Democratic Party was in turmoil heading into 1973.

My new friend, Robert Strauss, the DNC Finance Chairman, told us he was going to run for chairman to restore the National Democratic

Party to the mainstream, by keeping the 'Three Georges' within the party. He meant George McGovern, George Meany, and George Wallace. His attitude was to duct tape the three Georges together through the reconstruction period thus keeping the liberals, conservatives, and labor unions under the same tent, increasing the odds of recapturing the White House in 1976. He promised me a level playing field and fair party rules. He lived up to that promise.

The race for chairman of the Democratic Party was very close as the liberals and party activists fought hard to keep control. Senator McGovern had named Jean Westwood as the chairperson at the '72 convention and she was seeking re-election. Strauss had the backing of the House and Senate, mayors, governors, labor, and the party centrists.

In the fall of 1972, I went to Washington, DC, in preparation for the election. My job was to help Strauss win the chairmanship and assure Governor Wallace a "Seat at the table," as Strauss promised the governor. Of the entire DNC membership of over 300 people, only three were committed to Governor Wallace. Strauss won the election by three votes! I always kidded him that he was chairman only as a result of the Wallace votes!

After the election, Chairman Strauss followed through on his promise to incorporate Governor Wallace into the decision-making process of the DNC. The first order of business was to elect the Executive Committee of the DNC. The group of 25 members was the day-to-day authority of the Democratic Party and set the policy and direction on the national level. Chairman Strauss offered a slate of members, which included me, to be adopted at the DNC meeting in Louisville, Kentucky, in early 1973. This slate was overwhelmingly elected, and for the first time ever, Governor Wallace had eyes and ears in the highest party council.

At the Democratic National meeting in Louisville, Kentucky, in 1973, after the McGovern debate, I was to be elected to the Executive Committee of the DNC to represent Governor Wallace, at the age of 23. The youngest person ever elected to the Executive Committee of the

DNC. *Jean Westwood was a committee liberal from Colorado and was the McGovern chairman defeated by Robert Strauss. I ran into her at the elevator, and she said she could not vote for me because I did not support McGovern in the '72 general election as the Democratic nominee. I said, 'Jean, let me ask you a question, if Governor Wallace is the Democratic nominee, will you support him?' She said, of course not, but that was different. That was the type of hypocritical logic rampant in the DNC.*

One major issue facing the Party was amending the delegate selection rules to reflect proportional representation. This was critical for a candidate like Governor Wallace because it diminished the influence of party bosses and insured that a candidate after reaching threshold level, (usually 10-15%) of the vote would receive delegates in direct proportion to the vote received. This would guarantee Governor Wallace's support nationally would be reflected in committed delegates at the nominating convention. We argued and fought over every comma and footnote but eventually hammered out rules that assured fairness. Unfortunately for Governor Wallace, Georgia Governor Jimmy Carter would be the biggest beneficiary of the rule changes in 1976.

During the years between 1973 and 1976, the Wallace campaign participated in every event held by the National Democratic Party. The 1974 mid-term convention in Kansas City, Democratic telethons in Los Angeles, and any other function where we thought we could make friends and influence policy. Also, during this period, the national campaign staff was growing, becoming more sophisticated in election strategy, and most of all raising money. I was promoted to Political Director and for the first time had a staff of young political operatives who fanned out across the nation to implement a national delegate selection strategy and solidify grassroots support. We put together a plan to compete for delegates in all 50 states and had the manpower and finances to implement the plan. Based on the Party rules and Governor Wallace's abilities, I really thought we could win the nomination in 1976, or at least had a fighting chance to compete nationally.

Unfortunately, many of Governor Wallace's supporters both nationally and locally were very distrustful of the Democratic Party and were still intent on establishing a third party in 1976. We had an uphill fight to convince skeptics that the Democratic primary process was the way to go. This hurt our momentum and solidarity and created friction among supporters. I remember people telling Governor Wallace I was a 'Liberal sell out' or 'DNC spy.' I knew Governor Wallace understood that a renewed third-party effort in 1976 would be doomed from the beginning, and he also knew the new Democratic Party rules favored a candidate with broad appeal and grassroots support, similar to his strengths.

Governor Wallace had a photographic memory. It was the greatest attribute in my opinion, and I have never seen anyone else come close to his ability to recall names, dates, events and vote results. He could tell you how many votes he received in any of Alabama's sixty-seven counties in any race he ever ran, and he ran in a lot of them! He could tell you how many votes he received in each state in the presidential races of 1968, 1972, and 1976.

The ability to remember each voter's name and details of their life is invaluable to a politician and Governor Wallace was the master. Many candidates think campaigning and "Pressing the flesh" is a chore and burden, to Wallace it was everything. He thrived on campaigning, sometimes having 5 or more rallies in one day, talking to everyone, remembering them and details of their lives at each stop. Calling a man or woman by their first name is an endearing quality and inspired tremendous loyalty.

I saw Governor Wallace do the same thing in Florida in 1972, talking with a supporter from 1968 and saying, 'Hello James, good to see you again. I remember seeing you in Daytona in '68. How's your wife, Mary, and your three children?' It was unbelievable the effect this ability to personalize and befriend a person had on their self-esteem and was invaluable.

Governor Wallace was a 'Perfect storm' of a politician. He was tireless, enthusiastic, a great orator, witty, had a photographic memory, and most importantly, had an innate sense of the pulse of the voters. He knew what to say and how to say it to get the desired effect. I always thought of him as a pure thoroughbred candidate, superior to all the other national candidates in ability, and if he was from Ohio or California, and didn't have the racial issue around his neck, he would have certainly been president already. One on one, he could outthink, outwit, and out campaign any other candidate.

The Florida Primaries in 1972 and 1976 were very pivotal for Governor Wallace in two stark and contrasting ways. In 1972, Governor Wallace entered the Florida Primary against a very crowded field of unknown candidates trying to gain traction for their campaigns. Florida was in Wallace's backyard, and we had it well-organized, and he received a whopping 42% of the votes against the national field. It was a huge blowout! The party rules allowed for 'Winner takes all' at the congressional district level so he received the vast majority, approximately 75% of the delegates. A far higher percentage of the delegates than the 42% of the vote he received. The 'Winner takes all' provision helped magnify Governor Wallace's landslide win in Florida but it would hurt his returns in other states, where the 'Winner takes all' provision rules were stacked against him. For instance, if he received 15% of the vote in a state with 100 delegates, he would receive none, having to reach a threshold of 20% to receive delegates. The DNC changed those rules to proportional representation for 1976, so Governor Wallace would receive 15 delegates in the example, and most importantly get to name them to insure candidate loyalty. The rule change would greatly help a candidate like Governor Wallace with widespread national support to reflect that strength in delegates at the '76 convention in New York City.

However, it had the opposite effect in Florida in 1976, the scene of his greatest triumph of 1972. Also, the Democratic candidates withdrew or ran limited campaigns there, leaving only Jimmy Carter to run against

Wallace. Their strategy was to let Carter knock out Wallace in Florida, and then gang up on Carter and knock him out later in the Midwest and New England states.

In 1976, Governor Wallace was doomed in Florida by the rule changes, the candidate conspiracy, and lastly by the press. They were poised to blast him as a 'Loser' if he received one vote or delegate less than in 1972. But the worst event occurred by chance in the Florida panhandle. Governor Wallace was boarding a plane after a rally and bumped his leg while being lifted onto the plane (he was in a wheelchair and paralyzed as a result of Bremer's assassination attempt in 1972) and he cracked a leg bone and did not know it until later. This was the death of the 1976 campaign as he was perceived as an invalid from that day on and never was represented as a viable candidate after that by the press. It was ironic to me that we had everything going for the campaign in 1976; money, staff, fair rules, weak candidates, and by chance we lost Governor Wallace's greatest asset, his vitality."

My grandfather, Henry Burns, "Mr. Henry," is what I called him.

Quarterback and Captain of the Clio High School football team in 1936.

With my boxing buddy. My father's left cheek is swollen from his latest match.

My father and his friend, Glen Curlee, taking a walk in Tuscaloosa, during their law school days.

Sergeant George Wallace with one of the B -29 pilots of his bombing crew.

Alabama state senate page: "Counting those votes and remembering."

Youngest member of the Alabama legislature at age 27.

My father would walk through a dirt field, wearing a suit to talk with a voter.

My father speaking to the folks, during the 1958 governor's race.

Cousin "Minnie Pearl" warms up the crowd at my father's 1958 kickoff rally for governor.

My mother, father, Bobbie, Peggy, and me at my grandmother's home in 1959.

"A man of the law."

1963 Governor's Inaugural Ball at Garrett Coliseum in Montgomery: His old friend, Oscar Harper, on the left.

First Inauguration of Governor Wallace, January 14, 1963.

President Kennedy and my father departing Air Force One in Huntsville in 1963. "There was tension in the air."

On the way to a briefing from the military on Vietnam in 1964.

*My father visits with President
Lyndon Johnson in Washington in
1964.*

*My father visits with his friend,
Chiang Kai-shek, President of Taiwan
in 1968.*

*Meeting with President of South
Vietnam, during his Southeast Asia
trip in 1968.*

*With Hubert Humphrey in
Montgomery in 1971.*

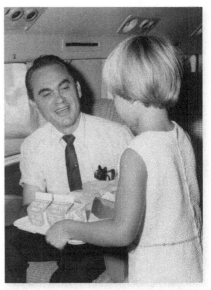

Visiting with Roy Acuff backstage at "The Grand Ole Opry" in Nashville, Tennessee, in 1964.

My sister, Lee, serves my father lunch on the 1968 presidential airplane.

My mother and father visit with comedian, Jack Benny, in 1967.

Three Alabama Legends: Paul "Bear" Bryant, my father, and Ralph "Shug" Jordan in 1971.

The classic, "Wallace Fire and Brimstone."

Mother as a beautiful young woman.

Mother arrives at the Capitol for her swearing in as Alabama's first woman governor.

The famous, "Turkey Picture."

Mother and my father, with Mayor of Mobile, Lambert Mims, the morning of her inauguration.

```
AB211
NSD644 NS MYB246 (A LLB274) PDB FAX
ATLANTA GEORGE WALLACE
THE CAPITOL BLDG. MONTGOMERY ALA.

ON BEHALF OF MYSELF AND MY CHILDREN,
WE OFFER OUR SINCEREST SYMPATHY AND
CONDOLENCES IN YOUR BEREAVEMENT. AS A
WIDOW, I AM ACUTELY AWARE OF THE AWESOME
BURDEN THRUST UPON A SURVIVING PARENT.
IT IS AS A CHRISTIAN MOTHER THAT I
EXPRESS MY FAMILY'S HEARTFELT SYMPATHY
TO YOU AND YOURS. WE SHALL OFFER OUR
PRAYERS FOR GOD'S CONTINUING BLESSING. I
WANT TO QUOTE ONE OF MY LATE HUSBAND'S
EXPRESSIONS OF HOPE AND FAITH:

"ONLY WHEN IT IS DARK ENOUGH CAN YOU SEE
THE STARS."

SINCERELY
MRS. MARTIN LUTHER KING JR. AND CHILDREN
```

Condolences sent from Coretta Scott King, for the death of Lurleen Wallace, May 7, 1968.

CHAPTER THREE

George Wallace, the Masterful Politician

SOME POLITICAL SKILLS OF GEORGE WALLACE

The days in the political wilderness for my father following the 1958 race and prior to the 1962 governor's race were filled with travel and organizing. It was obvious that he was extremely depressed for a time after the 1958 loss, but he pulled himself together and hit the ground running. One of the first things he did was to contact all of Governor Patterson's supporters and work to get them on board for his race in 1962. My father was notorious for reaching out to people who had been his political adversaries and working to bring them over to his side.

The stories are legendary of his calling people and building personal relationships with them. I have heard stories over the years from people who did not intend to support him. He would call them and as they would tell me, "He was just so damn charming that I could not resist." That is a political skill that is invaluable, and those same persuasive qualities served him well as governor. I have told the story of his dialing a wrong number and start to talk to the person even though he realized he had misdialed. When the person on the other end of the phone realized it really was Governor Wallace, they of course were thrilled and then the conversation would begin. Let's say perhaps this person lived in Jackson County. Well, my father invariably would know as many people in Jackson County as the person to whom he was talking. He would ask about their family and find all kind of connections with this Alabamian and have a fine twenty-minute conversation. He would end by saying, "Tell everyone, hello, and call if I can help you. I love Jackson County." What is significant about this call was that he had the genuine patience and need to talk to folks and was truly interested in how everyone was doing. The people he talked to knew this and that endeared my father to them.

HIS SPEAKING ABILITY

As my father's reputation grew, his speaking schedule across the nation picked up and he drew demonstrations for and against him wherever he appeared. As he traveled, his agenda included a strong law and order stand, tax relief for the middle class, reining in a Washington bureaucracy out of control, winning the war in Vietnam conventionally, and halting the political games being played in Washington with the war. These and so many other issues and positions he embraced captured the imagination of the voters from all across the nation. Not only were the issues important to his increasingly expanding base of support, but it was also his speaking style coupled with the message that moved and stirred people in a visceral way.

Dr. Billy Graham, who was a dear friend of my father, once told him, "George, you are one of the finest orators of the twentieth century," at which time my father replied to Dr. Graham, "No, Billy you are, because your message of hope through salvation is much more important than any political message I convey."

My father had a unique way of speaking straight to the real concerns of the working-class voters of the nation with the ability to articulate their concerns and inspire them at the same time. George Wallace became to millions of Americans the very embodiment of their frustrations. He had the charisma and energy as a public speaker that moved audiences of thousands to a level rarely seen in American politics.

HIS UNDERSTANDING OF PEOPLE

On occasions my father would say, "Son, people are funny." This quote would come after perhaps a conversation he had with someone or an experience I had related to him about someone. To me, it revealed a sense of humor that he attached to the human condition. In politics, people come at you in all kinds of ways. Many of the people who surround you are sincere and dedicated to the causes to be fought. On the other hand, there are those who are motivated by a sense of self-interest only, and that at times can be easily recognized or it might take time for it to reveal itself. There are subtleties involved in that many hold a combination of both motivations. While they are loyal to the message and cause, they are at the same time looking for opportunities for economic gain. All this is part of human nature, so a successful politician has to sort through all of the idiosyncrasies of those who surround you. You must be careful and have a good read on the deepest motivations of the people closest to you. He once told me, "Son, sometimes it is your friends who will get you trouble. You know your enemies are after you but you have to watch both your friends and enemies."

HIS MENTAL FOCUS

He had a unique way of tossing things aside mentally and putting them out of his mind as insignificant. This was a manifestation I believe of his thinking and dreaming larger than most people do. It was just in him, and when his time arrived, he was comfortable and confident on the national stage. With all the scrutiny and criticism he received, he faced it with the aura of a man possessed by his beliefs and devotion to those beliefs.

People saw this, felt this, and responded to it, and thus the Wallace phenomenon was born.

As observant and focused as my father could be in certain areas of life, he became easily distracted in other areas, especially when he went into deep thought as he so often did. I believe we can safely assume that the deep thought into which he had entered was political in nature. There were times when my father was driving and smoking his cigar and was oblivious to anything around him. He was in deep thought as he passed people on hills to Mother's horror as she would tell him to be careful. Or, he would take a curve too fast as Mother once again made her displeasure known. I am not certain today if he ever heard any of her eloquent admonishments. He was an interesting man to have driving you around, and to this day I have not ridden with anyone else who drives an automobile quite the way he did. And I hope I never do!

My mother and father had an accident on their anniversary many years ago while on their way to eat oysters at a popular oyster bar near Clayton. It seems that a bridge was out and the flares that had been set off to warn motorists had been extinguished by the rain, and thus there was no warning. They plunged into a creek at which time the car turned over and the front windshield ended up on the creek bank. They emerged from the car fortunately unhurt and waved down a passing farmer for assistance. What was indeed fortunate was that my sister, Bobbie Jo, was planning on going, but did not go at the last minute. Mother told Bobbie the next morning, while braiding her pig tails for school, that she and her father had been in an accident the night before. What Mother knew was that had Bobbie gone she would have been sitting in the back seat, and easily could have been thrown from the car and seriously injured or killed.

MY FATHER AND HITCHHIKERS

One more story about my father's driving habits concerns how he would, over the years, pick up hitchhikers as we were riding down the road. They were usually young men, many of whom looked to be down on their luck, and many were from the Barbour County area. My father would ask them about their families and then talk to the young men about what they were doing and what their plans were for the future. My father would actually lecture them in a way that did not seem like a lecture at all. He spoke to them in a kind and caring way about the need to get all the education they could. He would tell them they could be anything they wanted to be if they would apply themselves and believe in themselves. I was always interested in what he had to say to the hitch-hikers [sic], and I remember he would give them a little money when he would drop them off.

THE FAMOUS WALLACE RALLY

I always looked forward to the campaign season although I am certain not as much as my father did. I don't think I will ever know anyone who looked forward to campaigning more than he did. This was a time when politicians moved among the people more than they do today. The sights and sounds I recall of Confederate flags, bumper stickers, the sound of country music and the Wallace girls, ready to pass the buckets for the dollar bills or whatever people could afford to give, are etched in my memory forever. It was truly a magical event. While other candidates in Alabama have attempted to hold political rallies, the main ingredient missing was a candidate with the charisma and dynamic personality of a George Wallace. His ability and innate talent to reach inside people and tap into their feelings about issues and the South is legendary, and all I can say is you had to be there to know the total experience. I watched my father over the years take an audience to a level that in some instances even surprised him. He had not only the capacity to relate to them and that he knew what they were thinking, he also would bring up subjects that perhaps they had not thought about and take them on a journey of discovery within themselves. It has been said that when he was on his game in the '60s, and speaking to an audience, they were about to have an unforgettable experience.

Technology has given us many things, but it has also taken away some of our richest political traditions and customs that gave politics its richness and flavor. Today, the focus is on the poll numbers and the media strategy, rather than a grassroots effort to see the people. It all comes down to who can raise the most money and buy the most media. For everything gained, there is something lost.

From town to town the advance teams would travel in station wagons with speakers attached to the top with Wallace signs and stickers covering the automobile. They were the town criers of a coming Wallace rally. The teams would drive all through the community and announce who the entertainers were and what time everything would begin. I recall an instance in 1958 when the rumor somehow got started that Elvis Presley would be there. I do know that increased the number of people who came, but do not recall how disappointed they were that Elvis was absent. It is ironic to note that years later, Elvis Presley would call my father quite often, especially after he had been injured. Elvis would offer my father any of his vacation homes around the world and said he would have his plane pick him up. He would tell my father that, "We Southern boys need to stick together." As a matter of fact, Elvis said he had placed a Wallace for President sign on the front lawn of Graceland during the 1968 campaign. I do not know if that is true but Elvis told my father that. Elvis also told him one night that he would like to spend five minutes alone with Arthur Bremer, the man had who shot my father.

The Wallace rally has become a large part of Alabama folklore. There will probably never be an event that captures the true nature of Southern politics as did a good old-fashioned Wallace Rally.

I will always see the faces in my mind of the people who came to the rallies. In James Agee's *Let Us Now Praise Famous Men*, the many pictures in Agee's work of the people of the South who had to endure the Great Depression, will give you some idea of the people I saw as a child. They possessed a quiet strength and a steadfast stoicism that spoke of what they had endured. The look in their eyes spoke of the harsh realities with which they had to live, and it left its mark on their face and in their soul. Embraced within this was the faith and goodness of a proud people and a people searching for hope. I believe my father gave them hope and helped to restore a lost sense of pride in being from the great Southland. As I moved among these people and felt their kindness and goodness I was transformed, and deeply affected by the experience. I know that as the years passed and I eventually became involved in public service, that experience never left me and shaped my actions while serving in public office.

He had arrived at the outskirts of the site of the rally an hour before sundown. As the band played, he would usher various leaders from the community into the back seat of his black Ford LTD and talk about what they might need and how he could help them. He would smoke his cigar and develop an intimacy with them they would always cherish. This was George Wallace at his best, in having someone close to him physically, and simply overwhelming them. As his legend grew, that aura became larger and more powerful, and it had a mesmerizing effect on people that was intriguing to observe. They felt as though they were in the presence of living history, and the connection he had with them was genuine.

As he looked out the window after the last local leader had left, he saw the people beginning to crowd around the stage, floodlights shining brightly on the sequined coat of the Grand Ole Opry star and lighting up the Confederate Stars and Bars as an Alabama breeze blew her gently in the night. This was his time. This was when he felt alive and at his best. He looked at the faces of the people through the blue haze of his cigar smoke, and he knew they were his strength. They had longed for someone to take them on a journey, and he was certainly doing that. He exited the car and as he started making his way to the edge of the crowd people, as they turned, recognized him and here they came. "There's the governor there, I want to tell him about my Uncle Huber and how he is doing. You see they grew up not far from each other," said a lady as she and her friends moved to intercept him. Another old man said, "Well there's George, I've always wanted to shake that man's hand." My father did not make it to the stage and he probably knew he wouldn't, but it gave time for Doug Benton to work the crowd into a heightened state of excitement as he talked about how Governor Wallace represents you. By the time my father hit the stage, the sun was going down and there was magic in the air. As he looked out over the crowd while strutting back and forth across the stage saluting his troops, his mind might have taken him back in time. He might have been thinking of how hard he had worked to get here and the sacrifices that were made by his family. I believe he also thought about his success, and realized he was touching people in a way that far transcended that of any contemporary politician in Alabama.

As the lights hit him, his black suit and black hair were shining as he took the microphone with an ease and command that spoke of his many years before the people. He told them how good it was to be with them again, and he slowly built them into a state of raw excitement. He hit them where they lived. He told them how for so many years they had been looked down upon and cast aside as irrelevant. They had been told they were backwoods Southerners who were unsophisticated and not as intelligent as the elite in the North. Here he was fighting for the South and the Southern people once again.

Who were their ancestors that others should question the blood running in their veins? Their ancestors were the great Anglo-Saxon people from Western Europe, who had built civilizations and birthed cultures with art and learning. George Wallace defended his people on national television and gave those national commentators, who were so disrespectful toward him, a good dose of Southern pride. He had tapped into a deep reservoir of resentment among Southern people, and I have often thought it was deeper than they realized. He, like no other, had become their champion and Alabama will never again see one of his kind. Here was the perfect example of the man, hour, events, and time in history coming together as though the stars were aligned for this moment in time.

He told them he was their instrument and that their critics were not trying to silence him, but rather they want to silence those of you here tonight. "It is those of you here tonight they fear, not me. They know that a movement has started in Alabama that has captured the imagination of working people all across this nation."

These topics brought roars from the crowd not only for their content, but his unique defiant style of delivery. Here was their hero and defender saying things they felt inside, and this man, George Wallace, was becoming in an historical context, John the Baptist, lighting the way for the ultimate savior of the modern conservative movement, Ronald Reagan. In many respects, these speeches, and his overall philosophy about the role of government in our lives, was the genesis for the Reagan Revolution. Who was to know at that time that in later years there would be discussions between my father and Ronald Reagan about them being a presidential and vice-presidential team in 1968?

THOSE FEDERAL JUDGES

One of his favorite targets were Federal Judges and the Federal Courts and this was always a topic that brought one of the loudest roars from the crowds. He would tell them: *"My friends, the Federal Judiciary in this country is out of control. They have more power over your life and the lives of your family and your property than all the legislatures and Congress put together. Why you wouldn't know a Federal Judge if you saw him walking down the street, but he has more control over your life than the Constitution intended. Thomas Jefferson, a great Virginian, warned us of an all too powerful Federal Judiciary. These judges are appointed for life my friends and it seems as though some of them have become so senile, they have lost their reason."* As the crowd would cheer, he would top it off with a story about Chief Justice Earl Warren. *"My friends, your governor was invited to a state dinner in Washington, DC recently, one of those black tie and tails shindigs, and in attendance was Chief Justice Earl Warren. I made mention in my remarks to the Chief Justice that I parted my tails the same way he did before I sat down. You see, Mr. Chief Justice, we know how to do that in Alabama.* At this the crowd would roar with laughter.

THOSE BIG CITY NEWSPAPER EDITORS AND THE NATIONAL MEDIA

He thoroughly enjoyed making fun of the big city newspaper editors. As he would tell his audience, *We [sic] have many of the editors making fun of us and what we represent ladies and gentlemen, but I want you to remember one thing about these ivory tower pundits. The opinions they write are just that, the opinion of one person. And that one person's opinion, assessment and judgment of things is no better than yours. As a matter of fact, yours is better because you work for a living, pay the taxes, fight the wars and maintain the stability and order in our society.* He would throw in a humorous aside during his speech in talking about some of the newspapers. As he would pick up a glass of water to take a drink he would say, *Now, my friends, for the benefit of the Birmingham News, I want them to know that this is water and not something else. If they don't believe it, they can take a drink of it, but I don't think they want to drink after me because they'd be afraid they'd get some of what I've got. Actually, what I've got would be good for them, so if they want a drink here it sets.*

He would then turn his attention to the national television commentators by saying. *I am reminded, and you have seen them, of some of these television commentators with their melodious voices sounding as though what they have to say has come down from the mount. Why they have about as much common sense as some of those pseudo-intellectual [sic] professors who can't park a bicycle straight.*

I want you to know tonight that this movement has captured the imagination of people all across this country. Your courage and patriotism give hope and inspiration to people from Manhattan to Malibu.

These so-called experts on everything are the same people who called Fidel Castro the Robin Hood of the Caribbean. Why, my friends, all you had to do was ask a good cab driver in New York City, and he would have told you Castro was a Communist by looking at him. When your governor spoke to the National Press Club in New York City, I asked them why they didn't have a woman as a member of their club. They told me it was not their custom or tradition, at which time I asked them why they were so intent on changing the customs and traditions of those of us in the South. My friends, they didn't give your governor the traditional gift as a token of appreciation for appearing before them. No, they didn't give me one, but they gave Fidel Castro one, so as far as I am concerned, they can take their gift and they know what they can do with it.

RECAPITULATION STORY

One of his favorite stories was the "Recapitulation Story." When he entered the three presidential primaries in 1964 in Wisconsin, Indiana, and Maryland he received a very respectable vote that surprised the so-called political gurus nationally, and within Alabama. Some of the large newspapers in Alabama even wrote that "Governor Wallace will embarrass Alabama and he will be made a laughingstock." The last laugh would be on some of the press when he received a huge vote in these three states upon entering their presidential primaries. In one of these states, he was at one time leading in the votes cast until about ten o'clock and as my father was fond of telling it, *The head recapitulator came on television and he said after a thorough recapitulation of the vote, Governor Wallace is now behind.* As the crowd would groan at the insinuation that Governor Wallace's vote had been tampered with he would say, Well my friends I don't know what recapitulation means, but if anybody ever tells you they're gonna recapitulate on you, you better watch 'em cause they're fixing to do something to you. This story always received a huge response, and it appealed to a Southerner's sense that we are on to you.

DO YOU HAVE CHANGE FOR AN EIGHTEEN DOLLAR BILL?

One of his favorite jokes was about the two traveling conmen from up north who found themselves on a rural country road in the heart of Alabama. They drove up to a country store where they saw a grizzled old-timer sitting on the front porch whittling.

They thought they would stop and pull a fast one on him by asking for change for an eighteen-dollar bill. They eased up to the front porch of the store while an old blue tick hound slept at the feet of the old man. "How you doing, old-timer," asked one of the men as they approached him. "I'm doing fine, what brings you fellas down South?" "Well, we were just hoping you could help us out old-timer and wondered if you could give us change for an eighteen-dollar bill?" The old man didn't hesitate in responding to them by saying. "Why I sure can, do you boys want it in two nines or three sixes?" From a psychological perspective this joke was a salve to the wounds Southerners had felt for too long. They had been looked down upon and were thought to be ignorant and unsophisticated. They had been taken advantage of and this bit of humor spoken from their champion released pent up frustrations.

As he finished his speech and told the crowd to, "Stand up for Alabama," the people began to surge to the front of the flatbed trailer, reaching up to him and trying to touch him. As he would lean over to shake hands, his security men would hold him by his belt to keep him from being pulled into the crowd. The shouts of, "We love you, Governor," and "You tell 'em, George," were almost deafening, as some youngsters actually climbed up on the trailer to shake his hand and hug his neck. The connection he had with the people was magical and is now legendary, and stories I hear even today by people who were at some of those rallies always take me back in time. They take me back to a time and place before so much of the pain that would make its way into our lives had arrived. But be certain, it was on its way.

As my father was shaking hands, people would hand him cards or a piece of paper with their name, address, and phone number and say, "We're for you governor so call if we can ever help you." My father would stuff those pieces of paper in his pockets and when he returned to Montgomery, they went into his ever-increasing database of supporters. That person would receive a letter from my father thanking them for their support, and inside would be an autographed picture along with an honorary certificate making them a member of his staff. The system the Wallace Campaign, over the years, had put into place was a well-oiled machine. It was the most efficient and comprehensive political organization the state of Alabama had ever seen. As my father was working the crowd following one of these stump speeches, the bumper sticker crews were hard at work putting bumper stickers on the cars of those who had attended the rally. The crews were set up at every intersection for several blocks circling the rally site, and as we would leave town, virtually every car to be seen had a Wallace sticker on it. I am reminded of the first hit by Charlie Daniels back in the seventies when he penned a lyric that said, "Why, they even went as far as tearing Wallace stickers off the bumpers of cars." At that time, wearing a Wallace bumper sticker on your car was almost a sacred act for many people. They wore it proudly as an outward sign of their innermost feelings about this man, George Wallace. The Wallace bumper sticker crews were fast, efficient, and convincing as they with a cloth in one hand, wiped the bumper clean, and with the other hand slapped a bumper sticker on. They would ask the driver if they needed any extras for their family and friends, and then move on to the next car.

THE END OF A CAMPAIGN DAY

As the car pulled off, he would be leaning out the window saying, "Thank y'all so much for standing with us. Lurleen and I love you; tell 'em hello, and goodbye folks." This being done he would lean back, light his cigar, and sometimes close his eyes as he thought about the day. He would have several more of these days in front of him, and many miles to go as the poet had told us before he could rest. He thought about the special projects he had discussed with the local leaders, and how he would need to let the various departments know to contact the local folks about the specifics and get it done. There were always people around him who took notes and followed up for him on these projects, but he never failed to follow up himself, to make certain it had been done.

He looked out the window as he traveled through his beloved Alabama, and as he looked upon the fields and the people going about their lives, he might have been thinking of his father and grandfather. His father and grandfather were the main influences in his life, and their words early in his life affected him profoundly. So much of what he had heard them talk about relative to the needs of the people had left a deep impression on him.

CHAPTER FOUR

Time of Contemplation

HIS REFLECTIONS ON THE ISSUE OF SEGREGATION

He took a long puff of his cigar, and as the orange glow lit up his face, it revealed sadness in his dark eyes as he gazed into the Alabama night and thought about this bargain he had made. He of all people had felt the deepest empathy for the less fortunate and the downtrodden and that included Black citizens of Alabama as well. It could be no other way because of his depth of feeling for all humanity.

I know he ached inside when he thought about the four young girls killed in the 16th Street Baptist Church bombing. Precious children's lives taken prematurely by mad men. He could have reflected on how after this act of hateful violence, militants had threatened his own children, and as he looked upon the lights of approaching cars, he might have imagined that this was the glow at the end of the tunnel that would light his way through the abyss in which he was now traveling. The abyss of the race issue and how there seemed to be such a distance between people and how he had been, he knew, a catalyst for some of this. He again leaned his head back and closed his eyes. It was late into the night now and he was exhausted. It would be good to get back to Montgomery and try and get a good night's sleep. As he drifted in and out of sleep resting peacefully, his body jerked when he thought of the segregation issue. It caused agitation in him as he considered the extreme emotions the issue brought forth in people. He had fueled much of this and the bargain he had made would take him on a journey of discovery within himself. The journey to be certain would be filled with all the elements this Faustian bargain of his choosing could bring. And from that journey, the lessons learned, I believe, are lessons that should be studied today as an example of how changing the heart ultimately leads to understanding and hope for the future of relations between people. With the racial divide we see today between people, the journey of George Wallace is one of the most enlightening and inspirational examples in American history of how we should approach this racial divide. What an irony this is, but how poetic. These destinations would be reached, but there would be much pain for my father physically, mentally, emotionally, and due to this pain, a spiritual awakening. Due to his familiarity with being on the brink of death, his heightened sensitivity for our common humanity would be his ultimate destination.

Knowing the momentum the Civil Rights movement had gathered and the volatility of the issue, especially in the South, he was torn about advocating the perpetuation of a segregationist society, one that he knew put him on the wrong side of history. He certainly knew how people felt about race and the reasons the issue ran deep with people. Blacks and whites had come from different historical cultures. He was cast in the role of being a divider rather than a unifier, and this went against everything he had done publicly and privately for his entire life until now. His life experience from the time he was a small boy was one of being taught that a segregationist society was in the best interests of all people both Black and white. There was part of him at one time that believed this, but time began to take its toll on such a belief because of his conscience, and his understanding that our common humanity must be nurtured and not starved. This ultimate conclusion was simply a revelation of who he truly was as a person. He was born with this, and he died with this.

He would ultimately in large measure transcend this issue with the life he would live and all he would endure, but for now he had become the embodiment of defending segregation. It was the race issue largely that had gotten him to this point, and it only confirms V.O. Key's assertion in *Southern Politics,* that race tends to always manifest itself in Southern politics. My father seized this issue early on with vehemence and a defiance that would set the stage for what was to come.

GEORGE WALLACE'S BRAND OF SOUTHERN POLITICS

The 1962 race for governor was a moment when the man and the hour met. George Wallace would be the next governor of Alabama and become a national political figure within a matter of months. Much has been written and talked about concerning the race and his position on the issue of segregation that propelled him into the governor's office. It has been written that following the 1958 race for governor, my father saw clearly that the issue of segregation was paramount on peoples' minds, so he took the hard line on this issue and drove it home in 1962. Whereas Governor Patterson had the stronger position on this issue in 1958, my father's decision to talk more about this in 1962 was a political decision. I recall my father saying that how in 1958 he would talk about education, economic development, roads, and other quality of life issues, and the people barely responded, but when you talked about the need to maintain a segregated society, as he said, "They stomped the floor." That was the burning social issue at the time, not only in the South, but also in other parts of the country. As time would pass, we would see that in many respects the people of the South, while struggling with the issue, would come to terms with it better than those in other parts of the country.

While there can be no legitimate reason for having a segregated society, it was the custom and social structure that prevailed at that time in the South and generally throughout the nation. The people of the South understood fully the need to do all that they could to raise the educational level and proficiency of the Black population. Until *Brown vs. The Board of Education* in 1954, the policy under which our society operated was based upon the Supreme Court ruling in the case *Plessy vs. Ferguson* in 1896 that gave us the "Separate but Equal" Doctrine. This was the policy, although any thinking person understood that black people did not truly have the opportunities necessary to provide them the education and hope necessary for success under the "Separate but Equal," ruling.

As my father's early career has been analyzed and studied there has never been a suggestion, other than from his harshest critics, that he held any ill will, malice, or racist feelings in his heart or mind toward Black people. The acceptance of the social institution of segregation in the South was not, as has been suggested by many writers and others who do not understand the Southern people, consistent or synonymous with hate or ill feelings. Now, there were some exceptions to that rule, but generally, the Southern people accepted segregation as they accepted the other norms and traditions in their lives. Their acceptance of it was part of their socialization and upbringing. Knowing my father as I did, I knew him to be a man of great compassion and concern for the underdog and downtrodden. As I have discussed before, his experience during the Great Depression growing up in the rural South molded and shaped him. The poverty and deprivation he witnessed and experienced as a young man in Barbour County, Alabama, gave birth to a profound empathy for the needs of all people, both black and white. Of all the people he saw who were suffering the most during the Great Depression, he realized it was Black folks who had the greatest burden to bear.

The inclination of much of our media culture and some historians today, is to focus only on my father's early positions, and not record an honest and complete assessment of his life and journey. An assessment in totality is how our lives are truly judged. It is at best intellectually dishonest and disingenuous that these critics, supposedly being the most insightful, reflective, and objective among us in their own minds, lose all those fine qualities when it comes to my father. Therefore, they become what they hold in such contempt—that is those who are biased, intolerant, and clearly less than objective. It seems they live in a hypocritical world, setting their own political agenda based upon ignoring the truth when it is convenient. That agenda in no way serves our country and the greater good. In thinking about this, I have always found it quite hypocritical that many pundits, editorialists, writers of history, and other shapers of opinion go to great lengths to rehabilitate Hugo Black and Robert Byrd. These men were both members of the KKK and uttered some of the vilest words about Black people you have ever heard. My father always fought the Klan, and I never heard him disparage a people the way Hugo Black and Robert Byrd did. They of course in their later lives disavowed their earlier positions, and the mainstream media took them under their wing and worked to reshape their image. I can hear my father now asking a member of the national media as frankly as he could, *You folks rehabilitated Hugo Black and he belonged to the Klan; I always fought the Klan, why don't you tell the truth about me?*

Politics in Alabama as in other Southern states has a special flavor and spice which is uniquely Southern and provincial. The Southern people have long held in high esteem those who seek to serve and do serve in public office. While there has been a national trend for some time, toward deep cynicism for those in public office relative to trust and confidence, I believe the Southern people and the people in Alabama still work to hold onto the most cherished ideals of public service, such as honesty, dedication, duty, and seeking the greater good for the long-term best interest of our people.

The words duty and faith have a special significance for me as I spoke of them while introducing my father when he took the oath of office for his fourth term as Alabama's Governor, in January 1983. I asked my father if I could introduce him to give his inaugural address in January 1983, and the following is my introduction of my father:

My Friends,

We are gathered together today on the steps of this state capitol, in an historic moment. We are witnesses, on this day and in this hour, to the greatness which truly binds all of us together as a people. For we are today, heirs to that first freedom which was heralded to the world at another time and in another place: That spirit of free men everywhere which had its birth in 1776.

We celebrate today not the victory of one individual over another, nor do we rejoice at one party's win over the other's defeat. Rather, we celebrate today the right to peacefully govern ourselves; We [sic] celebrate the freedom to democratically choose who from among our own ranks, shall be asked to lead. We celebrate the right of every citizen, regardless of race, religion, age or station in life, to enter into the workings of this Republic and cast our votes in accordance with the dictates of our own hearts. We celebrate the right to determine, without fear and without hesitation, what our own destiny shall be as God gives us the light to see that destiny.

You, the people of Alabama, have determined that these next four years are years of challenge for our state. You have determined that they are years that will require the best that is in each of us if we are to overcome our many problems. And you have determined that they are years in which stagnation must be converted into organized effort; despair must be converted into hope.

The man I am honored to introduce in this hour is no stranger to hope. He is no stranger to faith, and in my own humble estimation and judgment, he is no stranger to his God.

My father, and your governor [sic] for the fourth time, has stressed on more occasions than my memory will serve, two overriding values in his life: His unending faith in the Lord, and his unswerving faith in the people of Alabama. And I know from my own personal experience that as he begins the tremendous undertaking of these next four years, he will rely heavily upon both.

General Robert E. Lee once said: "Duty is the most sublime word in the English language. Always do your duty. You can never do more; you should never seek to do less."

The man who appears before you on this inaugural day to receive the oath of office as governor will do his duty, God willing. I know that in doing so, he seeks your encouragement, your continued support, and constant prayers.

It is now my privilege to introduce to you my father and your next governor, The Honorable George C. Wallace.

It is part of the beauty and goodness of the Southern people and is manifested in a Southerner's desire to look with hope toward the future with greater confidence in our system—more so than do some in other parts of our country. This is a real indicator of the belief and devotion Southerners have in our institutions, values, rule of law, respect for authority and the divine inspiration of our Constitutional principles. This belief and mindset make the Southern people unique and fiercely patriotic. The value system which they adhere to and seek to instill in their children is fundamental in its inextricable link between Constitutional principles and the Christian ethic. This philosophical value system is rooted to a large extent in the Southerner's history of confronting and overcoming deprivation, whether it was following the "War Between the States," the Reconstruction period, or during the Depression South that Franklin Roosevelt spoke about, when he called the South, "The nation's number one economic problem." These major experiences in the life of the South were felt to the very soul of the Southern people, and generation after generation spoke of these things with deep passion.

In my father's 1963 inaugural address, he spoke of the Southern people when he said, *We remind all within hearing of this Southland that a Southerner, Peyton Randolph, presided over the Constitutional Congress in our nation's beginning, that a Southerner, Thomas Jefferson, wrote the Declaration of Independence, that a Southerner, George Washington, is the Father of our country, that a Southerner, James Madison, authored our Constitution, that a Southerner, George Mason, authored the Bill of Rights and it was a Southerner who said, "Give me liberty or give me death," Patrick Henry.*

Southerners played a most magnificent part in birthing this divinely inspired system of freedom, and with God as our witness, Southerners will save it. The great writer, Rudyard Kipling, wrote of them, that: *There in the Southland of the United States of America, lives the greatest fighting breed of man, in all the world.*

Over the years, the good people of the South were referred to and depicted as mentally slow and backward via movies and television, and Southerners held a deep resentment for those who perpetuated these stereotypical myths. This was an affront to the dignity of a great people, and clearly ran counter to the understanding that some of the finest minds the country had produced were from the South. The often-mean-spirited portrayal of Southerners by Hollywood producers and directors is due largely to a political and philosophical agenda on their part, which is obviously contrary to the very essence of who Southerners are. Of the many burdens placed on the backs of those from the great Southland, this is just one more thing we endure, with the knowledge and understanding that our truth will be the ultimate victor.

There was an attempt early on by some in the media to correlate his positions with a mean spirit and almost primitive intent. This always brought forth his ire and disdain, because of the historical experience the South and Southerners had endured over time. My father, more than most, connected deeply with people about this feeling, and he fought back hard publicly in defending the genuine goodness of the Southern people. In doing this, he tapped a reservoir of pent-up desire within the innermost sanctum of the Southern people, and as so many people have told me over the years and continue until this very day, "George Jr., your father made me proud to be a Southerner."

Historically, there had been Reconstruction injustices perpetuated on the South, along with punitive measures such as, "The Chicago Freight Rates," that had been imposed on the South into the 1950s that contributed to economic hardship. These economic sanctions imposed on the South coupled with a condescending attitude many, but not all, "Northerners" had toward our region of the country, brought forth the fighting spirit of the people from the South. They had been waiting on their defender and an advocate of the truth about who and what they truly were.

As I have mentioned, some of the finest minds our country has produced have come from the South, and that trend clearly continues today. Of all the names of accomplished Southerners one could name, we need look no further than Thomas Jefferson who was truly a renaissance man and a man of Virginia. As John Kennedy on reflecting upon the great minds who had dined at The

White House said, *Of all the gatherings over the years of great minds to dine at the White House, the most wisdom and intelligence ever to grace the White House dining room was Thomas Jefferson when he dined alone.* In truth, if you look at the Southern culture over time it is found to be one of great sophistication and learning. Again, as my father so often said, *The people of the South are just as refined, intelligent and cultured as the people of any part of our country and we are proud of our history.* This said it all! He had, in just one sentence, captured the very essence of what the people of the South were feeling and had always wanted to say. He would lead and they would follow him anywhere, and they would together change the political landscape of the country. His leadership brought forward a movement in the country that became the genesis of the modern conservative movement in our country. It would reach far beyond the region of the South, as it would captivate people from all over the country, and in the final analysis become one of the most exciting political movements in American political history, and thus make him an international figure.

NEW YORK TIMES REPORTER GOES WITH MY FATHER TO CLIO

So, we have a *New York Times* reporter who has come to visit my father and they take a trip to Barbour County so the reporter can see the old home place and be introduced to some of the home folks. The time frame of this visit would have been in 1963 after his, "Schoolhouse Door" stand, so the reporter had great trepidation and grave doubt about my father and what he was all about. As would happen, while they were traveling Highway 82 east to Clio, they were passing a country store with four young tough-looking Black men standing outside the store. When my father saw them, he told the trooper to pull the car into the store. Before the car had stopped, he had jumped out and briskly walked up to the young,

Black men, shook their hands and asked them, "How you fellas doing?" They immediately surrounded him, shaking his hand and telling him how good it was to see him, and they were glad he had come home. My father asked about their families, calling many of them by name, and told them if there was ever any way he could help them to let him know. It was like old home week, family reunion and quite a spectacle for a *New York Times* reporter to see. As my father got back in the car after telling the men goodbye, he turned to the reporter and asked, *"Do you do that in New York City?"* The reporter was shocked and asked my father if he was not apprehensive about doing that and my father responded, *"No, you see the races in Alabama get along much better than you realize, and better than in some other parts of the country, including where you live in New York City."* He always noted what he considered certain hypocrisy by some members of the media who sought to perpetuate the idea that the only feelings between the races in the South were animosity and racism. It simply was not true, and history would prove that the ultimate transition from segregation to integration in the South was much more peaceful and understanding than in some other parts of the country.

My father knew as the rest of the country was learning that, in many, if not all cases, the real animosity and violence over the issue of race was revealing itself in other parts of the country more so than in the South. The real breakdown of law and order that occurred in other parts of the country such as Watts and Detroit, with race riots and the number of people killed spoke of a need for some members of the media to look at themselves and where they lived before judging the people of the South too harshly. This was a sermon my father preached and it resonated deep within the people of Alabama and always received a warm response even from audiences in other parts of the country. He found that the people of the country looked to the South for hope and inspiration and that being Southern was not a matter of geography, but rather a matter of the heart. He was fond of telling audiences over the years that, *You've never really heard the song "Dixie," until you have heard it sung in Polish, the way we heard it in Milwaukee, Wisconsin, the other night.*

SOUTHERN HEROES AND LOST CAUSES

It was a period of the South continuing to fight some of the same constitutional and philosophical battles that had been fought for so many years. It would be the last stand for causes and principles that were inherent within Southern culture. The social tradition and custom of separating the races some believed could be accomplished with more opportunities afforded to Blacks under the "Separate but Equal" ruling in *Plessy vs. Ferguson,* but the *Brown vs. Board of Education* ruling in 1954 made that strategy moot. As has been talked about, the "Separate but Equal," doctrine clearly had not been complied with by the letter or the spirit of the law in all those years before, and to suggest that Blacks had equal opportunity under the *Plessy vs. Ferguson* ruling was ludicrous on its face.

It would all be too late even when my father took his most controversial positions that defined him for many years. The issue of segregation was the political fuel that propelled him onto the national political stage, and while I believe he realized he would ultimately be defeated in the courts on the issue of segregation, I don't know if he could even imagine the profound redemptive and reconciliation, and forgiveness overtures that would ultimately follow when his journey took him to Dr. Martin Luther King's Dexter Avenue Baptist Church where he said, "I was wrong." From that point forward, the affection, understanding and forgiveness he received from the Black community helped restore his soul. This early fight for segregation would be lost as he probably knew it would be, and I believe he was glad when it was all over.

This conjured up fond memories of General Robert E. Lee and President of the Confederacy, Jefferson Davis, and many other heroes of the South, who the people of the South held in such high esteem. As leaders of the South, Lee and Davis in defeat understood the need to work to bring our country together and heal the wounds that had caused such pain. Likewise, one-hundred years later, my father and the South would experience a similar battle with segregation as an issue and following the dismantling of the social institution of segregation, my father also sought to heal wounds and build bridges among all people. George Wallace, Robert E. Lee, and Jefferson Davis all accepted their own individual defeats and political defeats with stoicism, gallantry, and an ultimate appeal to the Southern people to work for understanding, fairness, and justice. These men epitomized Southern manhood and were and are idolized by Southerners. There is a certain redemptive quality for the Southern culture of having fought the gallant fight and even in defeat finding heroes.

WALLACE POPULISM AND HIS VIEW OF THE ROLE OF GOVERNMENT

The authors, political writers, and pundits in seeking a definition of what captures the Wallace philosophy tend to define it as populism. I believe that puts us in esteemed company with the likes of Thomas Jefferson, Andrew Jackson, Theodore Roosevelt, and William Jennings Bryan. They understood as we do, that the greatness we have achieved as a people has not come from government, but rather from a free people in a free society who love their God, church, family, state, and institutions. These are our people who hold everything together and provide stability and order in our culture and society. Our hope rests upon them, and posterity awaits our decision. The death of the common man will violate and destroy the sacred covenant between our Founding Fathers and our posterity, and we do this at our own peril.

The deliberations in Philadelphia in 1787 were intended to craft a document that would be a living breathing testament to the sacredness of individual liberty, human freedom, and the rights of man. The earlier *Articles of Confederation* did not provide enough cohesion for our fledging country. Because of that, the individual states had their own trade policy, military units, monetary exchange, and other examples of independent policy that prevented them from working together with the other states as would be necessary. The *Articles of Confederation* prohibited a too strong Central Government, and the reason for this was based upon the experience of our framers with the tyrannical policies of King George III. However, witnessing the failure of the *Articles of Confederation* to accomplish what was intended, the framers convened in 1787 and established, "Checks and Balances" and our *Bill of Rights,* the first ten amendments, within our Constitution, so as not to allow any branch of government to be all powerful and omnipotent. This masterful concept has served our Constitutional Republic well, and the debates that occur from time to time relative to powers of the different branches are a healthy exercise for our country.

The central issue concerned the states and the powers they would retain, and how to blend those sovereign rights and powers with the power of the Federal Government. This debate has manifested itself in several instances in our history and was a contributing factor in bringing the War Between the States.

My father's era, in a political sense and from a Southerner's point of view, held dear to the proposition that the sovereignty of the states was explicitly given to the states in the 10th Amendment that reads, *All powers not expressly delegated to the Federal Government,*

nor prohibited by it are expressly reserved to the states and the people.
This steadfast belief beat deep within the hearts of the Southern
people, especially because of their fate at the hands of history.

Their apprehension and distrust of the Federal Government
was ignited by my father in a way that is now legendary. He was
one of the folks, he spoke for them, and they knew it. He became
the very embodiment of resistance to the encroachment of the
Central Government on the lives of our people in many respects.
Of course, the Civil Rights movement was the focal point of this
fight regarding states' rights, and it, more than any other issue in
our country's history, has tested the relationship between the states
and the Federal Government.

The story is well-documented of his "Segregation Forever"
speech and the "Stand in the Schoolhouse Door," but I am hopeful
that as time passes, his entire life's journey will be considered and
studied, because I have often thought that if he was a leader in
the "Old South," he was a leader in the "New South" as well. His
journey was a journey we all took. His coming to understand the
need for change was an understanding that the South and nation
came to understand, so the journey was made by us all.

I grew up in a segregated society as a young boy in the 1950s
in Barbour County, Alabama. There was total segregation between
Blacks and whites at that time as there was in most sections of the
country. I recall as a young boy walking around with my father in
downtown Clayton and how, as I have already mentioned, he knew
and talked to everyone. I recall that he treated everyone, Black and
white alike, with the utmost respect and that made an impression
on me. He was known as a fair and good man who cared for all
the people. Because of his inherent concern for everyone, I believe
in later years, during the turmoil of the Civil Rights era, he was
saddened and hurt by the portrayal of himself as someone who
was a racist and harbored hate in his heart. This myth to a large

extent was perpetuated by his enemies who sought to distort for their own political reasons his positions and his message. His message during this period ultimately was to allow the states to determine their own destiny relative to their local democratic institution. Within the power of self-determination would be the power to establish a time frame for the integration of Southern society. I know that my father believed integration was inevitable, and clearly, he used the issue to gain political power. Now that he had gained political power, he could have to live with this bargain he had made.

Herein lies the dichotomy of my father's political climb to national prominence. His entire political career up until the 1962 governor's race had been predicated on helping the less fortunate of all races. Now, because of the segregation issue, he was perhaps making a Faustian bargain for power, at the expense of many of those for which he had the most empathy.

I have always found it fascinating how many of our older Black citizens tell me that, "We knew Governor Wallace had to take those positions so he could help us." When you consider some of his earliest populist programs and reforms such as free textbooks, creation of the two-year college system, historic pay raises for teachers, including all our Black teachers, and new and expanded industry, it is understandable why many Black folks would make such comments. These initiatives helped Blacks as much or more than whites in Alabama. In addition, I think it speaks to the fact that they knew he was not a racist, but rather a politician. His earliest positions were political positions and were not based upon ill will, malice, or hate. I have always believed that because of his dynamic personality, aggressive stance against federal encroachment and his high-octane speech delivery, there were many who genuinely misunderstood the man and his mission. Still there were critics who because of their own agenda totally misrepresented his motives and positions. Part of their agenda was to continually represent Southerners as illiterate, mean-spirited, violent, and intellectually challenged. The reasoning for this is very clear in that if Southerners are portrayed in this light given the fact that they hold dear conservative values, then obviously their thinking must be flawed. There is a political agenda at work here that you can see in living color even today in so many ways when Southerners are portrayed in the movies and television. The great irony to me is that while the liberal elite seek to denigrate a great people, ironically it is those very people's values and willingness to fight for our country that will save our country and allow for those who seek to denigrate our region the freedom to do so. I am reminded of a quote I read years ago about the Southern people that reads: "Living is not all of life, dying is not all of death, I would rather live a short life of principle, than a long life of compromise."

My father's personal and political dilemma from an historical viewpoint was how to make certain the conservative message he carried across the country was what resonated, rather than his earlier position on segregation. I believe he felt as though the early years in many respects clouded the modern conservative message that made him a national figure. It is ironic that without his earlier political positions, he might not have been elected Governor of Alabama, and consequently would not have had the forum especially later in life to highlight the cultural change the South and our country had experienced.

Many national columnists and authors such as George Will, David Broder, Paul Greenberg, and Dan Carter to name a few, have written that he was the grandfather of the modern conservative movement blazing the trail for Ronald Reagan. Dan Carter, the eminent scholar from Emory University wrote in his book, *Politics of Rage,* that, "*George Wallace had more influence in shaping and molding the political environment than any other 20th century politician.*"

EMBRACING THE INEVITABLE—THE ISSUE OF RACE

It was the issue that caused him the most discomfort, yet he chose to rise to power with it. The race issue was the one issue that people were passionate about and he believed he had to embrace it. In so doing, I always sensed he had done it with regret. The issue of race was inextricably linked to the issue of "States Rights," and the sovereignty of the state to determine its own destiny, based upon the will of the people. His time had come, and he rose to power on the backs of the least among us, the Black folks of Alabama. These were people he had grown up with, understood, and had the most compassion for because of their plight as poor Blacks in the rural Depression South.

He would find himself in situations where people would say the cruelest things about Black people, and he developed over time, because I know that kind of hate talk made him uneasy, the ability to move the conversation to the Constitutional issues he was raising. I can hear him saying, *"Now, now folks, our fight is not with anyone, (Blacks), it is with the Central government trying to run every aspect of our lives and subjecting us by federal edict to all kinds of social engineering experiments.* Turning the conversation away from hate talk and attacking the Federal Judiciary satisfied the urges of the people without acknowledging their venom. He was bobbing and weaving as he did so well when he was a boxer. Passions ran deep on the issue of race, and there were times when he allowed himself to be drawn into conversations to satisfy the boys, and in so doing probably made statements he regretted even at the time.

It is interesting to note that after the initial "Segregation Forever" speech and the "Stand in the Schoolhouse Door" he with great fervor turned his attention to the Constitutional questions concerning state and federal relations. The great concern our Founding Fathers had concerning an all too powerful Central government was his standard speech. He made the argument, as that issue became linked to the 1964 Civil Rights bill, that there were provisions within the bill affecting private property rights, labor laws, and essentially engineering peoples' lives and businesses.

He ventured onto the Ivy League campuses in 1964 when he ran in three presidential primaries and lectured the students on the Constitution and the intrusive provisions of the Civil Rights bill, and in many instances so impressed the students with his knowledge and intelligence, that while they still did not support him, he won a grudging respect from them. And that included interestingly enough some of the professors. Their expectation of him early on was that he would be a redneck from Alabama who hated Black people. What they found was an articulate and reasoned man, who while taking the extreme opposite view from what they held, they nevertheless observed someone who was well-versed on the Constitution, and not some backwoods wild-eyed redneck. He, to the surprise of the many he encountered during these trips, represented and presented himself with dignity, intelligence, and a sense of sophistication that must have baffled them.

In thinking about those early days, I believe he worked to separate himself from race while still holding on to it somewhat, because so much of his early political base, frankly, was made up of people who thought only about race. He was able to begin to transcend race on the national scene when he talked about and hit a nerve with people concerning law and order, the federal bureaucracy, tax exempt foundations, playing politics with the war in Vietnam, foreign aid to those countries who as he said, "Turn and spit in our faces," and several other issues that no other politician on the national scene addressed quite the way George Wallace did.

Along with his message was that famous Wallace charisma that he had fine-tuned in the countryside of Barbour County, Alabama.

The reaction he had received from the home folks was now the reception he received all across the country to the amazement of all the national pundits. He had hit a nerve, and the train had left the station. It would gain momentum like very few national movements have in our nation's history and it of course came to an abrupt life changing end, in a Laurel, Maryland, shopping center parking lot on May 15, 1972.

When I consider the many changes destiny placed on my father, I am reminded of the quote that says, "Everything is revealed in its own time." I believe much was revealed to him as he lingered at death's door for so many days following his shooting, and the near-death experiences he had in the years following his shooting. He was a changed man inside and out, and he lived his life now as the man he really was and had, I believe, longed to be for so long. You could see it in his face as though he was relieved and his soul had been restored.

I recall a quote from Governor Lester Maddox of Georgia, who was one of his contemporaries, after my father's visit to Dr. Martin Luther King's church [sic] on historic Dexter Avenue in Montgomery, Alabama, in 1979, when my father told the congregation that he had been wrong about segregation and asked for their forgiveness. Lester Maddox said, "Well, Governor Wallace was lying then when he said he supported segregation, or he is lying now when he says he was wrong." As I think about that, I find that Lester Maddox missed it completely, and was probably incapable of understanding, because of his own personal racist views, anyone who would profess to having been wrong in supporting segregation.

His pilgrimage to Dr. King's church in 1979 was for him a sacred one. Stephan Lesher's book on my father, *George Wallace, American Populist* describes the moment. *Most dramatically he appeared unannounced at the Dexter Avenue Baptist Church in Montgomery, the church whose pulpit Martin Luther King Jr., occupied when he kindled the modern civil rights movement. And what made it more meaningful than any of his other acts of contrition was its timing, late in 1979, almost a year after he had left office and nearly two years before he decided to seek the governorship again. The visit was unannounced; there was no press; Wallace, two years from seeking office again, had no immediate political design. The singular symbolism of the moment must have pulsed through the congregation, "I have learned what suffering means. In a way that was impossible before (the shooting), I think I can understand something of the pain Black people have come to endure. I know I have contributed to that pain, and I can only ask your forgiveness.*

As my father's aid pushed him up the aisle, a member of the choir broke into a chorus of "Amazing Grace" while members of the congregation reached out to touch George Wallace with love, understanding and forgiveness.

The Alabama writer, Diane McWhorter, a self-described Wallace adversary, put it succinctly: *George Wallace may have said the three words probably never before uttered consecutively in the Old Confederacy: "I was wrong."* She could have added "or in the North" and cited such people as Earl Warren, who never apologized in his lifetime for his role in interning Japanese Americans during World War II.

My father knew, as our country needs to know today, that understanding and tolerance toward one another no matter our race or ethnic background, is the key to better days for our country when it comes to the issue of race. I believe strongly that it is as much a matter of the heart as it is a matter of the mind.

THE SIXTEENTH STREET BAPTIST CHURCH

Four beautiful children had been killed. On a beautiful Sunday morning, the holiest of sanctuaries, The Sixteenth Street Baptist Church in Birmingham had been shattered by a bomb. The blast took the lives of four precious little girls, and it also took some of my father's life. He was totally devastated and moved among us with deep despondency and sadness. This was not what he wanted at all. Was he to blame for the killing of innocent young girls worshipping on a tranquil Sunday morning? Was his rhetoric such that he was the cause of this, as so many of his national critics had claimed? This was not how it was supposed to be. He had always been a champion of the people and in his heart of hearts he loved all Alabamians, both Black and white. It could be no other way based upon his upbringing and what he had seen all people experience during difficult times in the South. His ambition and the bargain he had made were bringing home consequences he never imagined.

The Constitutional issues he had been raising relative to the sovereignty of the states as outlined by the Founding Fathers, led him into a direct and historic confrontation with the Federal Government. And all along the way, I believe he regretted that the issue of segregation was the cornerstone of this historical debate concerning the encroachment of the central government on states' rights.

The Black issue, the issue of segregation, and the deep feelings people had about separation of the races was of such historical precedent that his participation in it was a matter of course in his mind in order for him to be elected Governor of Alabama. He was the embodiment of resistance to the Federal Government intrusion, especially in the form of the Federal Judicial edicts, on the lives of his people. A large part of his rallying cry during those days was the Federal Courts, and in discussing this he always would quote Thomas Jefferson, James Madison, and other Founding Fathers who warned us about an all-powerful Federal Judiciary that would eventually thwart the will of the people. These issues took on a more powerful tone and significance due to the emotions that ran so deep concerning the segregation issue. The Constitutional questions being raised, standing alone without the race issue would have been significant enough, but that was not to be, and now he was caught up in one of the most historic cultural changes in our country's history.

Inside he knew, he had to know, the times would be changin' and to everything there surely would be a season. In many ways, the walls were closing in around him and Bob Dylan's words, "They'll shatter your windows and rattle your walls, for the times they are a-changin'" might have circled in his mind as he thought about the walls he had erected. Those walls would eventually come down by the forces of cultural change, brought on by his public recognition of our own common humanity. A bond that he had recognized, but in making his arguments in his defiant way, had been cast in such a light that it would be many years before the world would eventually come to know George Wallace the man. The man his family had always known.

That would be much later, but now it was said by some that the blood of four innocent young girls was on his hands. We had a home on Lake Martin that my father had bought for Mother after he became governor. Mother had grown up swimming and fishing in the Black Warrior River near Tuscaloosa and loved the water. Having a home on the water would give her and our family some sense of peace amidst all the controversy and hate that had come our way. I remember spending time at the lake during events such as my father's standing in the schoolhouse door, the Selma to Montgomery marches, and other times when the level of animosity toward our family had reached a level where the security personnel believed it best that we be in a secluded spot. Thus, our lake house became a haven and source of protection during some difficult days.

I recall a story my brother-in-law, Jim Parsons, told me about our time at the lake shortly after the 16th Street Baptist Church bombing. Jim was on our pier and my father came walking down alone and asked Jim how to operate the boat. Jim explained that you start the motor in neutral, push the throttle forward or pull back depending on which way you want to go. My father told Jim, thank you, cranked the motor, and took off across the lake. It must have been an odd sight for Jim to see my father driving the boat, as Jim was wondering where in the world he could be going. We could recall only a few occasions when my father had been in a boat, much less driving one, but there he was. Because of the horrific nature of the church bombing, he became the figure certain militant groups indicated they would harm. The church bombing, more than any other event during that time, caused a melancholy look in him that I will always remember. He had that melancholy mood with him as he rode around Lake Martin and pulled along piers to talk to people. I have often wondered what people thought as Governor Wallace pulled up to their dock and started talking to them. He had gone to the people all his life on land, so it was natural that he would take it to the water.

As he talked with people around the lake, the church bombing was all people seemed to talk about. My belief is that he was searching for someone to tell him it was not his fault. To have them say, "Why Governor that's not your fault, you didn't do that Governor." As much as he wanted to believe that and in a practical sense he knew that was true, something kept whispering to him, asking him was he to blame. No amount of time on the water talking to people would resolve that question for him. Only his conscience and much soul-searching over the years brought him a certain shrouded peace.

BLACK ATTORNEYS IN JUDGE WALLACE'S COURT ROOM

There are stories from prominent Alabama Black attorneys, who practiced law in front of my father when he was a circuit judge which speaks to and reveals the man he was and his feelings about Black people.

J. L. Chestnutt, a prominent, Black Civil Rights attorney from Selma, Alabama, relates the story of a case he had in my father's courtroom in the early 1950s. Mr. Chestnutt's clients were some poor, Black farmers who were in a dispute with some large landowners being represented by some high-priced attorneys from Birmingham. The attorneys for the landowners would refer to Mr. Chestnutt and his clients as, "Those people," rather than Mr. Chestnutt and his clients. When this happened, my father told the counsel for the landowners to approach the bench, and he told them that they would show the proper respect to Mr. Chestnutt and his clients in his courtroom, or he would hold them in contempt of court and put them in jail.

Another story related by Fred Gray, a prominent Black Civil Rights attorney from Tuskegee, Alabama, concerned how my father made certain that Mr. Gray and his Black clients had food brought to them during the lunch break. This was due to segregation and the fact that they could not eat in the restaurant in downtown Clayton.

My father was a fair man and that made him a fair judge. He never had a decision overturned by an appellate court, and that is quite a tribute to his knowledge of the law. As a judge, he always had sensitivity for the poor and less fortunate, and his decisions reflected this. It is ironic that the very nature of my father that sought to help others was so misconstrued in his later years by his position on segregation. That issue more than any other defined him and try as he might, he never would be able to change that.

Such a dramatic change in social norms and traditions that integration brought to the South and the nation, made for a charged political environment, and he took full advantage of it. In talking with Governor John Patterson, who defeated my father in 1958 because of his hard line on segregation, he recently told me that it did not take him two weeks during the 1958 governor's race to fully realize that the issue of segregation was what was on the minds of the voters. My father's position as the moderate on the issue of segregation was one in which he believed a more gradual timetable in dealing with the issue was the policy to adopt. This was clearly not the policy the voters wanted adopted and he learned from that. That one cultural change was the flash point within the body politic that propelled him to a position where he was ultimately able to help those he had been accused of seeking to in many ways harm. He had to, for a time, turn his back on the very people he most wanted to help. He would eventually return to the spirit of his judicial robes, return to his roots, and continue to seek fairness for everyone.

Even during these times there was a reaping of the harvest grown from the roots of his populist planting. His desire in terms of education and economic policy was to lift all our people. John Kennedy's quote that, "A rising tide lifts all ships," was the centerpiece of his administration. I recall a story related by my friend, and famed Civil Rights attorney, J. L Chestnutt, who talked about how his mother planned to vote for my mother in the 1966 race for governor. He recalls the shock and disbelief he felt when his mother told him this. When he asked her why she planned on voting for the wife of the man he had fought so vigorously in the Civil Rights arena she replied, "Son, do you realize that during Governor Wallace's administration, teachers have received annual pay raises every year for the last four years? And also, son, because of Governor Wallace, our children now get free textbooks!" And as it just so happened, Mrs. Chestnutt was a public school teacher, and she knew in her heart of hearts that he cared about her and wanted to help her. It was watching his actions coupled with an instinct that the races have with one another in the South, probably more than any other region of the country that enabled Mrs. Chestnutt to see, hear and know the real George Wallace. I have often thought that one of the major factors in the equation that allowed our people to have a greater understanding of each other was the land. The South was agricultural and all races historically worked the land together over the years, so consequently people were in close proximity to each other. The very laws of nature dictate that because of this, you get to know people as people and not simply as a race of people.

One of the most intriguing comments over the years, I have heard from Black Alabamians was their belief that my father took his early positions on segregation so he could be in a position to help them. I have had Black citizens tell me that they knew George Wallace was not a racist, because they knew the man. This was clearly not true for most Blacks throughout the country, but the Black folks in Alabama were much closer to him and as they watched him, I believe they knew the truth about who he was.

The suggestion over the years by some that the relationship between Blacks and whites in the South was one only of employer and employee tends to cloud other things that were going on. Clearly and as any thinking person in the South knew, the cultural change between the races was on its way. Of course, there were people who believed, and there are some even today who believe that we should have separation of the races. That would not be right or just, would not be practical, it is not to be, and we must find as much common ground among races as possible in order to survive as a nation. The issue of race and all it entails has been with us for thousands of years.

Simple paternalism has been put forward by some to describe the historic relationship between the races in the South. This paternalistic relationship as they would have you believe was one that put whites and Blacks in a relationship having no substance beyond employer and employee. That is absurd on its face. I grew up in the South, I live here and I know of many examples of true and genuine love and affection between the races. There are those who always suggest that this relationship was phony, disingenuous and that the only consideration whites had was the comfort Blacks could bring to their lives and the economic interest to be derived from Black labor. You had to live in the South and experience the relationship to fully understand how much sincerity existed between the races due to their very personal and close environment. You could not live in this setting and not develop feelings for people of all races and backgrounds. To suggest that none of that existed, questions an entire peoples' ability to care and that is not fair. Political agendas have always been a part of the attack on the South by some, just as politics played a major part in my father's early position on the issue of race. He was defending a social custom and tradition that had existed for many years for Southerners, as well as people in other parts of the country, but the change now on the horizon would teach us many things about ourselves as a people and a country.

The completion of this arc is Shakespearean and drama of the first order and the profile of his very public, personal, and political journey mirrored the journey our culture was taking. We all hold regrets inside ourselves and we each in our own way seek to come to terms with those regrets. His ambitions ran deep and were an obsession, and I have often thought that here was an example of the man and the hour meeting. At a particular point in history, issues arise and an individual will emerge who addresses those issues in a manner so unique and powerful as to capture the imagination of the country. His leadership qualities and style of standing and delivering sent shock waves through the political establishment. His story is one of triumph and tragedy and through both he emerged an enlightened and better man.

THE NATIONAL SPOTLIGHT—HIS STAND IN THE SCHOOLHOUSE DOOR

The schoolhouse door incident was the moment when my father became a national political figure and received continuous invitations to appear on the national network news programs. Invitations to speak on college campuses across the country also began to arrive, and suddenly he had become a national figure. My father stressed to the people of Alabama and the people of the nation that he sought to raise Constitutional issues as to who should control local democratic institutions in Alabama, in this case, the University of Alabama. Should the states or the Federal Government be the last authority in determining the integration of The University of Alabama? The states' rights issue and the sovereignty of the states was an issue of which the people of Alabama and the South were especially sensitive. The sentiment was evident during the Constitutional convention of 1787 as the Founding Fathers feared a too powerful Central government. This sentiment was pronounced following the War Between the States when the Radical Republicans under the leadership of Thaddeus Stevens were punitive in their positions toward the South and her people. President Andrew Johnson was almost impeached because of his policy of conciliation toward the South, which ironically was the very policy Abraham Lincoln had adopted before his death.

Because there had been such violence at Ole Miss and in Little Rock, Arkansas, when those institutions were integrated, my father was determined that there would be no violence at the University of Alabama. To accomplish this, he went on statewide television for several nights and urged the people of Alabama to stay away from the University. He told them that he would represent them and raise the constitutional questions that needed to be raised. Because of this my father was fond of saying, "We had absolutely no violence at the University of Alabama, why there wasn't even a sprained ankle." He knew that the national press would have a field day if there was any incident at the university. They would like nothing more than to cite the violence they always seemed to enjoy fostering about the Southern people. My father was well aware of this and did everything he could to maintain law and order and was successful.

Over the years I have spoken to many of my father's closest advisors during that period about the dynamics of his stand in the schoolhouse door. There has been speculation over time by some that it was an orchestrated event worked out between my father, President John Kennedy, and Attorney General Robert Kennedy. The scenario was simple: My father would block the Federal Marshals; the Alabama National Guard would be federalized, and my father would step aside having kept his commitment to the people of Alabama. The fact is there was no prearrangement. A documentary made years ago shows footage of President Kennedy in his rocking chair in the oval office talking with his advisors and asking questions such as: *"Do we physically remove him if he decides not to move? How do we handle this?"*

There are documented conversations that went on between President John Kennedy, Attorney General Robert Kennedy, and other aids about my father's stand in the schoolhouse door and how they should handle this. The following are excerpts from Stephan Lesher's book, *George Wallace, American Populist*, which outline very clearly that there was no prearranged plan between my father and the Kennedy administration relative to the "Stand in the Schoolhouse Door." The following conversation in the oval office between President Kennedy, Attorney General Robert Kennedy and Burke Marshall, Assistant Attorney General demonstrates very clearly several dilemmas for them.

The first step, Robert Kennedy said, would allow the governor to sidestep disobeying the court order; Katzenbach would confront Wallace while leaving the two students in a nearby parked car. That way, Wallace would not technically be barring the students from entering. "Then if he still refuses," Kennedy continued, "Nick Katzenbach will say we've got this court order and we have to go through on a legal basis; he's made the test and this matter should be determined in the courts, it shouldn't be determined out here. He's had the opportunity and should let them go through or otherwise we are going to have to take other steps, because these students are going to attend the University of Alabama. And then if he still doesn't move, then we'll try to get by him." The president looked skeptical. "Pushing?" he asked. "By pushing a little bit," Robert Kennedy said. There was a long silence.

Just as the attorney general was concerned about the idea of lifting Wallace and carrying him out of the way, the president was troubled by the thought of any physical contact. "Try to walk around him," he said firmly.

Wallace arrived at Foster Auditorium [sic] at 9:53 a.m. He climbed out of his car and walked alone down the asphalt path lined with state troopers in riot gear—helmets, pistols, gas canisters and truncheons. Wallace nodded to some of the 150 state patrolmen who were ringing Foster Auditorium and made a special effort to greet many of the 400 reporters who crowded behind the specially drawn white line. Everyone was perspiring in the already broiling sun. But then, Wallace went inside an air-conditioned office, stripped off his jacket, and sat down to read that morning's copy of the Montgomery Advertiser. Katzenbach was late and showed up at 10:48 a.m. Jones rushed inside to summon the governor, who donned his suit coat, walked briskly to a lectern set up in front of the entrance to Foster Auditorium, set his speech before him, and allowed Jones to loop a microphone around his neck.

As Katzenbach emerged from an official car, Malone and Hood remained nervously behind. "That was the only time I was really apprehensive," Malone recalled later. "I had in mind the situation at Ole Miss. I sort of expected things might be worse." Katzenbach flanked by a marshal and a U. S. attorney approached Wallace who abruptly raised his left hand in the manner of a traffic cop. Katzenbach and the others stopped. The deputy attorney general identified himself and said, "I have a proclamation from the President of the United States ordering you to cease and desist from unlawful obstructions." Then crossing his arms across his chest and beginning to sweat in the direct sun, Katzenbach leaned toward the governor and said, "And I've come here to ask you for an unequivocal assurance that you will permit these students who, after all, merely want an education at a great university . . ." Wallace cut him off in midsentence. "Well," Wallace said his voice flat and hard, "You make your statement, but we don't need for you to make a speech. You make your statement." Katzenbach grew increasingly uncomfortable . . . "I'll make my statement, Governor, I was in the process of making my statement. I'm asking from you an unequivocal assurance that you will not bar entry to these students, Vivian Malone and James Hood, and that you will step aside peacefully and do your constitutional duty as governor." Wallace simply ignored Katzenbach's request and said, "I have a statement to read." He then launched into a thousand-word statement that kept Katzenbach and the others sweltering in the heat for fifteen minutes. He began by saying that as the governor and chief magistrate, he was representing, "The rights and sovereignty" of Alabamians. He continued: "The unwelcome, unwanted, unwarranted, and force-induced intrusion upon the campus of the University of Alabama today of the might of the central government offers a frightful example of oppression of the rights, privileges, and sovereignty of this state by officers of the

Federal Government. This intrusion results solely from force, undignified by any reasonable application of the principle of law, reason, and justice. He continued on and finally closed by saying. I hereby denounce and forbid this illegal and unwarranted action by the central government. He stepped back sharply as if to punctuate his closing assertion."

It took a moment for Katzenbach to realize that Wallace had finished. With his arms still folded across his chest, he said, "Governor Wallace, I take it from that statement that you are going to stand in that door and that you are not going to carry out the orders of this court and you are going to resist us from doing so. Is that correct?" "I stand upon this statement," Wallace said. A disdainful smile crossed Katzenbach's lips. "You stand upon that statement," he repeated. "Governor, I'm not interested in a show. I don't know what the purpose of this show is. I am interested in the orders of the court being enforced. That is my only responsibility here. I ask you once more. The choice is yours. There is no choice that the United States Government has in this but to see that the lawful orders of this court are enforced." Wallace stood mute, his jaw jutting belligerently. Twice more Katzenbach asked Wallace to remove himself, but the governor, standing rigidly, stared past him.

Shortly before 3:00 p.m., Al Lingo rushed into the room to tell Wallace that a hundred federalized troops were only minutes away. Wallace donned his suit coat and walked back outside. This time Katzenbach remained out of sight. General Graham, accompanied by four armed enlisted men, stepped vigorously along the path. Graham, tall, straight-backed, dressed in combat drab with the Confederate flag of the Thirty-first Division (called the Dixie Division) stitched to his breast pocket, stopped three feet in front of Wallace, saluted and said, "Sir, it is my sad duty to ask you to step aside under orders from the President of the United States." After a moment's hesitation, Wallace snappily returned the salute and said, "General, I want to make a statement." "Certainly, sir," Graham replied, and moved to one side. Glancing at notes scribbled on a calendar pad, Wallace characterized the federalization of the guard as an *"Unwarranted . . . bitter pill" for Alabama guardsmen to swallow and called on Alabamians to remain "Calm and restrained." He concluded by maintaining, "Alabama is winning this fight against federal interference because we are awakening the people to the trend toward military dictatorship in this country. We shall now return to Montgomery to continue this constitutional fight." He turned and walked quickly to an awaiting state patrol car."*

There it had been done. He had kept his commitment to the people of Alabama about standing in the doorway, and he also kept a commitment to the state as well as to himself that there would be no violence. The Stand in the Schoolhouse Door was a symbolic test in my father's mind, to demonstrate to the country the extremes to which the Federal Government would go to bring about social change.

While these events were occurring, I have often wondered what my father was thinking. He had to know that the Civil Rights movement had become a force of nature, and to attempt to hold it back would ultimately not succeed. But, after these present-day battles had been lost, in what realm would he operate? As history has shown, as time passed, he stressed what the truth had always been, and that was his fight had been with the Federal Government not against Black people. He was strategically moving away from the issue and would ultimately find other issues as a presidential candidate that would help define him again. But, it would always be the race issue that would define George Wallace more than anything else in the minds of people throughout the country. It would take years of suffering, reflection, and his very public apology for the world to know him as he truly was.

My father indicated years later that he had made a mistake in saying "Segregation Forever," in his first inaugural address, and he wished he had not stood in the doorway of the University of Alabama. He believed it had harmed Alabama's image and his own image and he had regrets about that. He told me one time in describing these two events that he had been, "Young and brash." These two events were so dramatic and made such an imprint on the minds of Americans that he would forever be associated with these moments and no matter what actions he took or explanations he gave, those images would be synonymous with George Wallace.

Robert Kennedy came to understand as observed by William Manchester. *"The Kennedys thought Wallace had been made to look ludicrous, and the country would see his posturing for the absurdity it was. But years later, Robert Kennedy came to understand that Wallace "Did not fear defeat as a political pitfall . . . In the past, defeat and a noble defeat . . . had a redemptive quality."*

SELMA—"BLOODY SUNDAY"

One of the most disturbing perceptions held by many over time relative to the violence at the Edmund Pettus Bridge in Selma, is that my father's orders were for the Alabama State Troopers to beat and tear gas the marchers in order to stop them. Nothing could be further from the truth as the facts reveal. I had the opportunity in 1997 to be a guest on Larry King's CNN program along with Mike Wallace of *Sixty Minutes* and the Reverend Jesse Jackson, to discuss my father's life personally and politically. The subject of the Selma incident came up when Reverend Jackson made the statement, "Governor Wallace ordered the troopers to attack the marchers." At this time, I told him he was wrong, and I recall how intrigued Larry King and Mike Wallace were at my statement. I explained that if you looked at his history of maintaining peace and tranquility when he stood in the doorway at The University of Alabama; especially given the deaths at Ole Miss and in Little Rock, Arkansas, it is clear that the last thing he wanted in Selma was violence. From a political standpoint, he knew the national media would have a field day if there was violence, because it would simply confirm what they broadcast nightly about the Southern people being racist violent rednecks, filled with hate. If you think about that and consider the great lengths he went to before the Schoolhouse Door stand to keep peace, why would he deviate from that position? Before the Schoolhouse Door stand, as I have indicated, he went on statewide television night after night telling people to stay away from The University of Alabama. He told them he would represent them and raise Constitutional questions to be adjudicated in the courts relative to the Sovereignty of our state. Before, during and after his Schoolhouse Door stand there was no incident whatsoever at The University of Alabama. He had The University of Alabama locked down with the strictest orders to maintain peace, and it was done. Now given this, why would he allow Alabama State Troopers and Dallas County sheriff deputies to beat marchers at the Edmund Pettus Bridge in Selma, Alabama, with the eyes of the nation watching?

Stephan Lesher's book on my father *George Wallace, American Populist* outlined clearly what Col. Al Lingo and Sheriff Jimmy Clark's instructions were from my father on the day before the march in Selma. These recollections are from Bill Jones who was my father's press secretary and who was present at the meeting.

Lesher writes:

Wallace summoned Lingo again on Saturday night; this time Lingo brought along Clark. "The meeting broke at midnight, twelve to fourteen hours before the events at the Selma bridge," Jones recalled. "And I know that Lingo and Jim Clark left the governor's office with instructions not to do anything more than to hold their nightsticks in front of them, and if the marchers pushed ahead, just to let them through. We thought the thing was in hand." Later, when a Montgomery television reporter phoned to ask the governor's reaction to the Selma clash, Jones was shocked. "Lingo violated the policy Wallace had set down." Actually, Wallace had asked Lingo to stay away from Selma altogether. "I ordered Lingo not to go to Selma," Wallace recalled, "because he had been taking pills for a bone marrow condition. I told Major John Cloud {a Lingo subordinate who would officially be in charge at the confrontation}, "Don't y'all let anything happen that will cause any sensationalism. If they want to march, go beside them and protect them."

When Wallace heard the reports from Selma, he was enraged, especially because Lingo had ignored his order to stay away from Selma. Wallace recalled, "Lingo went anyhow, and I think he may have been one of the ones who caused the trouble."

Bob Ingram in writing for *The Montgomery Advertiser* wrote: "Wallace is no fool and he learned the hard way that both he and the state suffer anytime anyone is injured in a racial clash in Alabama . . . Knowing this . . . Wallace is the last man to encourage undue force." Bob Ingram was actually in the governor's office with my father when they heard the news of the violence at Selma. Ingram wrote and described how he had never seen a man as enraged as he saw my father when he learned the news of the violence.

The violence that occurred at Edmund Pettus Bridge in Selma will to a large extent always be associated with my father. In talking with people over the years about this, I have been surprised at the number of people who just believed that he had ordered the troopers and deputies to assault the marchers. When I explain to them what really happened, they are surprised, and invariably indicate that their perception was based upon what the news media had reported.

Little known to many is that there were certain rogue groups and individuals who could cause harm to the marchers along the highway. This was of great concern to my father as he so indicated to President Johnson at the time. When the march proceeded, the Alabama State Troopers and other law enforcement officers walked the tree lines along the highway to make certain there were no snipers. There had been early reports that the marchers could be in real danger, and this was of grave concern to my father.

In thinking about the Selma to Montgomery march and the violence there, I am reminded how during my father's last years he called Congressman John Lewis from Georgia on more than one occasion, and expressed his sorrow at what had happened, and how he had not intended for the violence to occur. Representative Lewis was in Selma, was one of the marchers, and had actually been beaten and tear gassed. As a victim of the circumstance, he indicates in his writings that my father's calls to him were ones of a man pleading for forgiveness and filled with contrition about what had happened. In my conversations with him late in his life, he would talk about this on occasion with deep remorse about what had happened, and I know he was saddened that so many over time would always believe he had given the order to brutally beat innocent people.

My sister, Peggy, went to Selma in 2009 to help commemorate the bridge crossing by introducing Attorney General Eric Holder. She gave an eloquent and moving introduction that spoke of our common humanity and the need to learn from the past in order to build a better future among all people. I was in Florida when she spoke, and I remember calling her a couple of days later and telling her how very proud I was of her. She told me how warmly she was received and of the love she felt among those in attendance. Peggy's presence in Selma was a moment of closure in many ways, and she represented our family with grace and dignity. The following are some excerpts from her introduction of Attorney General Holder:

"I want to thank Congressman Davis for his kind remarks and his many years of friendship to my husband, Mark, our children and myself. I am truly humbled to be here today to join with you in commemoration and in celebration of the many men, women and children that joined together and remain united in the struggle for freedom and equality in America.

I am honored to have been asked to bring remarks on the occasion of the introduction of the Attorney General of the United States."

"In the spring of 1965, as clouds of hatred and violence thundered across the South, a brave band of believers walked across the Edmund Pettus Bridge and into history. With heads held high, they, along with many of you, carried the flag for freedom while holding the souls of those who had gone before them close to their hearts. They prayed for a day in America when justice would run down like water and righteousness as a mighty stream. In the darkest moments they never gave up on their common belief in the inherent goodness of mankind.

"Watching from behind the gates of the Alabama Governor's Mansion, I knew in my heart that their cause was just, but unlike them I feared to let my voice be heard. For many years, I wandered in a world of indifference until I heard the voice of Barack Obama calling for a refreshed and invigorated America. He inspired me to believe in myself and to join with millions of others who laid claim once again to faith and pride in America.

"As the daughter of George Wallace, I realize that my children and my grandchildren will always live in the shadow of the stand in the schoolhouse door for that is as much a part of their legacy as is their grandfather's journey to redemption on his own road to Jericho.

"But today, not as a daughter or a wife but rather as Peggy Wallace Kennedy, I lay another stone upon the foundation of a legacy of my own so that one day my children and grandchildren will bask in the glow of the story of the day when their mother and grandmother joined hands with people from all walks of life, all races and creeds and walked across the Edmund Pettus Bridge in the dawn of a new beginning where hope, honor, truth, and dignity will light our way.

"Attorney General Holder, a native of New York, is married to Dr. Sharon Malone, a native of Mobile and a graduate of Harvard and Columbia Medical School. Dr. Malone's sister, the late Vivian Malone Jones, has become an icon of the civil rights movement. In 1963, she and

James Hood integrated the University of Alabama following a bitter battle between my father, Governor George Wallace, and the United States Attorney General, Robert Kennedy.

"Mr. Attorney General, one of the most poignant memories of my father in his later years, is of the night in 1996 when he and Vivian Malone met for the second time in their lives. As they sat together in the Alabama State Capitol building in Montgomery, he praised her for the role she had played in the American Civil Rights Movement and how she had done so with great dignity, grace and courage. As my father's eyes welled with tears she reached out to him in a gesture of friendship and forgiveness."

I know my father would have been proud of Peggy for continuing his legacy of seeking love, understanding and brotherhood among all people. Peggy's journey to the Edmund Pettus Bridge was a moment that is historic and lasting, and in essence conveyed to the world the genuine heart and soul of our father.

TO THE EXCLUSION OF ALL ELSE

You must understand that one of the main reasons for my father's success as a political candidate was his one-dimensional approach to life. He lived for politics to the exclusion of all else. While others in the political arena were playing golf, fishing, hunting or otherwise pursuing an interest for a mental diversion from politics, my father did just the opposite. He never stopped working on strengthening his campaign organization in Alabama and across the country. He was notorious for staying in touch with his supporters often, not just as a campaign approached. His relationship with his organization, whether at the state or national level, was close, personal and their loyalty was steadfast.

I remember going to our lake house for some relaxation and Mother and our family would enjoy the water and tranquility that comes with that setting. Now on the other hand, when my father would come to the lake, he could never seem to relax. I think on occasions he tried, but there was always a newspaper there or the telephone and his mind went from relaxation with the family to thinking that there was so much to be done. Given this he would tell Mother, "Lurleen, honey, I think I'll head back to Montgomery and meet with some people." She understood him and knew that politics was his life and his obsession, and thus his leaving was certainly nothing new to her, the years had taught her to live with it.

As the years went by, especially his later years, he would express his regret that his ambitions caused him not to be with us more as we were growing up, but then he would say, "I wanted the family to be proud of me." It is true that he wanted that, and we were proud of him, but he knew in order to do the things he was doing that many sacrifices would have to be made, and on a fateful day in Maryland, his own life was almost sacrificed.

SUPERNOVA ACROSS THE POLITICAL UNIVERSE

When I consider my father's career, it amazes me how quickly it took on a national dimension. He went from being a candidate for Governor of Alabama in 1962 to a presidential candidate in 1964, and a major third-party candidate for president in 1968. By 1972 as a candidate in the Democratic primaries, he was leading in popular votes and delegate count on the day he was shot. All of this happening within a span of ten years. He was always a man in a hurry and when he came on the political scene, his masterful talents as a politician took him to great heights but also took him personally to the depths of despair. The one thing he loved the most would eventually cause him the most pain.

Historically, you will find individuals who have achieved great things in their careers, and one thing many of them have in common is their one-dimensional approach to the pursuit of their ambitions. How could we have known that the events in our lives would take us not on a gentle journey, but rather one streaking across the political universe like a Supernova.

SPIRIT OF THE SOUTH

The Spirit of the South and the people who inhabit her land have been an inspiration to the rest of the country for generations. I have seen this firsthand when I traveled all across our country during the time my father was seeking the presidency. From all parts of our country, I have seen the looks on the faces of people longing for someone in whom they could believe and follow. Their longings were answered by George Wallace who voiced their deepest concerns and moved them to act upon their convictions by giving him support from all across the country.

I recall campaigning in Massachusetts for my father in 1972 at a time when there was considerable momentum for the Wallace campaign. One of our coordinators arranged a street walk for me in Boston with a man who owned a vegetable stand close to downtown Boston. I can see and hear him now as we walked the crowded streets, and like a carnival barker he announced that Governor Wallace's son was right here and would like to shake your hand and meet you. This man was an Italian and had more personality than anyone I think I have ever met, and he knew virtually everyone. His voice boomed for blocks, and I remember the Secret Service agents becoming a bit nervous as people gathered and the excitement grew. I remember the comments I received from people wishing my father well as they voiced their support. The various accents took a while for me to grow accustomed to as well as the overall demeanor of the people, which seemed to be more outgoing than I was accustomed. Southerners tend to be more reserved and possess a certain stoicism within their personality. These personality traits and other distinctions distinguish us from other parts of the country, and for me as a young man it was quite an education to experience new people in other sections of the country. What I found was that while there are some differences in accent and personality, the underlying core belief in our country and all it represents knows no region but is rather the strand that binds us together and makes us one people.

CAMPAIGN CROWDS ON THE NATIONAL SCENE

The crowds that turned out to hear him during these campaigns were massive and passionate. He had struck a nerve with the great "Silent Majority" as President Nixon called them, and his message resonated in a visceral way. His famous line, "There's not a dime's worth of difference between the National Democratic Party and the National Republican Party," would bring roars from the crowds. He would tell them they are like, "Tweedle Dee and Tweedle Dum."

The Madison Square Garden rally in 1968 resulted in the auditorium being completely full and loudspeakers being hung on the outside of the Garden for the thousands to hear who could not get in. The law enforcement personnel said it was the most excitement at the Garden since Franklin Roosevelt's nomination for president.

The division within the Democratic Party is evident today as the more moderate element seeks to find the center, while the more liberal element risks alienating itself from the center. This same philosophical divide was evident and prevalent during the 1972 Democratic primaries, and the clarion question among the National Democratic Party elite was, "What do we do with Wallace?"

HIS BATTLE WITH THE CRITICS

There is a famous quote from Theodore Roosevelt from a speech he gave to the Hamilton Club in Chicago, Illinois, entitled,

The Strenuous Life, on April 10, 1899. In the speech he said: *"Far better it is to dare mighty things, to win glorious triumphs, even though checkered by failure, than to take rank with those poor spirits who neither enjoy much nor suffer much, because they live in the gray twilight that knows neither victory nor defeat."* This quote more than any other captures the spirit of my father as a modern-day gladiator. He, more than any other person I will know in this life, enjoyed much, suffered much, and gave me the greatest gift one can give, when he helped me understand forgiveness and the real meaning of brotherhood.

What makes his life even more wondrous is that he touched people in a way that transcended politics. He spoke for them exhibiting qualities they admired in a man and a leader. His intelligence, personality, including his fighting spirit, his sense of humor and his willingness to stand up for them ignited their spirit and lifted their hope.

From the very beginning of his national career the "Elite left-wing media," as he called them, did everything they could to discredit him even to the point of very personal attacks. In thinking about some of these critics, I recall Marshall Frady's book, *Watch out for Wallace,* that had a grotesque caricature of my father on the front cover with a Swastika as the cleft in his chin. One irony here is that my father was fighting the Japanese and Germans in World War II risking his life, protecting the Bill of Rights, so Marshall Frady would have the right and freedom to denigrate and slander my father with impunity. What was so revealing was the way in which some of these critics would level such personal attacks against him in an effort to destroy him. We have heard the phrase, "Politics of personal destruction." Well, my family lived with this for many years.

Marshall Frady's suggestion that my father made my mother run for governor and because of that experience, her condition was compromised and thus her cancer was much more difficult to fight, is absurd on its face. Mother thoroughly enjoyed campaigning, and as I have stated, she realized a potential within herself that I do not think she knew existed before the campaign. The campaign was her road to a level of self-actualization as she gained confidence and felt a growth within herself. She basked in the love the people of Alabama so freely gave to her. This experience gave her strength because of the deep affection the people of Alabama had for her. If anything, the experience strengthened her as she was surrounded by so much love and admiration, and that became like a medicine for her.

Her relationship with the people is endearing and enduring. To suggest publicly that my father would knowingly and willingly risk my mother's health for political gain was only one of a myriad of mean-spirited and false attacks my father and family had to endure for many years.

SPARRING WITH THE NATIONAL MEDIA

As Elizabeth and I travel the state, inevitably someone will relate one of the famous stories about my father's appearances on the Sunday morning national news programs, such as: *Meet the Press, Face the Nation,* and others.

The most famous story, and the one people relate to me the most, concerns an exchange between my father and one of the panelists interviewing him, who after becoming increasingly frustrated with my father's ability to hold his own, blurted out, "Governor, you must think you are the smartest man in the country." At this point my father responded in a calm but matter of fact manner by saying, "No, I don't believe I am the smartest man in the country, nor do I believe I am the smartest man in Alabama, but one thing is certain, I am the smartest man on this television program today." These exchanges would leave the interviewers flustered and raising their voices and, in some instances, almost becoming uncivil. While doing this, they were playing right into the political hands of George Wallace.

As the people of Alabama and around the nation saw this, they liked what they saw. For Southerners, it was a way to strike a blow for freedom, in their minds, at "Those who had looked down their nose at us for so long," as my father would put it. Here in George Wallace was a man who stood up to and bested the elite media and others who sought to disparage the Southern people. As they watched him, they were proud of how he handled himself, and they were quite amused at the inability of the interviewers to handle this man from Alabama.

I was talking to a barber recently in Montgomery who moved to Alabama from Georgia many years ago, and he related a story to me about his father who was dying of cancer. He told me that the only thing that could get his father out of his sick bed was when George Wallace was to be interviewed on national television. He told me that the way in which George Wallace defended the Great Southland gave his father inspiration and energy. I have heard similar stories from people all across the nation.

On another occasion, he was questioned by Anthony Lewis, of the *New York Times* about the murder by hanging of a Black man that had occurred in Alabama the prior year. The insinuation and inflection in the voice of Mr. Lewis was since Alabama was my father's home, then, in some way, my father had been responsible. My father responded to the Lewis query by telling him that he had been devastated by the murder and had offered the largest reward for any information leading to the arrest and conviction of those who had committed this heinous act, and he would not rest until they were brought to justice. At this point, my father's great counterpunching skill came to the fore. He then asked Mr. Lewis if he was a resident of New York City where the interview was being held. Mr. Lewis answered yes, and my father told him that on the way to the studio, he read in the *New York Times* that there had been nine murders in Mr. Lewis's hometown the day before. His question to Mr. Lewis at this point pierced the veil when he asked, "Mr. Lewis, murder is murder, so how do you explain yours?"

My father's appearance on *Meet the Press* after Mother's election as governor in 1966 brought a unique exchange between my father and Lawrence Spivak. Mr. Spivak was the moderator of the program, and an interesting historical note is, that as the years passed, they developed a close personal relationship forged out of mutual respect. Lawrence Spivak had come to know my father as a bright, articulate, and reasoned man, who was not the stereotypical Southern governor depicted by so many of Mr. Spivak's colleagues. In questioning about Mother's tremendous victory in defeating nine men without a runoff in the Democratic primary, and then winning in a landslide in November against the Republican candidate, Mr. Spivak said that her large percentage of vote from Black Alabamians in November was only because historically they voted Democratic, and she of course was the Democratic nominee. In essence, they were not voting for her, but simply supporting the party, therefore the votes for her were not that significant. My father bristled at this as he was extremely humbled and gratified at the large Black vote and responded accordingly. He stated to the panelists and the American people by saying, "Well, Mr. Spivak you say that, but just because you say it does not make it true. I don't have a crystal ball and I cannot read peoples' minds because I am not that smart. All I know is that they voted for her, and you can reason any way you like, but you cannot remove the fact that they voted for her and that is what you would really like to do."

When I consider some of his harshest critics during this time and throughout his life, I am reminded of a lyric in Don McLean's

"Vincent," when he wrote, "They would not listen, they're not listening still, perhaps they never will."

MISS BERTIE PARISH AND *THE CLAYTON RECORD*

My father was asked one time on *Meet the Press,* after the interviewers had become increasingly frustrated with his ability to counter their barbs on national television, what he read to keep up with international affairs. Lawrence Spivak, the moderator of *Meet the Press,* asked the question with a condescending tone and my father's response was classic. He said, "Mr. Spivak, I read my hometown paper, *"The Clayton Record,"* published by Miss Bertie Parish and she keeps me informed on international affairs, what do you read, Mr. Spivak?" Following the program, it was reported that the Kremlin in Moscow subscribed to *The Clayton Record* to see what newspaper Governor Wallace was reading. Clearly, my father was well-versed in international affairs as he read deeply and widely about the geo political [sic] landscape, but he enjoyed having a little fun with the interviewers who, so early on, underestimated him.

Let me tell you now about Miss Bertie as she was called, and her husband, Tom. They were owners and publishers of *The Clayton Record* from 1960 until 1998 when their daughter, Rebecca, became the fourth publisher. Miss Bertie's family, the Gammells, had owned the paper since 1915. The paper has a circulation of about 2500, is not a large newspaper, and has a Mayberry quality about it that takes you back in time. To this day, I subscribe to it and look forward to reading it. It is a weekly paper that includes all the local news of a rural Alabama community. The farm news and local happenings as well as school news is included. You will often read about relatives who are visiting family in nearby, Clio, Louisville or Texasville who have driven down from Charlotte for the weekend. The front page has a section about flowers blooming, hummingbirds arriving or the first touch of spring. Weekly papers of this kind all across Alabama are wonderful to read and by doing so you get a real sense of the kind of people who are Alabama.

Bertie and her husband, Tom, have a daughter, Rebecca, who while growing up I thought was the most beautiful girl I had ever seen. They also have a son, Ed, who still resides in Clayton, and actually portrays me in the annual play *Wallace/The Clayton Years* held every year at the Clayton High School auditorium where we started in school.

Following the death of her parents, Rebecca took leadership of the newspaper and has continued the tradition of her parents. Rebecca has always been active in the community and today serves as Clayton's mayor. Her husband, Billy Beasley, is an Alabama State Senator and successful pharmacist in Clayton in a building where years before my father had his law office. They are dear friends who are devoted to the town of Clayton that will forever be my home.

Rebecca and her family will always be special to me. When I am with them, I go back in my mind to a much simpler time before all the turmoil. Back to those long summer days of my childhood in Clayton.

CONSUELLA "CONNIE" J. HARPER—A SAINT AMONG US

Now let me tell you about my friend, Connie Harper. Connie Harper is a Black woman from Montgomery who started the Central Alabama Occupational and Industrialization Center, {OIC} over forty years ago. Her vision and passion was to work with at risk young people by helping to prepare them for a productive and meaningful life.

Her relationship with my father was very special to him and the way in which they met and how their relationship grew is fascinating. In 1968, during the time following Mother's death and after the 1968 presidential race, Connie went to see my father at his office in Montgomery. She told him of her mission to work with young people who were headed in the wrong direction, and that her vision was to provide job training and job placement and other services to students up to the age of twenty-one who are unemployed, underemployed, unskilled, or semiskilled. OIC also works with students who dropped out of school or were expelled, in preparing them to pass the GED. Over the years OIC has successfully assisted over 20,000 young people. In addition, OIC has built homes for those who are living in shacks or public housing.

Connie went to visit my father and at this time he was not governor and was in no position to help her officially, but listened carefully to her dream to help especially those Black, young people who had no hope. Because my father was so moved by her and the concept, he gave her all the money he had on him, which was two twenty-dollar bills. At this time, Connie was actually going into the pool halls and bars in mainly black neighborhoods and talking to the young men about their futures and how they needed to go to school and prepare themselves for the future, rather than hanging out on the streets. She would go anywhere and proclaim her message and my father heard her message loud and clear. He told her that if he was elected governor in 1970 to come see him as he would like to help her.

In January of 1971, following my father's inauguration, a reception was held in the governor's office and a long line of visitors spilled out into the corridors of the capitol all the way to the rotunda. Connie stood in line and when she got close to the governor's office where my father was greeting people, he saw her stick her head in the office door. In seeing her, he said, "Why there is Connie Harper, Connie come in and let me introduce you to everyone." Connie said that some of the men around him looked shocked and wondered who this lady was. They knew she was someone special because of the way my father greeted her and talked to her. He told everyone around him including his cabinet members who she was and her mission and that his administration was going to put her organization into the budget and help her anyway and every way they could. The rest is history and Connie Harper has told that story all over the country to audiences from Washington, DC to Los Angeles, California. She told me there were times when she would talk glowingly of Governor Wallace and how he truly and genuinely cared about her program and the help and hope many young black students were receiving, and how instrumental he had been with the necessary funding. She relates that there were some Black leaders around the country who were not pleased that she was complimenting my father, but she told them they did not understand him as she did.

Connie Harper has won many awards for her service to our community and has helped thousands of young people realize a better life through education and belief in them. She and my father were close friends who knew that education was the key to success, and Connie Harper continues today with her great work and our community is better because of her.

THE DEMONSTRATORS

As my father traveled across the country, and given the volatility of the times, he became a magnet for demonstrators who often became violent and sought to hurt him. When he entered the three primaries in 1964, he often spoke on Ivy League campuses where he would lecture and speak on the Constitution and the issue of States' Rights. In many instances, demonstrators would rush the stage and the police would have to fight them back. Apples and oranges with embedded razor blades would be hurled at him and as he was trying to enter or leave a building he would be spit upon and cursed. I recall when he was trying to leave the Harvard campus how the demonstrators attempted to hit him with signs that read, "Free Speech." I guess that meant free speech for everyone but him. I have always found it interesting that some at the Ivy League schools, those institutions so famous for their intelligence and enlightenment, would react to him in a manner totally inconsistent with what they preached and taught. This hypocrisy became evident to people all across the nation as they saw, in the reaction my father received, their universities being controlled by such radical elements. There were several instances where his car was almost turned over and the Secret Service feared for his life. There were instances when his security detail had to pull their pistols to hold people back, when they were outnumbered. My father had a lot of fun with the protesters and he became famous for knowing how to handle them better than any other candidate. He never became flustered and seemed to enjoy the opportunity to banter back and forth with the protesters. As they would shout obscenities he would respond, "You know those four-letter words, how about some other four-letter words like, SOAP and WORK, I'll bet you don't know those do you?" When he said this, the crowd would roar. It was brilliant in its simplicity. On occasion, he would look at the protesters shouting their obscenities and tell them, "I can take anything you anarchists can dish out, you remember that." He said one time to the protesters, "With all the aid and comfort you punks give to our enemies in North Vietnam you ought to be tried for treason, and when I'm president you will be."

I recall a campaign rally in Kalamazoo, Michigan, in 1972, where at least 20,000 people attended and it was a great success. As was the case most of the time, there were approximately 300 demonstrators down front who sought to disrupt the event. As I always did, I helped to open the rally by playing three or four songs with Grand Ole Opry star, Billy Grammer, to help warm-up the crowd. As I was playing my first song, "Gentle on my Mind," the protesters shouted obscenities at me, and were generally uncontrollable. Many times, the protesters would find some of my father's supporters attacking them and the police would have to intervene. There was always the very real possibility that a full-scale riot could occur. As I was playing my first song, the shouting continued. When I finished, I turned my attention to the protesters and told them, "When I was growing up, my parents gave me a book to read entitled, "How to Behave in a Crowd," and I believe y'all need to read it." At this, the 20,000 supporters went absolutely wild and shouted the protesters down.

We found out later in reviewing pictures of the campaign speeches that Arthur Bremer, my father's assailant, was in one of the first few rows at the Kalamazoo appearance with his ever-present sardonic smile.

CHAPTER FIVE

Campaigning for the Presidency of the United States

THE 1968 CAMPAIGN—THE AMERICAN INDEPENDENT PARTY

There is normally a moment in time when a spark is ignited to launch a movement. There were several such moments leading up to 1968 but none more significant than my father's appearances on the national television news programs. As discussed in Stephan Lesher's *George Wallace, American Populist* his appearance on *Meet the Press*, on April 23, 1967, was the moment when he said, *"There is more chance that I will run, than I will not run,"* and was the closest thing to date of an announcement. On the program, he indicated that he was, *"Not a racist, that he did not dislike any person because of the color of their skin, that he did not recommend segregation in any phase of our society, in any state in this union."* But rather *"That the states . . . continue to determine the policies of their domestic institutions themselves, and that the bureaucrats and the theoreticians in Washington let people in Ohio and New York decide for themselves . . . what type of school system they are going to have."* He went on to say: *"There is a backlash against big government in this country."* In elaborating he said: *"This is a movement of the people, and it doesn't make any difference whether leading politicians endorse this movement or not. And I think that if the politicians get in the way . . . a lot of them are going to get run over by this average man on the street . . . the man in the textile mill, the man in the steel mill, the barber, the beautician, the policeman on the beat . . . the little businessman . . . They are the ones . . . Those are the mass of people who are going to support change on the domestic scene in this country."*

The impact of his words was stunning. People from all across the country loved what they had heard. Here was a political figure representing himself and his cause in a dignified and thoughtful manner. His delivery was confident and spoke to the core of what millions across the country were feeling. He had, in essence, stripped away all the propaganda that had been fostered about him by the national media, and people saw for themselves who and what he really was. From this appearance, millions across the nation started talking among themselves and the intense interest manifested itself in his receiving thousands of letters per week. Letters of encouragement, speaking invitations and contributions poured into the governor's office in Montgomery.

One example highlighted in Stephan Lesher's writing cites a homemaker in her mid-forties from San Francisco, California, by the name of Mary Marshall. *She said that as she watched "Meet the Press," in the living room of her small single-level stucco home. "I was so inspired by him," she said, "I got up and wrote him a letter and drove down and mailed it that same day. I told him I believed there were certain times in history for certain men. "This is the time and you are the man to lead us." Mary and her husband, Carl, a worker in an oil-company refinery, were concerned, as they put it, about law and order, welfare cheats, Communists, hippies, and the decline of public education and public morality.*

His 1968 campaign as an independent candidate for president and the strength it gathered was a mystery to some of the pundits and media, as they looked at my father only through the prism of race. However, in many respects he had hit on issues that far transcended race as Susanna McBee wrote in *Life Magazine: Wallace's primary pitch seems targeted dead center on middle-class and on lower-middle-class whites. Here lie resentments about high taxes, inflation, and crime, along with the sullenness of people who feel that they are left out in the cold while the country's leadership pampers the undeserving and shiftless. Both North and South, Wallace appears to be tapping a powerful underground stream of frustration and discontent.*

There was something going on in the country and my father had tapped into it in a visceral way that touched people deeply. Marshall Frady, certainly not an admirer of my father, probably put it best when he wrote: *Power to him [George Wallace] does not lie in the traditional equations of press and business and political establishment support. He operates outside the conventional political wisdom, has bypassed the classic brokers of political power and could only be called a revolutionary. If the cliché were ever true of a significant political figure in this country, he has nobody but the people . . .and just how many of his people there are in this nation is, aside from the dishevelment he may cause the normal presidential election process, the most unsettling specter raised by his candidacy. It's doubtful any other recent national figure has operated with the uncanny and total and undistracted instincts for the primitive dynamics of the American democratic system as Wallace has. His formula is almost childishly naïve: power lies with the folks and nothing else.*

The 1968 campaign was of historical significance for many reasons not the least of which was that it put the National Democratic Party and the National Republican Party on notice that there were millions of Americans who were feeling deep discontent with both national parties. This was the moment when he coined the phrase, "There's not a dime's worth of difference between the National Democratic Party and the National Republican Party."

Third party movements in our country have always been born from discontent among a certain segment of our voters, and my father's 1968 campaign had tapped into that feeling and frustration. As we all remember or have studied, 1968 was one of the most volatile years in our nation's history. With the assassinations of Martin Luther King Jr. and Robert Kennedy, coupled with the near riots at the Democratic convention in Chicago, the country was in turmoil. The Vietnam war was an issue that divided our country, and while it was an unpopular war, millions of Americans believed we should support our troops, allow the military to wage the war and stop playing politics with the lives of our troops.

Many of the cultural changes occurring in our country at the time left many Americans bewildered about many of the young people, often their own children, and they questioned why their attitudes about conventional values were so contrary to those embraced by their parents. The "Hippie" movement and the "Make Love Not War," sentiment expressed by many young people and others struck the "Greatest Generation" as out of touch with reality. Their parents had faced the Great Depression and World War II and having won both, knew how difficult life could be, and they wanted their children to share in, and appreciate the prosperity their sacrifices had brought. What they got was an anti-materialism, anti-military philosophy born from the idealism of youth. To be young, fighting for causes and seeking to make the world a perfect utopia is a luxury largely, reserved for the tender years. What many of these young people came to know later in their lives as they matured was that while our system of government perhaps plods along, at the very least, it is designed to move in the direction of righting wrongs and seeking justice. It does not fly as the angels do, but it does seek the better angels of our nature. The beauty of our system is that it allows the moral consciousness to rise to a level that will then manifest itself in action to right our course. Government's response is not always the answer, but eventually the policy we set should reflect the intent of the framers. Human beings are not perfect, so our efforts in many regards will be flawed; however, our Constitution's design that recognizes the Rights of Man should be the principle upon which we base our decisions.

The famous quote among many young people from those years was, "Don't trust anyone over thirty." There was a disconnect not only in our country politically, but also between many parents and their own children. I am reminded of Dylan's words when he wrote a few years earlier, "Come mothers and fathers throughout the land, and don't criticize what you can't understand, your sons and your daughters are beyond your command, your old road is rapidly aging, so get out of the new one if you can't lend your hand, for the times they are a-changin'." The times would be changing not only for our country, but for my family in ways we could never imagine.

I have fond memories of 1968 when I traveled with my father and played with, as I have mentioned before, Billy Grammer of the Grand Ole Opry, other Nashville stars and musicians and also, my rhythm guitar player, Steve Morgan. We would open the Wallace rally whether it was in Pittsburgh or California. I would play several songs and talk to the crowds as I looked into their faces. I remember while performing thinking how much hope he was giving so many, but how much hate he also caused to rise up in others.

The supporters of my father and his cause worked themselves into a frenzy as he tapped into their frustration and became the champion for whom they had longed. There were times when, as I would look into the eyes of some of the demonstrators who would be shouting obscenities at me while I was singing, I would wonder how they could allow themselves to be so violent and obscene. Many, if not most of the demonstrators, were college-age youngsters, and I would wonder while looking at them if at another time and in another place some of these young people and I could have been friends. We probably shared some of the same favorites when it came to music and other college-aged trends of the day. We were so close to each other in some ways, yet so far from one another in other ways.

There has always been speculation as to whose campaign my father's third-party effort hurt the most in 1968. Was it Nixon in taking working class voters with conservative values who believed they had been forgotten by both of the national political parties? Or was it Humphrey when George Wallace received support from rank-and-file union members all across the nation, to the chagrin of many labor leaders around the country? The leaders of the various unions across the country were supporting Humphrey, but George Wallace had been a friend of organized labor in Alabama, and his message appealed to the conservative values of the average working man. So, in essence, George Wallace was taking votes away from the base of both National Political parties and caused Nixon and Humphrey both to adopt a strategy of saying, "We know you like what Governor Wallace is saying but he can't win." That did hurt him with some supporters, but even given that, the 10,000,000 votes he received, and the five Southern states he carried almost threw the election into the House of Representatives. The famous miscue of General Curtis LeMay, my father's running mate in 1968, I believe was the blow that kept the election from being decided in the House of Representatives.

GENERAL CURTIS LEMAY AND THE NATIONAL PRESS

Leading up to the press conference where my father would introduce General Curtis LeMay as his vice-presidential running mate in 1968, my father and his staff briefed General LeMay repeatedly about what to expect, as they knew what the national press would try to do to General LeMay during the question-and-answer period. They told him that the media would work to maneuver him into a discussion concerning the use of nuclear weapons in Vietnam. The discussion described in Stephan Lesher's book, *George Wallace, American Populist*, went as follows:

"General, you are used to giving orders and they would always be obeyed. But in this case, we are out here among a bunch of hungry media wolves and they want to trap you into saying you would drop nuclear bombs. One of them is going to ask you a question like this: "If the United States is in danger of being obliterated from the face of the earth, would you drop nuclear bombs? Of course any man would say, yes, I would drop a bomb to save our country from being annihilated. I would certainly drop a bomb. But you don't give that answer. The answer you give is this: Listen my friend, you are asking a purely hypothetical question . . .that would never have to be decided because we are going to be so strong under President Wallace that no nuclear bomb will ever have to be dropped in our administration." My father told him that it did not matter how many times they came at him with that question couching it in various hypotheticals, to never waver from the policy of winning the war conventionally, which again meant there would be no use of nuclear weapons in Vietnam.

Given General Curtis LeMay's background and temperament, which is legendary in Air Force history, it is no wonder he was unable to follow their instructions so his baptism into the world of national politics was a disaster. The media knew exactly how to approach him, and they did so with a vengeance. The beginning of the press conference was my father introducing General LeMay and talking about what a great patriot he was, and the major role he played in helping to win the air war over Japan during World War II. This obviously fell on deaf ears as the national press treated him with contempt and bombarded him with questions including those questions concerning nuclear weapons of which he had been warned. He was asked the question, "General LeMay if the use of nuclear weapons would assure victory in Vietnam would you use them?" General LeMay replied, "I would use a rusty knife, nuclear weapons or whatever it took to win." At this time, my father walked to the side of General LeMay and told the media, "Now General LeMay did not say we will use nuclear weapons in Vietnam," at which time General LeMay waved my father off and launched into a monologue about nuclear weapons and what happens when they are used. It was a disaster and my father dropped overnight in the national polls from around 24% to 14%. General LeMay's wife was crying as they entered the elevator and she told her husband, *"Curtis, Governor Wallace told you repeatedly not to say that. Do you know what you have done?"*

Certainly, my father knew what he had done, and from that point forward the newspaper articles referred to this great patriot as, "Bombs away LeMay." This was a classic case of taking a career military man, especially one with the demeanor of General LeMay and placing him in an environment that was totally foreign to him. He either did not understand the elementary art of politics, or his disdain for the liberal media was such that he lost control of himself. Perhaps his lesson was that the art of war is different than the art of politics. Either way the damage had been done.

Prior to the debacle at General LeMay's press conference, the polls were showing Wallace at 24%. The Lemay matter as well as Nixon and Humphrey stepping up their rhetoric that: "A vote for Wallace is a wasted vote, he cannot win," was having a negative impact as well. My father received 14% of the vote cast in November 1968 with a total of 10,000,000 votes. If he had received one more vote per precinct on average in the country, the election would have been sent to the House of Representatives and my father's role would have been significant there, in determining who the next president would be.

Our friend, Jimmy Rane, was one of his campaign aides with the Secret Service detail that drove my father to the airport in Philadelphia the next day, and he said my father got into the backseat and as he was smoking his cigar he said, "I should have known a general wouldn't take orders from a sergeant." My father of course had been a sergeant in the Philippines where General LeMay was the commanding general who planned the B-29 bombing missions over Japan of which my father was a part.

General Curtis LeMay was a great American and a great patriot who loved this country and was dedicated to the principles that have made us great. He was not a politician, but rather a military man who had given his life in service for his country. He was simply out of his element, and to the national media a caricature of what was wrong with our military at the time. The unvarnished truth is this; General Curtis LeMay understood as few do the horrors of war. He understood that in war there is a brutality that challenges all that we strive for in terms of goodness and kindness toward our fellow man. He understood that there are times when you have to go through hell to preserve Freedom. For that, he was lampooned and disparaged as a deranged mad bomber, when in fact his strategy in the Philippines during WWII as the Commander of the B-29 bombing campaign over Japan, was a spectacular success. It seems I never heard the press talk about his great contribution in winning WWII. I guess it just got by them.

THE FEAR OF WALLACE—NIXON'S SOUTHERN STRATEGY

Following the 1968 campaign, the Nixon White House developed, because of the tremendous success and support my father received in 1968, what they termed, "The Southern Strategy."

In essence, this was taking many of the issues my father had talked about during the campaign and working them into the Republican party agenda. Nixon and his people were very concerned about my father's popularity and what that could mean in 1972 if he ran as a third-party candidate that year. Nixon's paranoia based upon the general consensus among the experts, was that Governor Wallace's popularity had grown to the point that he would be a real threat to Nixon's re-election bid in 1972.

Of all the years in modern history, 1968, and the turmoil it brought to our country domestically and internationally, was unprecedented. The sixties brought us a cultural transformation challenging conventional traditions, customs and values. It brought with it a divide in our country that ran deep within people and provided an environment where my father's charisma and dynamic speaking style would thrive.

Following the 1968 campaign, my father wrestled in his mind about whether to seek the governor's office in 1970. He had come off the 1968 campaign and mother's death that same year had left him exhausted mentally, physically, and emotionally. While he wrestled with the thought of running again, I believe in his innermost self he knew he would. Being governor would give him the forum to run for president in 1972, and the governor's office was where he needed to be.

Following his victory in 1970, the Nixon investigation began of my father and family tax history seeking to find something to damage my father politically. The Nixon camp was truly frightened of my father's future political plans in 1972. In looking at it, George Wallace was the only candidate who could possibly cost Richard Nixon the White House, so the Nixon administration set out to destroy George Wallace. They sent $400,000 dollars to my father's opponent in 1970 to try and defeat him. When you consider what that kind of money is worth in today's dollars, you realize just how desperate they were. None of these tactics worked, and my father, after being elected in 1970, was poised to be a major force to be reckoned with during the 1972 presidential year. The night of the runoff as my father made his victory speech, he had some fun with the Nixon camp by stating, "I'm just sorry I don't have Nixon to kick around anymore." This was in reference to the comment Nixon made the night he lost the California governor's race in 1962 when he said to the press, "I know you'll be sorry you don't have Nixon to kick around anymore." The Nixon operatives would, my father believed, use another tactic that included having him shot.

Over the years, political pundits have debated what caused my father to abandon the American Independent Party to run as a Democrat in the Democratic primaries during the 1972 presidential election season. There has been speculation that the Nixon administration's attempted intimidation of my family and our friends led my father to run as a Democrat rather than as an independent candidate. The theory here is that in running as a Democrat, he would either be successful in the primaries and go to the convention in Miami with enough delegates to be the nominee, or he wouldn't. The Nixon operatives believed that the depth of George Wallace's political appeal was mostly regional and provincial within the South, but as was soon to be seen, his popularity soared all across the nation. The Nixon operatives reasoned that having George Wallace participate in the primaries would mean there would be no third-party effort to take votes away from Nixon in November. While this was their thinking, who knows what he would have done, had the democratic bosses at the convention used their tactics to deny him the nomination, or a place on the ticket even though he was in a strong delegate position. He could have bolted again with a large percentage of the population on his side which would have been motivated and dedicated to support another third-party campaign. They would have followed him anywhere, and the Nixon folks knew this. Their thinking was that with Wallace as a marginal candidate, the Democratic hierarchy would handle George Wallace, but as it turned out he was much too hard to handle. To suggest that my father ran in the Democratic primaries in 1972 due to Nixon intimidation is clearly wrong. Before the 1972 political season, Nixon had done everything he could to stop my father and nothing worked.

CHARLES SNIDER—1972 NATIONAL CAMPAIGN DIRECTOR

Charles Snider was named the 1972 Campaign Director following the 1968 effort and was instrumental in developing a good working relationship with the National Democratic hierarchy. On a personal note, prior to the 1972 effort, Charles was still active with the Wallace Campaign and my father asked him to assist me with my musical pursuits. Charles and I traveled all over the country together and had some wonderful times, and I will always be grateful to him for his help. He was instrumental in helping me sign with MGM Records in Los Angeles and with Buddy Lee Attractions, the largest booking agency in Nashville at the time.

Charles's wife, Nancy, is the daughter of James and Sybil Simon who were friends of our family for many years. Sybil was especially close to Mother and her, along with Mary Jo Ventress, Catherine Steineker, Juanita Halstead and a few others, were her closest friends. Sybil was in our home as much as a member of the family and we felt she was. Nancy's brother, Jimmy, is a few years older than I am and went on to become assistant Director of the CIA. Also, Jimmy and his mother and father nurtured my interest in the great game of golf. Sybil used to tell an amusing story that was associated with Mother. As first lady of Alabama, Mother had a state trooper driver who went with her everywhere she traveled. Given this, when Mother and Sybil went to Normandale shopping or other functions they traveled this way. One day, Sybil went to Normandale by herself driving her own car, did her shopping and returned to her car, opened the back door and got in. It only took a moment or two for her to realize she had driven herself to Normandale, and that she was not with Mother riding in the back seat. Now she had to figure out a way to get out and get in the front seat without someone seeing her and thinking she had lost her mind. Sybil and her family are special people to us.

Charles was exactly what the Wallace Presidential Campaign needed and at just the right time. When Charles was appointed by my father as Director of the Wallace Campaign, he was a very young man with a successful construction business, but he sold his business and set to work establishing a first-rate campaign organization.

Charles brought on board Alton Dauphin, my father's brother-in-law, who was married to my father's sister, Marianne. Alton was a bright, articulate man with a winning personality who helped motivate the Wallace folks all across the country.

One of the first things Charles did was solicit the writing brilliance of Joe Azbell who had been in the newspaper business and had the unique capacity to pen a phrase that summed up what George Wallace was saying. Joe's son, David, is a friend of mine and is involved in governmental affairs and is as bright and thoughtful as his father. The correspondence was overwhelming, so Charles set up an organization to sort and go through the mail and update the over one million names they had in the database following the 1968 campaign. In addition, Joe Azbell put together a newsletter he named, "The Wallace Stand." This newsletter updated the faithful on current affairs and Governor Wallace's positions and was a great way to solicit campaign contributions. At the same time, speaking engagements poured in and a schedule had to be kept for my father.

My father's secretary at this time was Sara Crumpton who lived just down the street from us. Sara was very close to Lee and in many respects along with my sister, Bobbie Jo, provided stability for Lee at such a tender age. Sara has two children, Cara Mia and Robert, who have remained good friends over time. When I see them, we always start reminiscing about the times we experienced together.

Leading up to the 1972 campaign, the head of the National Democratic Party was Lawrence O'Brien who was a Kennedy associate from the earliest days in Massachusetts. His attitude toward my father was one of disdain, and he at every turn was dismissive of the Wallace influence nationally and presented an Ivy League elitist attitude toward the Wallace campaign.

An example of the arrogance of Lawrence O'Brien resulted from his influence on the apportionment of the California delegates based upon proportional formulas that worked against my father. Charles met with O'Brien and argued that the credential committee's ruling was based on the party's reform rules of fair apportionment, rules that should have taken precedence over the prior decision of the California Democratic party to conduct a winner take all primary. O'Brien curtly told Charles, "You are playing in the major leagues; you can't change the rules of the game after it starts." Charles rejoined, "Yes, sir, but this is the first ballgame we've been in where the umpire gets up to bat." O'Brien snorted, said he would consider their views and left.

While this was going on, Jimmy Faulkner, one of my father's closest confidants, was meeting with Humphrey and as Faulkner remembered: "I was received very warmly by Humphrey and Humphrey saying: "Wallace would be good for me and I think I would be good for him." Humphrey went on to say: "We would make a winning team." Humphrey added that should the convention vote the next night to give McGovern all 271 California delegates, the idea of a Humphrey-Wallace ticket would be moot. The opinion among the insiders at the convention was without O'Brien's sleight of hand in working the California delegation, McGovern very well would not have received the nomination and it would have been a Humphrey-Wallace ticket.

The treasurer of the National Democratic Party at that time was Robert Strauss, an old Texas protégé of Lyndon Johnson. Strauss understood immediately the appeal and influence George Wallace had, and that it was not just a regional influence. Understanding this, Charles was able to work through Strauss and develop a relationship and thus make certain the Wallace Campaign was treated just like all the other campaigns, notwithstanding the desires of Lawrence O'Brien. Except for the California delegation matter, Strauss delivered, and would become Chairman of the National Democratic Party during the 1976 campaign. Going forward, when Strauss became chairman of the party, following the 1972 election year, he worked very closely with Charles and Mickey Griffin to ensure that the Wallace positions were considered thoughtfully and honestly at the national committee level. Strauss understood that my father had far transcended the issue of race and was a national figure with a huge following. Strauss clearly wanted George Wallace to be a part of the Democratic party and not bolt to a third party, because of the ramifications that would bring.

Having known Charles for all these years, I have watched him in virtually every circumstance a political organization and campaign can put you in. He has the diplomatic skills of a Secretary of State and the cool under pressure that always served us well. He at the same time could be a bulldog, look you straight in the eye and as my father would say, "Put the hay down so the goats can get it." Coupled with his ability to operate well in any setting, he had the organizational skills and the political acumen and instincts that put him on a wave link with my father like no other.

After the 1972 campaign, Charles kept the organization together and raised millions of dollars for what everyone knew would be the 1976 campaign. It was the finest and most organized national campaign in the country, and we were poised to really make a run at it in 1976. We had everything we needed that year, but as we were soon to see, the wheelchair always got in the way.

One of the most significant contributions from a politically strategic standpoint, was Charles' real belief that my father should run as a Democrat in 1972. Charles believed that the third-party route had run its course. He told my father this and they both finally agreed that was the route to go, and as history has shown that was the best route until Laurel, Maryland.

One of Charles' primary goals was to raise money for the campaign. As Stephan Lesher points out in, *George Wallace, American Populist: Charles contacted Richard Viguerie who was a fundraising guru and a staunch conservative. Viguerie had made a name for himself in 1970 when he raised money for G. Harold Carswell, a rejected Nixon nominee for the United States Supreme Court, who was running for the U.S. Senate. Charles and Joe Azbell met with Viguerie and worked out a deal where Viguerie would utilize the three million names in the Wallace Campaign data base [sic], and by refining it, determine those who were willing to consistently donate.* When my father was taken out of the race due to the assassination attempt on his life, Viguerie had raised millions of dollars, the most effective fund-raising operation among Democrats to that point in the campaign.

One of the major national issues leading up to the 1972 presidential season was the issue of forced busing of school children from their neighborhood schools to schools in many instances miles away. The Supreme Court ruled in 1971 that it was constitutional to transport children out of their neighborhoods for the purpose of dismantling a racially dual school system. This Supreme Court ruling caused outrage all across the country by parents and many other Americans who viewed this action as destroying the neighborhood school concept. Through the Supreme Court's edict of social engineering, my father took up this issue and became the nation's leading advocate against forced busing. Nixon's response to the Supreme Court ruling was mixed when he said he supported it but did not believe busing for integration was in the interest of better education. That would not work with the parents whose children were being bused. This was George Wallace's issue and he seized upon it. Lesher's work points out the confidence he exhibited when talking to the press during this time: *"Who ever heard of a good old boy from Barbour County having the impact I've had? All I'm trying to do is help the president and attorney general . . . to do what they say they want to do . . . and that's stop busing. That's all I'm trying to do . . . just make these judges stop toting our kids all over creation."* Then with what a reporter described as a quick wink and a sly smile, he asked, *"How am I doing?"* The consensus among reporters, politicians, and government officials who were watching Wallace's early campaigning was that he was doing fine.

His popularity leading up to 1972 caused President Nixon to call on him for the purpose of dedicating the Tennessee-Tombigbee Waterway. But Newsweek opined. *It is safe to assume that the president's main motive was to show his face and muster his forces in the midst of George Wallace Country.* This obsession continued even after the assassination attempt on my father when, as was revealed during the Watergate hearings, there was a plan discussed to plant George McGovern campaign literature in Arthur Bremer's apartment, for law enforcement to find during their investigation.

WALLACE, THE REAL THREAT TO NIXON

The only real threat to Richard Nixon was George Wallace. The mass appeal he had with the "Silent Majority," was growing every day, as there was no one on the scene who had the charismatic appeal he had. He touched and moved people in a way that must have been truly frightening to the Nixon White House. They knew that there was no one in the Democratic Party who came close to having the Wallace appeal. They had to wonder when, as they believed would happen, the leadership of the National Democratic Party denied Wallace the nomination, would he then mount a third-party effort, which if he did would devastate the Nixon re-election bid. For the Nixon White House, George Wallace simply would not go away.

Nixon talked about the "Silent Majority," and ironically this majority of middle income and average working people were beginning to let their voices be heard, and they were moving in mass to George Wallace. The time between his 1968 third party [sic] effort and leading up to the 1972 election, brought huge amounts of mail from across the nation that spoke of his increasing popularity. Much of the mail contained financial contributions that allowed him to travel and keep his organization together. He continued to speak across the country, and the campaign staff were kept in place as they stayed in touch with his many supporters in every state.

It is interesting to note that not only did the Nixon White House work overtime to try and stop George Wallace, the national news media as well did all they could to try and discredit my father and his efforts. I was talking to a retired CBS reporter in the summer of 2007, a man who had covered my father's campaign for CBS News during that year. He told me he had been instructed to try and find out anything negative to report concerning Wallace. He said they were especially interested in finding him saying something that would confirm the perception they continually fostered that he was a racist. The national news media worked tirelessly to create this image of my father, even after he had largely transcended the issue of race. He was now connecting with the people of the country on domestic and international issues. Nothing would work against him because he had filled a void in the hearts and souls of the American people, and they were overwhelmingly responding to his message.

There is an interesting story about a campaign rally in Tuscaloosa during the 1970 governor's race. Given that the national media did all they could to show my father in an unfavorable light, he took every opportunity to poke fun at them during his rallies and in interviews. Their coverage was prejudiced to the point they reported half the number attending rallies, distorted his positions on several issues, constantly brought the race issue up and generally did all they could to convey an image of him on the nightly news that fit their agenda. Back to the Tuscaloosa rally: Following this rally while he was shaking hands, Robert Shelton, who had once been the Grand Dragon of the KKK in Alabama, appeared and shook my father's hand. This was a point where people were all around you seeking to shake your hand, expressing their support, and generally caught up in the excitement of the moment. As Shelton shook my father's hand my father recognized him and he noticed that ABC News correspondent Sam Donaldson had his camera man shoot footage of this brief exchange. Immediately, my father knew what would be done with the footage. He knew that they would put it all over the national news and have a headline that said, "Wallace meets with Klan members." At this point he turned to Lloyd Jemison and simply said, "Get that film." Now you had to know Lloyd Jemison to fully appreciate his loyalty to and love for my father. Lloyd was a huge man with the strength of a bear and a quick wit who would have taken a bullet for my father. Lloyd approached the camera man and told him he wanted the film, at which time the camera man told him he couldn't have it. Lloyd told him that there were many uncertainties in life but one certainty was that he was going to have that film, at which time he took the camera and pulled the film out as the cameraman tried to resist. As I understand it, Sam Donaldson protested and generally made a scene, but the footage did not appear on the national news. While this was extreme, it was to me a small measure of justice extracted from some of the national media who were determined to put my father in a negative light, even going as far to manufacture a story that was not true. David Dick who was with CBS News covering my father's campaign in 1972 recently shared with me his feelings about my father. He told me that he had come to admire, respect, and develop a genuine regard for my father personally. He told me that he had seen a glimpse of my father's heart and soul and he knew there was no hate or racism there.

His candidacy became a national movement, the likes of which had not been seen in many years. It took on a momentum that led me to believe, in the days leading up to the shooting, that there was no way he could be denied the Democratic nomination. Because of the crescendo that was building with the popular vote and his delegate count, as he moved through states like a conquering army, barring anything catastrophic, he would be the nominee. The catastrophe was waiting on him in a Laurel, Maryland, shopping center parking lot on May 15, 1972.

GARY SINISE AS GEORGE WALLACE— ANGELINA JOLIE AS CORNELIA

The comprehensive movie about my father's life *George Wallace* which was directed by John Frankenheimer premiered in 1997. You might recall Frankenheimer had won an Oscar directing, *The Manchurian Candidate.* The production on my father took some dramatic license with some facts, but in essence captured the man and the times in which he lived. For portraying my father, Gary Sinise won the Cable ACE Award for Best Actor in a Movie or Miniseries. He also was awarded the Primetime Emmy Award for

Outstanding Lead Actor in a Miniseries or a Movie. He received the Satellite Award for Best Actor—Miniseries or Television Film, and the Screen Actors Guild Award for Outstanding Performance by a Male Actor in a Miniseries or Television Movie. He was also nominated for a Golden Globe for Best Actor—Miniseries or Television Film. In addition, Angelina Jolie, who portrayed Cornelia, received a Golden Globe award for Best Performance by an Actress in a Supporting Series, Mini-Series or Motion Picture Made for Television. She was also nominated for the Emmy Award for Outstanding Supporting Actress—Miniseries or a Movie. The raw ambition and burning desire to be successful was the prism through which the viewer watched my father, and the ultimate impact of the movie nationwide was that millions of viewers came to understand a man they had never known.

Gary Sinise was quoted as saying that his portrayal of George Wallace was one of the most intriguing parts he has played thus far in his career. The movie not only focused on my father's early career but took the viewer on an odyssey of his entire life and all he did to bring people together especially in his later years. A national poll following the movie found that over 85% of viewers around the world indicated that after watching the movie they had an entirely different opinion of this man, George Wallace.

CORNELIA

1972 was George Wallace's year. He had won back the governor's Office in 1970, and then married Cornelia Folsom Ellis, the niece of former Governor, Jim Folsom. She was twenty years younger and a striking and beautiful woman. With her raven hair, dark complexion, and athletic build, she and my father made a handsome couple and an interesting team and were termed the King and Queen of the Red Neck Riviera by some members of the national media.

Cornelia was the niece of Governor Jim Folsom who my father had supported and campaigned for as his South Alabama coordinator in the 1946 race for governor. My father, newly elected to the Alabama legislature, and Mother met Cornelia when she was seven years old at a function at the Alabama Governor's Mansion. As my mother and father were leaving the mansion, they noticed a little girl peering at them from the top of the mansion's staircase. Mother had actually seen her and pulled my father along as they climbed the staircase to say hello. They hugged Cornelia and how was anyone to know that my father and this little girl would be married in 1970.

Cornelia had grown into a ravened-haired beauty and had lived an interesting life as a country music singer touring with Roy Acuff in Australia and studying voice and dance in New York City. She was an accomplished water skier at Cypress Gardens where she met and married John Snively III whose father had built Cypress Gardens. She was outgoing with big dreams, but now found herself in her early twenties leading a rather dull life in Florida, and it was not quite the life she had envisioned. After the birth of her second son, Cornelia and Snively divorced and she moved back to Montgomery to live with her mother, Ruby.

Back in Montgomery, she and my father started dating and while they attempted to keep it discreet, it became a well-known secret in Montgomery political circles. I recall following my father's election as Governor in 1970 and prior to moving into the Governor's Mansion, Cornelia was visiting my father in the home Mother had chosen for us years before. My mother had been and always would be the love of his life and no one could ever take her place but, but as has been said, "Life is for the living" and he was still a young man.

A funny story related to their courtship occurred one afternoon in the spring of 1970. I was in the kitchen with my friend, Dicky

Whitaker, when my father came walking in as animated as I had ever seen him. He was almost giddy and if I had not known that he didn't drink, I would say he had been drinking. He engaged me in conversation about this and that and was uniquely and demonstratively interested in how my life was going. Anyway, after a few minutes of this, the doorbell rings. At that, he looks at Dicky and me and says, "Someone is at the door let us go see who it is." We followed him to the front door and as he opened it he exclaimed, "Why it is Cornelia, come in Cornelia, what a surprise!" He introduced me and started telling her about all my great attributes, and then introduced Dicky and started telling her about him. You see we were supposed to think all of this just happened when she had planned to come over all along. We might have believed it, but for my father's bad B-Movie performance. Dicky and I still laugh about that today.

She was a striking woman with tanned skin, dark hair and eyes that took it all in. She was comfortable and confident and made you feel special. These were some of her unique qualities that made her such a good campaigner for my father. There was a certain panache about her, and just a special way in which she carried herself.

I was eighteen and a senior in high school in 1970, and when I thought about him marrying again it just seemed to me that he should not be alone. Never was there a time when I thought of her trying to replace Mother. That was not in her mind or mine but it was clearly in the minds of some who were close to my father. I remember thinking that, and during my thoughts, all kinds of feelings were being made known about their marriage among family and friends. There were those who understood and wished him well in whatever he chose to do in his personal life. At the same time, there were those who I believe viewed Cornelia through a prism that still held a picture of Mother and they resented anyone, as they saw it, trying to replace Mother. I can understand that and appreciate their affection for Mother, but what seems to have been lost during this time was what my father wanted. After all, he had been through during the past two years; he deserved his own personal life and the satisfaction of making his own choices. I believe the personality contrast between Mother and Cornelia was difficult for some of our friends to embrace initially, and feelings among many were intense about the marriage.

Of course, their marriage was tested when my father was shot in Laurel, Maryland, and life changed for both forever. Cornelia was still a very young woman and my father understanding this had told her that they should get a divorce so she could begin a life again with someone who was not paralyzed. She protested, but as time would tell, he was right and a divorce would have prevented much turmoil in their lives in the next few years. They stayed together, but as time passed it took its toll on their relationship for all the reasons my father envisioned. They eventually got divorced and while it was acrimonious at the time, as the years passed, he helped Cornelia in many ways when she needed it. They had been through so much together that he would always feel a bond with her. She had a difficult time after the divorce in many ways, but eventually found peace and happiness living near her sons in Winter Haven, Florida. She had her family now and a certain peace that had eluded her in her younger years. Cornelia died at age sixty-nine in 2008 and Elizabeth and I attended the funeral. Following the service we visited her three sons Jack, Jim, and Josh. They are all doing very well with families of their own and Cornelia was very proud of them as we all are.

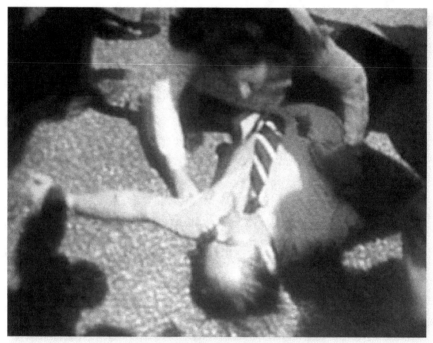

George Wallace was in his second term as Alabama's governor when he announced his third run for the presidency ahead of the 1972 Democratic primaries. His presidential aspirations came to an abrupt halt on May 15, 1972, when Arthur Bremer shot him during a campaign stop at a Maryland shopping center. Wallace survived but was paralyzed from the waist down for the rest of his life. The day after the assassination attempt, Wallace won the Michigan and Maryland primaries but he was unable to campaign and keep up the momentum and ended his bid in July.

.P.O. Drawer 4419
Montgomery, Alabama 36103-4419
(205) 834-1400

Gov. George C. Wallace

August 2, 1995

Mr. Arthur Bremer
Annapolis, MD

Dear Arthur:

Your shooting me in 1972 has caused me a lot of discomfort and pain. I am a born-again Christian. I love you. I have asked our Heavenly Father to touch your heart, and I hope that you will ask Him for forgiveness of your sin so you can go to Heaven like I am going to Heaven.

I hope that we can get to know each other better. We have heard of each other a long time.

Please seek our Heavenly Father because I love you, and I am going to Heaven, and I want you to be going, too.

Sincerely, your friend,

George C. Wallace

GCW:hh

P.S. Please let Jesus Christ become your Personal Savior.

THE TROY STATE UNIVERSITY SYSTEM
Troy   •   Dothan   •   Montgomery   •   Worldwide

147

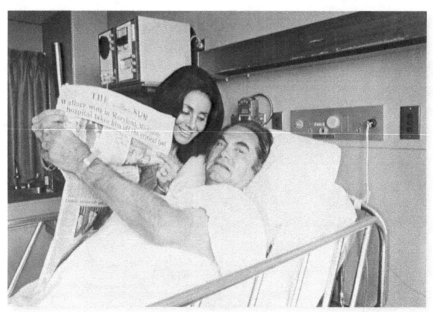

After his shooting, a hospitalized Wallace holds up a newspaper touting his victories in the Maryland and Michigan Democratic presidential primaries.

The crowds were large and the momentum was building.

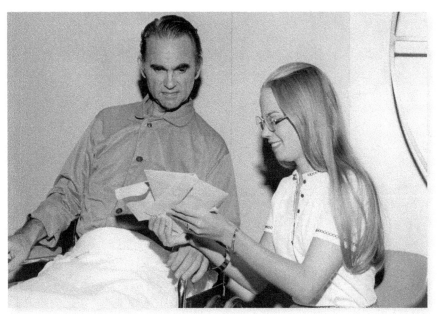

My sister, Peggy, sharing get-well cards with my father at Holy Cross Hospital in 1972.

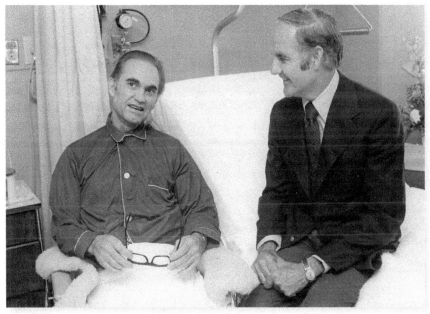

My father with Senator George McGovern at Holy Cross Hospital in May of 1972.

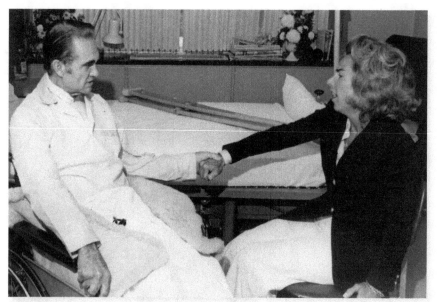

Ethel Kennedy, widow of Robert Kennedy, visits my father at Holy Cross Hospital in May of 1972.

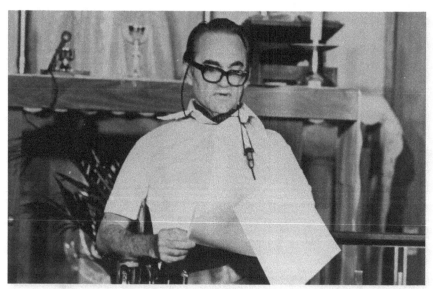

My father reads the 23rd Psalm at the chapel service the day he leaves Holy Cross Hospital on his way back home to Alabama. "Yea, though I walk through the valley of the shadow of death, I will fear no evil: For thou art with me."

A family photo with Cornelia and her two sons, Josh and Jim.

*My father with Senator Barry
Goldwater and Postmaster General,
and fellow Alabamian, Winton
Blount in 1974.*

*With Senator Edward Kennedy in
Decatur, Alabama, in 1975. "They
were all coming to see him in
Alabama."*

*My father with President Jimmy
Carter at his inauguration in 1977.*

*With Vice-President George Bush in
1983.*

My father visits with British Prime Minister Margaret Thatcher at 10 Downing Street in London in 1984.

My father welcomes President Reagan to Alabama in 1986.

Elvis Presley, the King of Rock and Roll, meets the governor in 1977.

With actress, Sally Field, who was in Alabama in 1977 filming "Smokey and the Bandit."

My father and Cornelia with Tammy Wynette and George Jones in 1975.

Tammy Wynette sings, "Stand by Your Man" during the 1982 campaign for Governor.

*First appearance on The Mike Douglas Show in 1971. (left to right) Mike
Douglas, me, my father, opera great, Beverly Sills, and actor Darren McGavin.*

My band, "Southern Stone," in 1975.

Alabama's Governor's Mansion—"My home for many years."

Family photograph at the Governor's Mansion in 1978.

Introducing my father at his historic fourth inaugural as Governor of Alabama, in January of 1983.

My father with Chinese officials and entertainers at a banquet held in his honor on his official trip to China in 1984.

Rev. Jesse Jackson shakes hands with George Wallace, seated.

Rev. Jackson meets with Gov. Wallace

By BRIAN O'SHEA
Associated Press

MONTGOMERY, Ala. — Civil rights leader Rev. Jesse Jackson met with Alabama Gov. George Wallace on Monday, saying the time has come for black and white leaders to "focus on common grounds, not on battle-grounds."

Wallace, who in the past inspired the anger of black leaders instead of handshakes, met with Jackson and black Alabama political leaders for what Jackson described as an amiable "summit talk."

Jackson, head of the Chicago-based Operation PUSH (People United To Serve Humanity), was in Montgomery as part of his "southern crusade" to register black voters. He also is considering a race for president, a job Wallace has sought four times.

"Historically, we have been at opposite ends of the political pole," Jackson said. "For us to have a summit meeting, a dialogue is to end a policy of nontalking. When people talk, they act, and when they act, they accomplish."

Jackson and Wallace also discussed "basic concerns," including the economy and "parity" for blacks in the political process.

He said Wallace is willing to support efforts to make voter registration easier, including a plan to allow school principals and librarians to register voters.

My father visits with Aldo Moro, Prime Minister of Italy in 1984. (Moro was killed by Red Brigade terrorists six weeks later.)

My father meets Pope John Paul II at the Pope's summer home in Castel Gandolfo, Italy, in 1984.

My father congratulating me upon being sworn in as Alabama State Treasurer, in January of 1987.

My father meets with Black mayors from around the country. The national Black mayors conference was hosted by Mayor Johnny Ford of Tuskegee.

He always sought out those who prepared the food and thanked them.

My father greets an old friend in Clayton on election day in 1982.

Official photograph of me as Alabama State Treasurer in 1987.

CHAPTER SIX

Assassination Attempt

MY FATHER'S DESTINY IN LAUREL, MARYLAND

Frankenheimer's production opens with the period when all is going according to my father's plans, and his style of campaigning had become a national phenomenon. He was winning primaries because he was speaking for the average citizen like no other had done for years. His appeal, to the chagrin of his most severe critics, was far beyond the provincial borders of his Southern home. He had touched that nerve in people and his message was a national message that fed on the discontent many Americans felt at the time, especially those Nixon wanted to call his own.

What could possibly go wrong? I recall having a real sense that something was going to happen. You could feel it in the air as it seemed to follow us everywhere on the campaign trail. From state to state the momentum was building, and the real optimism in the air about going to the Democratic National Convention in Miami with enough delegates to assure the nomination as the Democratic nominee in 1972 was felt by everyone in the campaign.

The Democratic bosses did not know what to do with my father, and the other candidates could not compete with the enthusiasm and excitement his campaign was generating. I remember one of my father's security men telling me that as they traveled with my father, they overheard many national politicians say to him privately, "George, keep saying what you are saying because you are right." My father would look at them and say, "Well you can say it too, why don't you say it?" At this, the politicians would look sheepish and not quite know how to respond, as my father glared at them. His complete candor and ability to get to the heart of the matter always fascinated me.

At the Democratic National Convention in Miami, Florida, only a few weeks after the shooting, my father summoned all his will and spoke to the convention delegates. He told the delegates and a national television audience that if they adopted the platform before them, the Democratic Party would lose by the largest margin in history. That is exactly what happened, and the Democratic nominee, George McGovern, did not even carry his own home state of South Dakota. He lost every state in the nation except for Massachusetts and the District of Columbia, two of the most liberal strongholds in the country.

The support received by my father would later be the support Ronald Reagan received as so many of the traditional political alliances and allegiances were questioned and the body politic was in transition. Most of the factors in the political equation were in his favor. The stars were aligned for him, and he was realizing his ambitions and his deepest desires and this was when George Wallace was at his best as a politician. How was he to know that at that very time, Arthur Bremer was stalking him, and plotting for just the right moment to kill him? My father knew the dangers and risks involved as he had felt the wrath of demonstrators over the years and had received more than enough hate mail for one lifetime. He did not need the Secret Service briefings to make him aware of the dangers that would face him. He had chosen this road, and with great ambitions being realized, the probability of an attempt on his life would be realized as well.

The volatility of the times in which we lived manifested itself in demonstrations and violence against my father all across the nation during his race for the Presidency in 1968. The year, 1968, was an especially volatile political year due to the social and cultural transformation that was occurring within our country. This, plus the controversy over the Vietnam War, made for an historic race for the presidency. If there was a year when I believed the real possibility of an assassination attempt would occur, it would have been 1968. The intensity of the demonstrations and the hostile and violent actions taken against him led the Secret Service at one point to ask that he carry a pistol in his coat. The reason being in case the Secret Service became separated from him he would then have some protection. He carried the gun for a couple of days and then gave it back to the Secret Service telling them he didn't feel comfortable carrying it. He told them he would take responsibility, which is the same thing he told the Secret Service on the day he was shot. He did not like wearing a bullet proof vest either, and after trying one for a short time he also returned it to the Secret Service. He did speak from behind a bullet proof podium, but when he moved from behind it he was extremely vulnerable. He was the most controversial figure of his time and the most threatened, but he accepted that fact with the understanding a statesman has when he knows he is representing something larger than himself. His journey was long and would be full of risks that had to be taken.

My father understood the very real possibility that he might be shot. He always believed that if he was shot, he would suffer a head wound and probably die from that. I do not think he ever thought about the possibility of being wounded and becoming a paraplegic until the day he died.

When the bullets pierced his body and he fell to the pavement, his life passed before him. He told us later that he realized what had happened and how serious his wounds were.

When he hit the ground, he turned his head to the left and kept his eyes closed for about twenty seconds so, as he told us later, to lead a possible second gunman to believe he was dead. His presence of mind kept him from going into shock, and according to his medical team at Holy Cross Hospital, probably saved his life.

As the scene around him became more chaotic, he told me of a peace and certain finality he felt. A Secret Service agent was kneeling over him and happened to have his gun that was drawn pointing at my father's head. My father reached up and pushed the gun to the side and told the agent, "I wish you wouldn't point that at me, I have been shot enough for one day."

The Laurel, Maryland, shopping center was a scene that found not only my father as a gunshot victim, but several other people in the shopping center injured as well. The head of the Alabama State Trooper detail, Colonel E.C. Dothard, who had always been like a father to me and had taken me to buy my first guitar, had received a flesh wound to the stomach. It was terribly painful but did not penetrate deeply and he was out of the hospital the next day. He had played an important role in my life and the lives of my sisters, and he was like family. As Dothard was lying on the ground being attended to, he was asking, "How is the Governor, is the Governor all right? Take care of the Governor." At the same time, my father had started looking around, and he noticed Dothard had been injured and he was inquiring about his condition. This was a testament to the close personal relationship they had developed over the years, going back to the time they had met in Clayton in the late 1950s. Their concern for each other was genuine.

As the scene around him became more surreal, Cornelia, who had been in a store in the shopping center, arrived and threw her body over his. In covering his body, his bleeding stained her dress. It would be several hours before she was to change clothes. He had been hit five times in the abdomen and in the arm and one of the bullets lodged against his spine, causing the paralysis he suffered the rest of his life. During the melee, the crowd had actually turned-on Arthur Bremer rather than trying to flee. The crowd helped to subdue Bremer and the Secret Service told us later how uncharacteristic that was of a crowd given the dramatic and dangerous situation. That spoke of the peoples' deep affection for my father for them to risk their own safety in wrestling with an armed man.

Arthur Bremer was subdued by the Secret Service and the Maryland State Troopers. One of the Maryland Troopers pulled his gun and pointed it directly at Bremer's head. Jim Taylor, the head of the Secret Service detail, knew the trooper was about to pull the trigger because he could see the anger and rage on the trooper's face. Taylor implored the trooper not to shoot and, I believe only because of this, Arthur Bremer's life was spared.

Was this how it was to end? Lying on his back in a shopping center parking lot seriously wounded by a would-be assassin. His feelings were reminiscent of feelings he had thirty years before when he was flying night missions over Japan. He knew how fragile life was, and now he was in for the fight of his life.

As the law enforcement personnel secured the area, Arthur Bremer was put in the back of a Maryland state trooper car and removed from the scene. While all of this was happening, the call had gone out for emergency help from the Laurel, Maryland, paramedics. The paramedic team that eventually arrived had been judged recently as the best in the nation, at a national paramedic competition. Their arrival took a few minutes that seemed an eternity, so David Golden, a member of my father's security team from Alabama, secured a station wagon, and was having my father put in the back to have him transported to the hospital. As they were lifting him to place him in the back of the car, the paramedic unit arrived and my father was placed in the emergency vehicle, started on oxygen and began the journey to Holy Cross Hospital in Silver Springs, Maryland.

As they started for the hospital and as my father lay on his back, he could see the tops of trees from the windows in the ambulance, and he described the feeling he had at this time as peaceful and serene as he thought he might now die. In looking at the treetops, he thought about how he and his brothers, Jack and Gerald, had climbed trees as children in Clio, and these would be the last trees he would ever see. About that time as he put it, "The pain set in." He described being shot similar to being cut deeply with a razor blade. Initially there is no sensation, but as the nerve endings begin to react to the penetration, the pain becomes unbearable. That was the time he started asking repeatedly for a pain shot. He said at one time, "I don't mind dying, just don't let me hurt like this." That pain would become his constant companion and bring him many lessons in life. The physical challenges his injuries caused at that moment, ultimately led him on a spiritual journey that would continue until the day he died.

HOLY CROSS HOSPITAL

After arriving at Holy Cross Hospital in Silver Springs, Maryland, he was met by a team of physicians led by Dr. Joe Schanno. Emergency surgery was performed for several hours on him because of the extent of his injuries. One of the major complications concerning his shooting was the fact that he had eaten approximately one hour earlier. He had eaten his usual meal of a hamburger steak, French fries, catsup, and iced tea. The doctors told us later that abdominal wounds are much more serious from an infection standpoint when the individual has a full stomach.

Doctor Schanno told me once, "If you are going to get shot in the stomach, make sure you haven't eaten." Because of this, he had to fight peritonitis which is a blood infection and is quite often fatal. He also had to fight abscesses from the infections brought on by the nature of his injuries. Dr. Schanno presented a watercolor to my father he painted several years ago, and Elizabeth and I have it hanging in our home and we treasure it. When I look at it, I realize the same hands that saved my father's life painted that picture.

He was paralyzed and a candidate for all kinds of infections and complications while he recovered at Holy Cross. The doctors told us later that because of his physical condition, he was able to provide the physical strength and will necessary to survive. They indicated that he had the cardiovascular system of a strong thirty-year-old. My father was a born athlete who moved with confidence and energy. If he was going up a flight of stairs he usually trotted up. He walked fast and didn't part the waves; he became the wave. When I visualize him walking, I often think of how he reminds me of Edgar G. Robinson and James Cagney. A pugnacious, confident, and defiant demeanor were his early trademarks, and now he would have to make, as a paraplegic, what would be for him a dramatic transition to a life with much less mobility and much more introspection.

That journey for him started on May 15, 1972, and the manner in which he, over the years, confronted the many challenges and changes in his life was in full view for everyone to see. I believe the lyrics in a song I wrote about his life speak of that: "And for the world its vision clear."

At the time of my father's shooting, I was in Tuscaloosa, Alabama, to rest for a couple of days and then rejoin the campaign. I had been traveling with him and helping to warm up the crowd at his rallies with the Grand Ole Opry stars. I was actually taking a nap and my friend, Cookie Motlow, whose family interestingly enough owns Jack Daniels in Lynchburg Tennessee, came into my bedroom to tell me of the shooting, and I will always remember that I awoke from just her presence. I knew something was wrong as she said in her soft voice, "Your father has been shot." I went to the television and watched the "Special Reports" on all the networks. About this time, the phone rang, and I was told the state jet would be in Tuscaloosa within the hour to fly me to Maryland. A minute later, there were two state trooper cars at my door ready to take me to the airport. I remember as the car was leaving the parking lot, students swimming at the apartment pool lining the fence and making gestures of reassurance to me, which I will always cherish. On the way to the airport, one radio report indicated that he had received a head wound and had died. That report was soon corrected and on the flight the pilots were in touch with the hospital and gave us updates. Our flight was what is termed a priority flight and means that the traffic controllers put you on a direct flight to your destination, and all other planes have their flight plans re-arranged to allow you the direct course. He was in surgery for over five hours, and we would be seeing him in the recovery room later that night.

I will never forget the look on his face when we walked into the recovery room. He was heavily sedated and I could see some of the stitches on his chest and stomach. He reached out to us with a look I had never seen. The look was of a man who had been to death's door and was back among the living being reunited with his family. That was the look I will always remember. We would be at Holy Cross hospital for a few weeks while my father continued to fight off infections and death. There was a hope that he would regain the use of his legs, but by listening to the doctors discuss it with us; I think I knew that he would never walk again.

He received many visitors including President Nixon, Ethel Kennedy, Shirley Chisholm, George McGovern, and other distinguished visitors once he regained some strength. He also received thousands of cards, letters, and flowers from around the world. The outpouring of sympathy for him was far-reaching and was a source of comfort for all of us at a time of extreme trauma for not only our family, but for the nation.

I have heard from countless numbers of people across Alabama that they remember exactly where they were when they received the news of the shooting. A good friend of mine, Randy Jinks, who is from Talladega County, told me he walked across a field his father was plowing to tell him the news, and how his father wept.

I RETURN TO THE CAMPAIGN TRAIL

As his condition became more stable, I traveled across the country to represent him at various functions including national television programs and events, intended to convey the message that he was still a viable candidate for the Democratic nomination. It is interesting to note that the day following his shooting, the Michigan and Maryland primaries were held. He won both of those primaries including carrying every county in the state of Michigan. For those who might put forward that he had received a sympathy vote, polls taken after the primaries, indicated that the shooting had caused some erosion of his support.

One of my roles while he was in the hospital was to do nightly interviews with the networks, to give the American people an update on his condition. It was important that a message of hope for his recovery be conveyed and that the people of the country knew of our hope for his recovery. As I have traveled over the years, I have had many people mention that my updates gave them a sense of comfort when they were seeking comfort.

I remember going to Lakeland, Florida, for an event held for him by Country Music Legends George Jones and Tammy Wynette. There were thousands of people present at this event, and I was to speak to the crowd after George and Tammy, who were married at the time, played a few songs for the people. I stood backstage with Tammy and as she held my hand, she sang a harmony part with

George while she was off stage with me. George Jones introduced Tammy and me and we walked on stage and the crowd went wild. Their affection and support for my father came forth like a rushing wind and as I spoke to the crowd their enthusiasm swelled to a crescendo. When I finished speaking, I walked through the crowd, to the consternation of the Secret Service, and the depth of feeling I felt as people reached out to touch me was beyond words.

MY FATHER LEAVES THE HOSPITAL—ON HIS WAY TO MIAMI

My father intended to be at the Democratic National Convention and to accomplish this President Nixon offered the presidential medical plane to fly him to Miami. The medical care and professionalism on the airplane were second to none, and my father was deeply grateful to the president for this kind gesture.

By virtue of state law, my father had to land in Montgomery, in order to assume the office of governor once again. Under Alabama law when a governor has been absent from the state for thirty consecutive days, the powers of the governor's office are entrusted to the lieutenant governor. To assume the power of the office again, he had to land in Montgomery, and when the time was announced for his arrival, thousands of people came to the airport to welcome him home.

Prior to leaving Holy Cross Hospital he attended a chapel service, and after a very emotional service he bid an affectionate farewell to the people who had saved his life. The nuns hovered around him like Mother Mary lifting him with their faith, a faith that was now his own. He was a changed man, not only from the bullets, but from a profound sensitivity for the sanctity of life.

I recently found the tape of his remarks to the crowd when he landed in Montgomery and while listening to it, and realizing he was giving it just a few weeks after suffering the kind of injuries he had received, found his delivery to be rather subdued and clearly emotional. This was his first speech and not only was he returning home which made for emotional moments but he had to make certain, to the extent he could, that he conveyed that he was still a viable political force going into the convention in Miami. He spoke of what he and the people of Alabama had represented together, and how they had given him the opportunity to speak for them. The essence of his remarks was that he was their instrument and he would continue to be, even though he had been wounded. They knew he was a man ready and willing to sacrifice his life in their noble cause, and in fact did sacrifice part of his own physical well-being in doing so. Knowing him as they did, they knew he would do it all again because his love for them was that strong. This was one of the most poignant moments in Alabama history.

THE 1972 DEMOCRATIC NATIONAL CONVENTION

The 1972 Democratic National Convention was held in Miami, Florida, and we stayed at the Fountain Bleu Hotel where the Wallace Campaign had several rooms reserved. My father's room was set up as a hospital room with all the medical staff present around the clock. The other rooms operated as campaign headquarters during the convention.

My father had decided to speak to the convention and that became the real buzz leading up to his dramatic appearance. What would he say? What kind of condition was he really in? These and other questions were being asked by everyone at the convention. He was visited by all the presidential candidates, the national networks and correspondents from around the world. We had to watch that he did not overexert himself, but he seemed to gain some energy from the entire atmosphere.

His speech was a dramatic moment for the convention, and I can remember how Tom Brokaw with NBC in covering the speech told the nation, "Here it is, this is the moment we have all been waiting for." As the state troopers and secret service lifted him to the platform, he fell forward but caught himself by extending his hand catching himself on the podium. I recall being startled at this thinking to myself that he would fall from his wheelchair. He did not seem shaken, and the resolve in his voice as he started his speech, I believe took many by surprise. I was concerned at one time whether or not he would be overcome by his emotions, but he held himself together and in check and did what he had to do. He spoke briefly of what he had been through and thanked the people for their prayers and concerns. He then turned to the matter at hand and that was who the nominee would be and what the platform would advocate.

As my father started his speech, I was standing with the Alabama delegation and heard a commotion above me. I looked around to my right and saw Jacqueline Kennedy Onassis and her entourage in the balcony standing up and leaving. I always thought that after all her family had been through, that this rude gesture on her part spoke of an insensitivity that is difficult for me to understand. Another commotion down front found Reverend Jesse Jackson and his followers attempting to shout my father down. There was a feeling at the Convention even among many delegates who were pledged to another candidate, that the behavior of Jackson and his followers clearly crossed the line of civil behavior and demonstrated a profound insensitivity to a fellow human being. There were a few in the auditorium who walked around with a paper mask of Arthur Bremer covering their face and I saw more than one of these masks grabbed by a Wallace delegate and torn to shreds. The vast majority of delegates gave him an extremely warm reception and they were captivated and stunned by who they were seeing, and what they were witnessing. They knew they were witnessing an historic piece of American political history, and they would tell their children and grandchildren about it. This being done, it was now time to return to his beloved Alabama. He had been away from her it seemed, for a long time, and now he was going home. In thinking about his journey back home and the affection so freely given by the people of Alabama, I wrote a narrative a few years ago that seeks to capture my families' feeling about Alabama, and how my father might have felt about going home.

GOING HOME

I was born in Alabama,
And my heart beats proudly underneath her skies,
The people of Alabama are a people of deep faith, Fierce patriotism
*   and grand nobility.*
They hold dear a sweetness of spirit and goodness of heart
Embraced by a willingness to devote fully of themselves,
To causes greater than themselves.
As I travel across Alabama,
I always look forward to those Sunday afternoon,
Spring time journeys that take me through small town Alabama,
This is where the spirit and essence of Alabama lives,
This is where the heart and soul of Alabama calls home,
The serenity and sense of community and brotherhood is felt,
Then I realize again and again, why I am so proud to be called
*   an Alabamian.*
When I reflect in my quieter moments on how good the people of
*   our beloved state have been to my family,*
I am humbled and honored beyond words,
It has been said that, "Friends are a gift from our Living God,

*And the warmth of their caring uplifts and sustains us during
our most difficult days and darkest hours."
And so it has been with the people of Alabama,
And for that and so much more I will always be grateful.
So to the people of Alabama, thank you for being who you are,
And what you are,
Always remember my mother's heartfelt feelings she shared with
the world,
About the people of our great state when she was inaugurated in
January 1967,
When she said, "Be proud to be called an Alabamian, for your
courage has nurtured the flame of freedom."
So bury me in her hallowed ground,
Underneath her skies and among her good people,
Because my heart will always belong to Alabama.*

He would return to extensive treatment and intensive physical
therapy and face an acceptance of a changed life as a paraplegic and
all the inevitable consequences that would bring. My father had to
adjust himself not only to the physical handicap he now had, but
he had to come to terms with the psychological acceptance of being
paralyzed. It took him some time to accept the paralysis, and he
experienced all the stages in that process such as denial, anger, and
depression. He had been such a physically active man, who was
always on the move, and now his life was changed forever, and if
he did not adapt, he would not survive.

Watching him over the years enduring the grueling physical
therapy and seeing the willingness to fight in his eyes was
an inspiration to all who knew him. Over time, he became an

inspiration to many paraplegics and quadriplegics who looked to him for hope, and as he started receiving calls and letters from people who were similarly challenged, he realized he would now be an advocate for the physically challenged.

I can hear him on the telephone talking to perhaps a young person who had become paralyzed by virtue of an automobile accident and telling them, "If I can be Governor of Alabama as a paraplegic, then you can finish school and accomplish anything you set your mind to." As I travel our state, I quite often hear stories from people about a family member he had called, and how much they cherished his call, and how it helped their loved one remain hopeful. I can see him now on so many occasions meeting with another person in a wheelchair, and how emotional those meetings were for him, because now he understood. All the suffering he had endured and continued to endure allowed him to understand the suffering of others in a way he never had before. The bullets had limited him physically, but they had also lifted him spiritually, and given him sensitivity for the suffering of others that was deepened.

FIRST STATE OF THE STATE ADDRESS FOLLOWING THE SHOOTING

As I have mentioned, he returned to Montgomery from the Democratic Convention in Miami to a changed life in so many ways. He would have daily therapy sessions for his physical paralysis, and he would have to counsel himself to a large extent to accept his now changed physical condition mentally and emotionally. While there was always hope that he would regain the use of his legs, the inevitable permanence of his paralysis was the mountain he now had to climb, and it would be quite a journey for him. One of the most moving moments in his life and political career was when he made his first State of the State address to the Alabama Legislature following the shooting. He could either give the speech from his wheelchair, or he could stand while braces were locked in place with a strap behind him securing him to the podium so he would not fall if he lost his balance. As he transitioned from the wheelchair to a standing position the crowd went absolutely wild at which time he told them, "I will always stand up for Alabama."

ARTHUR BREMER

I have always believed that because of the tone and mood set by Richard Nixon, that some of his campaign operatives demonstrated no reluctance in breaking the law. The testimony in the 1974 Watergate hearings revealed a deep paranoia about the Wallace strength.

There were people around Richard Nixon who were true desperados and would do anything to secure Nixon's re-election. Statements made by Watergate conspirator, G. Gordon Liddy such as, "I would take a bullet on Pennsylvania Avenue if it meant the presidency for Nixon," sums up the 'win at all costs' mentality that had penetrated the Nixon camp.

As I have over time reflected on the attempted assassination of my father, the question as to who financed Arthur Bremer's travels around the country for months as he stalked my father, still lingers. There has never been an adequate explanation of how Bremer could lead the lifestyle he did, such as staying at the Waldorf Astoria in New York City, flying around the country, renting limousines, going to massage parlors and otherwise leading a lifestyle that an unemployed waiter normally would not have the resources to afford. This and so much more challenges the reasonable standard. We will never know unless and until Arthur Bremer decides he will talk. Only time will tell, and only Arthur Bremer can tell it.

People have asked me for years if I have ever met Arthur Bremer. The answer is no, although I attempted to communicate with him in 1993. I wrote a letter asking that we meet and hopefully discuss the shooting or anything else he would want to discuss. Because we are about the same age, I hoped that would provide a degree of commonality that could conceivably lead to a meeting and conversation.

I wrote the letter with the assistance of two FBI agents from Montgomery, and in working with them they brought in a gentleman from the FBI Academy at Quantico, Virginia, to help draft the letter. This man was the nation's expert on how to approach a man with the frame of mind of Arthur Bremer. He, for example, had been asked to be the consultant on the movie *Silence of the Lambs* with Jodie Foster and Anthony Hopkins. The tone and appearance of the letter were very important given, as we came to understand, the mindset of Arthur Bremer. His psychological profile indicated that he was extremely paranoid and contemptuous of authority at any level. The expert from Quantico has quite a reputation for understanding the criminal mind, and how to approach an individual of this nature in order to gain some of his confidence. The goal is to give them some comfort level, possibly enough to pull off a meeting. The letter had to be written on plain white stationery with no letterhead that spoke of authority, whether it was simply my name or a home or office address. In addition, the letter must attempt to put Bremer at ease about what we would discuss and that nothing would be talked about that he did not wish to discuss.

I was briefed on two occasions by the agents and in a conference call with the expert from Quantico, Virginia, concerning how to talk with Arthur Bremer if the meeting happened. Given Bremer's frame of mind and his psychological profile, I was taught how to have a conversation with him. To the extent I could, I was to respond in a manner that made the same point Bremer made. An example would be that if he said to me the weather is nice, then my response, albeit with different words would be the same sentiment.

You seek to build a bond and allow him enough comfort where he might be led to talk about the shooting. It would take all the diplomacy skills I had to pull it off, but I was convinced I could do it. Ironically, I had asked the FBI agents if my talking with him about music would be a good idea. My thinking was that since we were the same age and music was such an important part of life for our generation perhaps that could be a bridge to communicating. The agents thought that to be a good idea but Arthur Bremer and I were never to talk of music or anything else. This was the first stage of seeking a meeting, and one where we would await a possible response. No response ever came, so at this point the two FBI agents went to Maryland to meet with Bremer and ask him if he had any response to my letter. As the two agents sat with him, they told me that he never answered them, then jumped on the bars of his cell and made noises like a monkey. When the two agents returned to Montgomery to brief me, I asked them what they thought his conduct meant. Their response was, "Mr. Wallace, we don't know what it means."

Arthur Bremer never responded to the letters my father wrote to him years ago forgiving him, or my overtures to talk with him. Bremer's self-imposed silence has been the subject of much speculation over the years, and the theory that he had help in his assassination attempt on my father is believed by many around the country. I do not believe we will ever know unless there is a classic death bed revelation by Arthur Bremer. It was always difficult for my father to believe Arthur Bremer acted alone. Bremer's travel for months with no visible means of support, and the several thousand dollars in $100 dollar bills in his possession when he was arrested, are only two major issues that lead a reasonable person to believe he had some powerful assistance.

My father accepted the final reports from the FBI and the Secret Service indicating that in their judgment Bremer acted alone. But over the years, my father would make the statement, on occasion in thinking about the assassination attempt on his life, "I see faces." I believe what he was saying was that he had people in mind who he believed were involved in his shooting.

We learned of reports over the years that speculated Arthur Bremer was seen on a ferry in Michigan, a state in which Bremer stalked my father, with a man who became famous later for participating in the Watergate crime and subsequent cover up. This man was the only one who never talked before he was sentenced for his participation in Watergate. He had indicated that he would take a bullet on Pennsylvania Avenue for President Nixon, and those who knew him said that he meant it. This man who knew so much and would not divulge anything about Watergate was G. Gordon Liddy. In my father's mind and heart, he always believed Liddy played a part in the assassination attempt on his life. There is an abundance of information, much of which seems credible to me on the internet, that leads a reasonable person to conclude that Arthur Bremer had help in his assassination attempt on my father.

The reason for my father's sense that there was more to the assassination attempt on his life than a deranged lone gunman has, in my judgment, been largely confirmed based upon the findings of scholarly research since May 15, 1972. A considerable amount of research has focused on Bremer, and relationships it appears he had with some of the Nixon operatives.

The following is an excerpt from a Christopher Ketcham article in the *Atlantic Free Press* in March 2007 titled *"Bigger than Watergate, The Conspiracy that Succeeded."* Mr. Ketcham has touched on some very pertinent questions and facts that have always concerned my family relative to the assassination attempt on my father. His research has been thorough and his sources are credible. Mr. Ketcham writes in his article:

Bigger than Watergate, The Conspiracy that Succeeded.

Mark Felt as Deep Throat counseled his listeners to "follow the money," advice that Woodward and Bernstein smartly heeded. There is another money trail from the Nixon years that has yet to be fully explored: It is a trail that suggests Richard Nixon/operatives within the Nixon White House ordered the 1972 assassination attempt against Alabama Governor, George Wallace, the populist agitator and threat to Nixon's incumbency. The bulldoggish Wallace himself candidly told reporters two years after the gunshots had paralyzed his legs and confined him to a wheelchair: "I think my attempted assassination was part of a conspiracy." That conspiracy, averred Wallace had its origins in the Nixon White House.

If we are to build a case for Wallace's charge against Nixon and/or Nixon's henchmen—specifically the key figures Charles "Chuck" Colson, the man who as White House special counsel once advised his president to firebomb the liberal Brookings Institution, who today is a powerful leader in the evangelical Christian movement. Everett Howard Hunt, the ex-CIA spook hired by Colson for 'black ops,' including the bungled Watergate break-in that occurred one month after the Wallace shooting; and G. Gordon Liddy, former FBI agent turned White House counsel turned dirty trickster under Colson, today a popular radio talk show host. We should rely on the two structural elements that commonly form an indictment for murder: motive and circumstantial evidence. The motive was clear. The circumstantial evidence is overwhelming.

The Motive

In the 1968 presidential election that brought Nixon to office on the slimmest of margins—Nixon defeated Democratic candidate Hubert Humphrey by seven-tenths of one percent—George Wallace as a candidate with the American Independent Party (AIP) carried an astonishing five states and 14 percent of the popular vote, some 10 million voters.

'Not since Theodore Roosevelt's Bull Moose Party emerged in 1912,' Newsweek noted, 'has a third party (the AIP) so seriously challenged the two party [sic] system.' The Wallace/AIP machine sparked a stomach-churning panic among Republicans under Nixon, given that Wallace had locked up a conservative Southern bloc that otherwise would have voted almost wholly for Nixon (four out of five Wallace voters told pollsters in 1968 that without Wallace in the running Nixon was their man by default; conservatives, Southern conservatives especially, could not countenance the Democratic presidential nominee Hubert Humphrey, a liberal Minnesotan). Conversely, if Wallace had carried 1 percent more of the popular vote in two different states, he would have denied Nixon the electoral votes needed for victory, throwing the contest into the Democratic-controlled House of Representatives, which was expected to install Humphrey.

As early as 1966, Nixon was telling Harry Dent, his southern strategist—who would later head an intelligence gathering operation against George Wallace that Nixon dubbed "Wallace Watch"—that Wallace was the man he 'feared most.'

In 1970, with Wallace topping out on the president's growing "enemies list," Nixon secretly taps into a $1.9 million cash slush-fund to help bankroll the campaign of Wallace's opponent, Albert Brewer, with infusions that eventually came to $400,000, a third of Brewer's entire campaign budget. Wallace is narrowly re-elected and fresh from victory goes on the road attacking Nixon in preparation for a 1972 run, again as a third party [sic] insurgent. The New Yorker pronounces him, 'an awesome and disquieting presence in national politics.'

Nixon in his typical fashion is wildly paranoid that Wallace will go it alone once again if he fails to mount a decent showing in the Democratic primaries. So, Nixon by 1972 lavishes another $600,000 to satisfy his Wallace obsession—this time to bankroll Wallace's campaign against Edmund Muskie in Florida. Nixon calculated that Wallace could in no way secure the nomination, but a solid series of primary victories would *keep him in the running as a Democrat, nonetheless. Nixon has now spent at least $1 million of his own slush-fund—and countless hundreds of thousands in government money—to quell the Wallace threat.*

In 1971, Nixon's henchmen under the leadership of Charles "Chuck" Colson—"tougher than hell, smarter than hell, meaner than hell," Colson was Nixon's go-to man for dirty tricks and later a key figure in the Watergate affair—even went so far as to attempt to purge American Independent Party voters from the rolls in California. This was in order that AIP, so successful when backing Wallace in 1968 would fail in 1972 to meet California's registration minimums for a spot on the ballot.

Wallace places well in some primaries—he wins Florida, for example, and does well in others, but always the question of whether he'd go the third party [sic] route darkened the future of the Nixon White House. The 'entire strategy' of Nixon's re-election, Nixon backer, Robert Finch, noted at the time, 'depends on whether George Wallace makes a run on his own.' A 1971 poll showed Nixon leading by four to six points in a head-to-head race with any of the likely Democratic nominees (Muskie, Ted Kennedy, Hubert Humphrey), a lead that dropped to a distressing one percent when Wallace as a third-party candidate was factored in.

The Assassin: The Strange case of Arthur Bremer

A nearly penniless busboy and part-time janitor, the son of an alcoholic truck-driver and depressive mother, Bremer in the two months before the assassination attempt suddenly went on the move, purchasing a blue AMC Rambler for $800 in cash. According to the Washington Post and Time Magazine, federal income tax forms discovered in his apartment indicated he'd only earned $1,611 the previous year, so the Rambler was an almost impossibly deep-pocket purchase. A month before the assassination attempt, Bremer flew to and from New York, where he chartered a helicopter over the city, hired a limousine, stayed at the Waldorf Astoria, and visited a high-rolling massage parlor. Bremer often earned less than $10 in a day. When he drives to Ottawa, Canada, three *weeks before the shooting, he stays at the exclusive Lord Elgin Hotel. He later purchases three guns for $80, a police radio, and binoculars. Wallace himself wondered publicly as to who bankrolled these excursions and purchases all paid with cash.*

Did Bremer have accomplices? According to investigative reporter Donald Freed, writing in the Los Angeles Free Press in June 1972, Bremer was seen on 'several occasions' talking with an 'older, heavy-set man' as they rode the route of a Michigan ferry back and forth. Investigative reporters, Sybil Leek and Bert Sugar, claim that Bremer's visit to the Lord Elgin hotel in Ottawa included a rendezvous with one Dennis Cossini, identified as a CIA agent. Cossini who had no history of drug abuse was found dead from a massive heroin overdose two months after the Wallace shooting. An eyewitness on the Chesapeake & Ohio Railway told the New York Times and the Associated Press that in April and May of 1972 he saw Bremer traveling by train across Wisconsin in the company of a well-dressed man who stood 6'2" tall, weighed 225 pounds and spoke with a New York accent. The eyewitness said the man talked heatedly about moving a political campaign—which campaign the witness could not say—from Wisconsin to Michigan. Was this the same 'heavy set man' from the Michigan ferry?

It is also of note that ballistics investigators in the Wallace shooting found disturbing discrepancies. Wallace alone was wounded in nine different places, while three other victims—a Secret Service agent, a campaign worker, and an Alabama State Trooper were each wounded once. Altogether 12 separate wounds were inflicted on that fateful day by a lone gunman firing a .38 caliber revolver that held only five bullets—magic bullets, one might assume. Yet, this wound count was entry and exit wounds, rendering the scenario entirely possible, though improbable. The New York Times, however, made note of the fact that 'four persons had suffered at least seven separate (initial entry) wounds from a maximum of five shots.' The Times noted there was 'broad speculation' as to how this could be—as logically, it was simply not possible without a second gun, or second shooter, in the mix. Added to the ballistics conundrum is a further mystery; several of the bullets recovered could not be matched to Bremer's .38 revolver (the experts, en revanche, claimed the bullets were too damaged for a positive identification).

A CBS News cameraman caught the events before and after the shooting and later provided the FBI a clip that reportedly depicted a man in the crowd near Wallace who resembled none other than G. Gordon Liddy, the Watergate break-in mercenary under E. Howard Hunt. CBS reporters from their film documentation alleged that Liddy 'led Wallace into Bremer's line of fire.' George Wallace told the FBI that he believed Liddy was standing directly behind Arthur Bremer.

Authors Freed, Leek, Sugar and others have suggested that Bremer had a control agent who was running him in the Wallace assassination project. The writers have speculated that Bremer was a programmed assassin, mind controlled by CIA handlers using psychedelic brainwashing techniques—massive doses of LSD and BZ coupled with hypnosis, perfected in government Cold War programs such as MK-Ultra and Operation Artichoke. There is no hard evidence to support a Bremer-as-a-Manchurian-Candidate scenario. Yet Bremer's disassociated behavior— his indifference, incoherence, his noted roboticism, and the 'silly grin' he consistently wore, raises questions. He writes in his diary that he would shoot Wallace in order to secure fame and publicity. But then, jailed and accused, he refused to speak to the press and, even after his conviction— he was sent to prison for 53 years—he has never talked since. 'I stand mute,' he said. Bremer's lawyer at the opening of the speedy five-day trial told the court that given the defendant's mental state—the eerie non-presence of the man—it is not surprising that 'some doctors will tell you even Arthur Bremer doesn't know if he shot Wallace.' When Bremer was arrested and charged, a federal officer noted that he was 'almost oblivious to what was going on.' Today Bremer spends his time in prison talking to 'inanimate objects,' though he has not been declared insane.

It was long rumored among CIA operatives that the public meltdown of the normally composed Sen. Edmund Muskie—the strongest of the Democratic contenders who doomed his candidacy by bursting into whimpering tears at a New Hampshire podium—was the result of LSD poisoning. Mile Copeland, a veteran CIA operative, writes in "The Real Spy World" that the CIA was asked (presumably by Republican operatives) for an LSD type drug that could be slipped into the lemonade of Democratic orators, thus causing them to say sillier things than they would anyhow. To this day, some of my friends at the agency are convinced that Howard Hunt or Gordon Liddy slipped such a drug into Senator Muskie's lemonade before he played that famous weeping scene.

Nixon's Dirty Tricksters: Colson, Hunt, Liddy and the Bremer Connection—Bob Woodward in 1972 chased through the labyrinth of the Wallace assassination story but failed to uncover definitive evidence of a White House-Bremer connection (at least nothing that satisfied his editors, who were difficult enough to convince that a sitting U. S. President and/or his closest aides would cover up a two-bit break in, much less attempted murder). Woodward at one point received an anonymous tip that a Watergate suspect had met with Bremer in Milwaukee, but he could find nothing to support the tip.

Two years later, in May 1974, Martha Mitchell, the estranged wife of the embattled U.S. Attorney General John Mitchell, visited George Wallace and his wife, Cornelia, at their home in Montgomery, Alabama. According to Wallace biographer, Dan T. Carter, Martha told Wallace an incredible story: John Mitchell, unnerved by what he believed to be a 'Colson-Bremer connection,' had repeatedly wondered aloud to his wife, 'what was Charles Colson doing talking with Arthur Bremer four days before he shot George Wallace?'

The Bremer break-in was another piece of the Wallace assassination puzzle. According to Woodward and Bernstein, Colson ordered CIA black ops specialist and author of spy novels E. Howard Hunt, who would quickly be implicated in the Watergate burglary that followed within weeks of the Wallace shooting, to enter Bremer's Milwaukee apartment and plant pro-Democratic literature to make the assassin appear a proxy for the McGovernite left. In any case, the FBI inexplicably failed to seal Bremer's apartment for a period of 90 minutes, during which time the place was stampeded by media and key evidence was reportedly removed and/or tampered with.

Meanwhile, in Bremer's car, a diary surfaced that was reportedly an accounting of Bremer's travels and thoughts in the two months before he shot Wallace, bearing on the pages the loud declaration that, 'I have to kill somebody' and 'I am one sick assassin.' But Wallace himself came to believe that the diary, with its bizarre admixture of sophistication and stupidity (complete with spelling errors so egregious they seem almost purposeful), was in fact a forgery. Its tone, he noted to reporters, 'contrived as though it was deliberately written to throw off inquiry into a possible conspiracy.' Gore Vidal in the New York Review of Books in 1973 came to a similar conclusion. Vidal's article, "The Art and Arts of E. Howard Hunt" traversed Hunt's long career as a spy novelist and concluded that Hunt likely authored the Bremer diary.

Seen in this light, one wonders if Nixon's payoffs to the blackmailing E. Howard Hunt (as much as $180,000 in cash at a time) served not merely to cover up the break-in at the Watergate Hotel—but to cover up a Hunt-Bremer-Wallace connection to Chuck Colson and the White House, a connection that ultimately might have signaled complicity in attempted murder.

Anecdotal evidence supports the notion of assassination plots being issued from the Nixon White House. A Boston intelligence operative named William Gilday as early as 1970 reportedly met with Nixon aides who recruited him for 'schemes ranging from dirty tricks to murder,' according to Anthony Summers, author of the "Arrogance of Power; The Secret World of Richard Nixon." 'Those (Gilday) was incited to kill,' Summers writes, 'included Senator Edward Kennedy and George Wallace.

The aides in question are unnamed here for legal reasons but Gilday has appeared to have knowledge of corroborating details—their nicknames, for example—and has provided reconnaissance photographs he said were taken with Kennedy's murder in view.' The Nixon White House Tapes suggest a Boston connection to Chuck Colson, who in conversation with a worried Nixon—who complained that operations that were 'very close to me' had been rife with mistakes—told his president that he would never betray him. 'I did things out of Boston,' Colson said, referring to '15 or 20 black projects.' 'We did some blackmail and . . . my God, uh, uh, uh, I'll go to my grave before I ever disclose it.'

Note that Nixon from the first news of the Wallace shooting became obsessed with the case, ordering the FBI to immediately force jurisdiction. Mark Felt, assistant FBI director under acting director and faithful Nixon appointee L. Patrick Gray, took charge in the critical first hours, but was quickly replaced by Gray, who would later help destroy Watergate evidence and was also pivotal in shunting the Bremer case out of the purview of the Watergate hearings. Gray briefed Nixon daily on the Bremer developments. Nixon stipulated that all evidence seized in Bremer's apartment be remanded to the White House rather than FBI headquarters, against protocol. All copies of the Bremer diary transcripts that had been provided the Secret Service and other agencies were to be surrendered and destroyed immediately. All records that the White House itself had even seen of the diary were to be destroyed. Nixon apparently felt the need to cover tracks.

The FBI re-opened the Wallace case at least four times in the years since Bremer's conviction, though these have hardly been extensive in their scope. In 1993, for example, the FBI conducted only one interview with an undisclosed individual and then once more retired the case (FOIA requests may reveal the interviewee). According to the FBI's case dossier, known as the WalShot Files, the agencies [sic] original investigation 1972-74 failed to explore key avenues of inquiry. The FBI under L. Patrick Gray refused to look at the wide-ranging information unearthed in the

Watergate hearings and possible connections to Nixon's dirty tricks bandwagon and Bremer. George Wallace, meanwhile had high hopes for the Watergate hearings, with UPI reporting in 1974 that Wallace felt the investigation 'would turn up the man who paid the money to have me shot.'

In 1992, George Wallace Jr., Wallace's son, requested the FBI and Congress re-open the case 'to learn if there is any truth to a report that the attack was discussed in the Nixon White House,' according to the Associated Press. 'My question is, did anyone else involved in Nixon's campaign have prior knowledge?'

According to Seymour Hersh, writing in the Atlantic Monthly in 1983, even Gerald Ford, on the eve of pardoning Nixon, demanded of Nixon's lawyer, James St. Clair,' Is there anything to it?' Asked Ford, 'Was the White House behind the Wallace shooting?'

Ironically, the one man that Richard Nixon, alone, and embattled, could now turn to was George Wallace, who carried enough influence to sway the votes of the Democrats who could save Nixon from the axe. 'George, I'm just calling to ask if you're still with me,' Nixon told Wallace. 'No, Mr. President,' Wallace replied, 'I'm afraid I'm not.' Nixon hung up, and turned to Alexander Haig, Nixon's chief of staff, delivering the famously echoed epitaph to his career; "Well, Al, there goes the presidency.'

'In reality,' observes Dan Carter, 'what provoked {George Wallace to refuse to help Nixon} was the ongoing refusal of the Nixon White House to divulge the details of the actions of Nixon and Colson on the night of the shooting.' What can we assume from this seemingly minor detail? Richard Nixon might have saved his presidency by fully disclosing to Wallace the truth behind the WalShot case; he instead opted not to. Perhaps, he feared such a disclosure more than the loss of the presidency. Perhaps he feared something worse than impeachment or resignation. Perhaps he feared a lifetime in prison for attempted murder."

While there have been many articles written concerning the possibility of a conspiracy, and there are many to be found on the internet, what was important was how my father accepted it. He rose above it all with forgiveness in his heart, and an acceptance of the inevitable crosses life causes us to bear. His acceptance of all these things led him to the most important "Cross," the one that lifted his burdens and gave him his final peace.

FAITH OF THE FATHER

When my father left office, in January 1979, he moved to a suburb in Montgomery known as Hillwood. In his neighborhood, the homes were modest and in a beautiful section of an upper-class neighborhood. The home was bought for him by his supporters before he left office in January 1979. I remember riding around with him one Sunday afternoon as he looked at the various shades of brick on homes. Surprising to me was that he had his own idea of the color of brick he wanted for the house, which was yet to be built. I recall thinking how strange it was to me that he had wanted to do this. It seemed out of character for him so I asked him about it and he told me, "Son, I'm looking for the shade of brick similar to that of my childhood home in Clio."

He lived on Fitzgerald Road that ran into Zelda Road and I always found that interesting as F. Scott Fitzgerald and Zelda were two of Montgomery's beautiful, intriguing, and creative people many years before. As I mentioned, the house was modest with an iron gate on the side of the house, and behind that in the carport, an office for the ever-present Alabama State Troopers, who protected him until the day he died. We always had a special relationship with the security men, and it was a personal relationship that transcended politics.

His bedroom was equipped as you would expect a paraplegic's room to be equipped. His bathroom was larger than the average bathroom, with special devices for his shower and other necessary needs of a paraplegic. His bed was a state of the art therapeutic and computer driven bed that continually shifted the air mattress that greatly reduced the possibility of his developing bed sores. One of the greatest threats to a paraplegic is the propensity they have to develop bedsores that in many instances can be fatal.

There was always the smell of cigar smoke when you entered my father's bedroom, and you would see a stack of books he had been reading. He had a large magnifying glass with a light attached that he could pull down from above his head to give him much larger font to read, plus more light. The reading material before him I always found fascinating. Over the years, he enjoyed political biographies, but as the years passed, he broadened his selection and I might find among other topics: Greek Mythology, Robespierre and the French Revolution, John Locke, the Federalist Papers, books on the Middle East, and several books on faith and religion. He especially enjoyed the books of his friend, Dr. Billy Graham. He had several autographed books from Dr. Graham and these books were instrumental in helping to strengthen my father's faith. There was one book Dr. Graham wrote about angels that my father talked about for years. Over the years, my father and Dr. Graham had more than one conversation about my father's role in World War II. My father agonized over the thought that innocent civilians could have been killed during his bombing missions over Japan. He was haunted for years with the thought that he could have participated in a raid that had in fact killed innocent civilians. This was the time Dr. Graham provided some comfort in that regard. Dr. Graham talked with him about how he had fought evil in the world to make it safe for individual freedom and human liberty. Dr. Billy Graham spoke to him of his duty as a member of the military, and how his mission was to only target structures and not people. Dr. Graham shared with him that he was a child of God and since he had accepted Jesus Christ as his Lord and Savior, all transgressions, intentional or otherwise, had been forgiven, and washed away. This was great solace to my father and Dr. Graham will always hold a special place in my heart for his friendship and willingness to minister to my father with such tenderness, insight, empathy, and love.

There was a therapy bed adjacent to the bedroom where, until his later years, he worked out with weights to help keep his upper body strong. This room also kept his medicines and the equipment that all paraplegics have to have. Hanging above his bed was the picture of an eagle that had been given to him by the Governor of Alaska many years before. Elizabeth and I now have it hanging in a special place in our home. The picture to me is symbolic of his life as he soared to great heights, just as the eagle does in the picture. To the left of his bed was a portrait of Mother, and over the years he would refer to it often. He would say to me as his voice broke the silence, "You know son, your mother was a beautiful lady and the people loved her." He would sometimes start to weep at that moment, and I knew he was going back in his mind, going back in time. She was the true love of his life.

The television in his bedroom was a gift from Governor Fob James who took office in January 1979. Governor James and his wife were always attentive to my father and visited him several times over the years. Once Mrs. James, on a return trip from Israel, brought my father some Holy Water, sprinkled it on him and they prayed together. That was a profound experience for him, and I can hear him now talking about the Holy Water from Israel.

Over the years, I would take people to visit my father. Some would be friends of mine and others would be people who had contacted me for a visit. It never failed that following the visit with my father no matter who I was with, they would comment, "George, you know there is a special feeling in your father's room." The special feeling, they were talking about was a peace and tranquility you felt from him that surrounded you and embraced you. My father had come to peace with his Lord, himself, his past, and his future. The feeling in his room on Fitzgerald Road was the presence of the Lord and the Holy Spirit.

MY FATHER MEETS POPE JOHN PAUL II

My father had met many national and international leaders during his time in public life, and their discussions always centered on public policy issues relative to domestic as well as geo-political concerns. This was the world in which he lived most of his life, and thus those were the issues that occupied his mind and heart.

As his life changed due to the assassination attempt on his life and his brush with death on so many occasions, he was changed as only someone who has sensed the frailty of life can understand. His faith was his friend now, and as it nurtured him it gave him insight and wisdom.

One of the greatest spiritual events in his life was his meeting with Pope John Paul II in 1984 during his last term as governor. His Chief of Staff, Elvin Stanton, was on the trip and relates the meeting and how powerful it was.

Elvin writes:

In the summer of 1984, during his last term in office, Governor Wallace led an industry-seeking trip to Europe and planned to meet with industrial prospects, government leaders, and Alabama soldiers who were serving overseas. The governor had a high regard for Pope John Paul II so his staff made inquiries through government diplomatic channels in Washington, as well as through the Archbishop's office in Mobile, as to whether the two might meet when the governor visited Rome.

Prior to the governor's departure from Montgomery, we were told that such a meeting with the Pope might be possible, but we would not know for sure until later. Governor Wallace proceeded with his trip, meeting Alabama soldiers in Germany, Prime Minister Margaret Thatcher in London, NATO Secretary General Joseph Luns in Brussels

Belgium, Italy's Prime Minister Aldo Moro, and many other government and business leaders in Europe.

At each stop the Governor would inquire, "Have we heard anything yet about the Pope?" Our staff would reply, "Not yet, but we're still in touch and we're waiting for an answer."

We arrived in Rome and checked into the Hotel Excelsior. One of the governor's security members, David Golden, and I were making advance arrangements for the scheduled stops in Rome. We had not heard anything from the Vatican yet. We returned to the hotel on Saturday to find that there was a message for me at the hotel desk. It was a hand-delivered white envelope, addressed to "Mr. George C. Wallace, Governor of Alabama. It bore an official Vatican seal on the back. Anxiously, I opened the letter and noticed that many of the words were in Italian; enough were in English that I could see that the governor had an invitation to meet with the Pope, "Tomorrow, Sunday, 12:00 noon, 21st July 1984." The invitation also noted that the meeting would be at the Castel Gandolfo, the Pope's summer vacation palace, a few miles south of Rome. We relayed the information to the governor, who of course was excited and pleased that the meeting had been arranged.

Golden and I had much to do and very little time to do it. State security policy was to never take the governor where we had not already been. While we had been to the Vatican, we had not been to Castel Gandolfo; it was a last-minute surprise. Hurriedly, we arranged with Italian police to join us for an advance visit to the Papal Palace. We were surprised by the guard's uniforms. They were dressed in flowing red, gold and blue brightly-colored tops and pants and beret-styled black hats. The guards showed us where we would park the governor's car and where we would enter the palace, but we were not allowed to visit the room before the actual visit.

On Sunday morning, our small motorcade with Governor and Mrs. Wallace, escorted by Italian police, journeyed south along hilly, winding roads leading high above Lake Albano to the Pope's summer residence *surrounded by beautiful gardens and villas. For hundreds of years, this site has served as a retreat for various popes. Only four of us, met by an escort representing the Pope, were allowed to enter the Palace.*

We were ushered directly into what appeared to be a medium-sized, high-ceiling meeting room with marble floor and door trim. There were several ornate chairs and marble top tables in various locations around the walls, and the tall windows were adorned with curtains and trimmed with valances across the top. Several pictures and ornaments decorated the walls and a statue stood on a three-foot high marble pedestal in one corner. We thought the room must be a waiting area, and that the Governor and Mrs. Wallace would be escorted into another room.

However, we were there only a few minutes before the Pope walked quite quickly through the marble doorway and went directly to the governor, who was sitting in the middle of the room in his wheelchair. Mrs. Wallace was standing by his side. The Pope was followed into the room by three attendants and a photographer.

The Pope who spoke good English reached out and grasped the governor's hand with both hands, greeted him and the two began to talk. The governor then grasped the Pope's two hands with both of his hands, and at one point as they talked, the Pope placed his hands on each of the governor's shoulders and they expressed their feelings with deep emotion. They met for about forty-five minutes and the Pope presented rosaries in small cases bearing the Vatican seal. Pope John Paul II spoke admirably of the governor and his courage, and the governor expressed his own appreciation for all the Pope had done for the cause of Christendom throughout the world.

One could not escape the irony of this poignant meeting. Both men were charismatic leaders who cared for those unable to fend for themselves. Both men were victims of assassination attempts. Both came perilously close to death. The governor was shot five times in a crowd at a Maryland shopping center in the month of May of 1972. The Pope was shot four times in a crowd in St. Peter's Square at Vatican City in the month of

May of 1981. Both were struck in the abdomen, both underwent hours of intestinal surgery, and both suffered severe blood loss. Both would-be assassins were apprehended immediately. In both cases, others were injured: three in the shooting of the governor, and two in the shooting of the Pope.

But the irony continues. Governor Wallace wrote to his attacker, Arthur Bremer, when he was in prison, expressing his forgiveness and telling him that he was praying for him, he loved him, and called upon him to seek forgiveness and salvation so the two could be together in Heaven. The Pope forgave his attacker, Mehmet Ali Agca, and asked people to pray for the man. He met privately with Agca in prison and sought his release. Bremer was sentenced to 53 years in prison but was released in November 2007 after serving 35 years. Agca received a life sentence, but was released in January 2010 after serving almost 29 years.

When I consider how, over the years, my father would talk about this meeting and how much it had meant to him, several thoughts occur to me about his life's journey. For all of his adult life he had sought to be a leader of men. His own personal strength, intelligence, confidence, and charisma were the tools he used as he climbed the political ladder. He at one time had been brash, confrontational, and a man very much in a hurry. He could never quite be still and was on the move constantly. You always had a sense when you were around him of his energy, and almost a sense of danger on occasion. His life had been one of such turmoil confrontation, joy, sadness, pain, and sorrow that his final journey had taken him to Christ. He had come to terms with his mortality and he got it right. He sought now more than any other time in his life, quiet and solitude so what a change grace had brought to him. This meeting with Pope John Paul II was not only a meeting of two men, but also two men's spirits embracing. They both had experienced bullets piercing their bodies and all the pain that caused them. But they both understood that to love even those who have sought to harm you, was the admonition from our Lord. Their examples of forgiveness and mercy are examples to us all.

CHAPTER SEVEN

Going Home

HIS RECOVERY AND REHABILITATION

In discussing my father's life with people over time, whether in a private conversation or making a presentation, they are intrigued to learn that he spent more years as governor paralyzed than he did before his injury. He was governor for five years and five months before the shooting and governor ten years and seven months subsequent to his injury.

The trauma of the shooting, the recovery and rehabilitation tested him in every way he could be tested. For my father to go from being a dynamic individual who moved around with such energy and prowess to being a paraplegic was extremely difficult at times. Coupled with his injury and paralysis, was the constant chronic pain he had to suffer due to the nerve ending damage the bullets had caused. The psychological blow was powerful, and he spiraled downward at times into deep depression. Once when he was feeling considerable pain, and wanted a pain shot from his doctor, the doctor for whatever reason said no. While I realize his doctors were concerned about his developing a dependency on Demerol and other pain medicine, there were many times when I wished they would give him some relief. Once in his frustration about the situation, and his doctor's refusal to give him a shot, he said, "Son, I can call out the National Guard, but I can't get a shot for pain." He suffered more than a man should have to suffer.

The depression and frustration he suffered with his condition, at times would have him look at the ceiling saying, "Son, I am in a heck of a shape." His condition gave way to some advocacy in the press and among his political enemies that he should resign from office. That was all it took! He got the old fire back and two years later in 1974 was elected Governor of Alabama for the third time. He had been challenged as he had so many other times in his life, and he prevailed.

The Secret Service stayed with my father in Montgomery for several weeks as they transitioned the operation of the new security technology to his Alabama security detail. At that point, they returned to Washington to assume other duties.

There was the need for a new car to accommodate my father's special needs as a paraplegic and to provide him with protection. General Motors in Detroit, Michigan, designed a special Lincoln Continental for him. The car was larger than the normal Lincoln Continental with more room in the back seat area to accommodate his paralysis. It had a special motor with superior power and a reinforced steel chassis. My father had always, prior to his shooting, been sensitive about riding in a car that he considered too luxurious. He preferred to ride in a Ford LTD and would have never considered riding in a Lincoln Continental before his injuries. His thinking was that people should not see you in a luxury car because you were one of them, and they needed to see themselves in you. Things had changed though and people probably seeing him in a car like this now thought that is the kind of car in which Governor Wallace should travel.

HE COULD HAVE BEEN ON BROADWAY

There are several ways to end a visit with someone in your office when you are in public service or in the private sector. To stand up and extend your hand and thank the person for coming is the standard practice. And, as you walk the visitor to the door, you both know the meeting has ended. Given that my father was now in a wheelchair and was seeking to end a meeting by having extended his hand perhaps three times and the visitor still would not budge, he knew he had to take stronger action. Make no mistake about it; he was in severe pain most of the time, so the days he could spend at the office when he was having a relatively good day were valuable. So here he is faced with a visitor he has been delighted to see, but it was now time for them to take their leave. This is the point where he rivaled Lawrence Olivier. In an Oscar-winning moment, he would jerk his head down so his hair would fall into his face and then look up with pain in his eyes to a very concerned visitor. At that point, my father would say, "I'm having some pain today; thank you for coming to see me." Well, the visitor at that point wanted more than anything to give him his privacy and let him recover from the muscle spasms so they left. Then the remarkable recovery was intriguing to watch as he straightened up, brushed his hair back, lit his cigar and you knew you had witnessed an Oscar-winning performance. Even before he was injured and after the injuries, he was a master performer whether he was on stage or not. I believe great politicians have this talent and politics to a large extent, especially given the virtual technology culture in which we live, has become more and more about media savvy. He was a master at this and one of the secrets of his appeal was a rawness and unvarnished truth that touched people. It was fresh, honest and spoke to their hearts with passion. He told me once in talking about public speaking that, "If you don't believe it; they won't believe it." It was that simple with him and that is how he always approached it. It was as though George Wallace was your neighbor and understood, like no one else, what you were feeling and what you believed.

His strength had always come from his relationship with the people of Alabama and their devotion to each other now would sustain him and give him the desire to carry on. Certainly, he wanted to improve and get better for his family and friends and we all knew that. We also knew that politics was in his bones and his very soul, and that would be the one medicine that would help him now more than any other. As he started moving among the people of Alabama once again, they greeted him with almost reverence. They had suffered with him on his journey and they were very proud of him. The love and affection from the people of Alabama at that time strengthened him and allowed him to endure. My family and I will always thank God for them.

After returning to Montgomery from the 1972 Democratic convention, the Secret Service installed very sophisticated technology around the Governor's Mansion that included infrared beams and state of the art cameras. Assassination attempts, in the minds of the Secret Service and his Alabama Security detail, did not necessarily end with the first attempt. Who could know if there was a conspiracy to ultimately kill my father? I even recall reports of threats to kill my sisters and me. H. Rap Brown, a renowned leader of the militant Black Panther Party, visited Montgomery during those tumultuous times and made the statement. "We're going to get George Wallace and then get George Jr." That was the moment in time for me that altered my teenage years because now on many occasions my constant escort was a plainclothes Alabama State trooper or a member of the Alabama Bureau of Investigation. It is always the unknown threats that security forces must plan for as best they can, and the real possibility of a deranged individual seeking to commit a copycat act had to be dealt with professionally and thoroughly. It only takes one person to cause havoc and great harm, and there is no room for error or omission in terms of precautions.

I recall late at night going into the backyard of the Governor's Mansion just behind the tennis court and sitting and talking to a Secret Service agent who showed me the tiny infrared beam that could barely be seen. As timed passed, during the campaign and after the shooting, I had developed a close relationship with many of the Secret Service agents, several who were not that much older than I was, and at various times I was able to have long conversations with some of them. And in so doing, made some good friends with wonderful memories of them I cherish today. I will always remember during those visits thinking about our backyard in Clayton where I would play when I was a young boy and reflecting on how different my life had become. The soil of my adult backyard was far different from the soil of my childhood home, where I would play in the clover under the clothesline while mother hung clothes in a slight breeze. The sweet smell of spring clover to a five- and six-year-old, as you rolled around in it, and talked to your mother while she hung the clothes on the line, became one of those gentle memories for me. The backyard of my youth was far different from the backyard for me now.

THE PAIN HE SUFFERED

From the day of the shooting until he died, he suffered constant chronic pain from the nerve ending damage the bullets had caused. In seeking to alleviate some of the pain, he had even put himself through an extremely dangerous surgery in Washington State in 1980. He also tried a medication called DMSO that was applied to the areas affected by the pain, and in some instances helped bring some relief. I believe the most help he received according to what he related to me, were the acupuncture treatments from a Chinese doctor in New York City. This always seemed to be a contentious point with some of our family doctors because of their Western mindset, but I believe the acupuncture treatments helped him the most.

His pain was so severe that it brought him to tears on more occasions than I can recall. He would tell me, "If I could just be paralyzed and not hurt, I would be the happiest man in the world." His suffering caused most of us around him to do more perspective thinking about our own lives, and the burdens we all were bearing. He made us all realize how truly fortunate we were. I never could remove my feelings of helplessness when I was with him. I wanted to take some of his pain and give him some ease and comfort because his suffering was so great.

Given this circumstance and considering whether or not to seek re-election in 1986, I knew what his decision would be. His conversations leading up to the day he made his dramatic announcement in the historic House of Representatives chamber at the Alabama State Capitol, were about how difficult it would be to serve and how he could not give a full measure of himself to the people he loved so much. His decision was based upon his consideration of them because the polling information clearly showed he could win again.

"I'VE CLIMBED MY LAST POLITICAL MOUNTAIN"

As I have mentioned, making the decision whether to be a candidate in 1986 for State Treasurer was in my mind predicated on what my father's decision was relative to seeking a fifth term as governor. I knew because of the time I had spent with him and the observations he made about his physical condition, and how it had worsened, that he would not be a candidate. He never came right out and said that, but as fathers understand their children, the children come to understand their parents. It was clearly apparent to me what his decision would be, and which of the two speeches he would give after arriving at the historic Alabama State

Capitol. As is in all cases when a popular candidate decides not to make another run, you have all types of people around you who for their own self-interest are always ready for another run. My father had some of those, but he also had so many around him who only wanted what would be best for him. Their deep affection transcended any political considerations. These are our truest friends. Our friends have given us the faith and strength to carry on, lifted us to great heights and honored us beyond my ability to convey my gratitude. In some small measure, public service has been a way to return some of the goodness the people of this great state have so freely and lovingly given to the Wallace family. So has been the friendship between the people of Alabama and the Wallace family, and for that and so much more I will always be grateful.

I rode with him to the capitol on the day he announced his retirement. Very few people know that he took two speeches with him. One speech was to announce that he would be a candidate for re-election. The other speech was that he would not run and that he had climbed his last, "Political Mountain." There had been intense speculation for weeks leading up to the speech, of what he would do and being the masterful politician he was, he kept everyone guessing until the moment he made his speech.

The House Chamber was absolutely packed with press representatives from around the world in attendance. There was a palpable feeling in the chamber of intense anticipation of what he would say, and everyone understood what an historic moment they were witnessing.

He started his remarks in a rather subdued manner, and from the outset I could see that he was feeling deep emotion as he spoke and was reflecting in his mind of all that he, Mother, and our family had been through. He spoke of his love for his state and her people, and then he reached the point everyone had been waiting for. He spoke of his prayer over the years that the thorn in his side, meaning the pain from his injuries, would be removed. And reminiscent of Paul who had prayed the same prayer, he realized it was not to be. Given that, and because he did not believe he could give fully of himself to the state he loved so dearly, he had decided he would not seek re-election. He then said, "The Lord willing I will be around a few more years, but for now I pass the rope and pick to another climber and I say, climb on, climb until you reach the highest peak, then look back at me for I too shall still be climbing."

The following is the complete text of his speech given that day:

My fellow Alabamians, I come to you today, with great humility and deep appreciation to the people of Alabama. They have honored me and my family more than they have honored any family in the state of Alabama.

They elected me governor four times and elected Governor Lurleen one time and my immediate family has been involved in state government about three decades, and I am very grateful.

We have shared good times and prosperous times. We have seen progress and we have been partners in the growth of Alabama.

But during the hard times, when we looked into the faces of the hungry and unemployed, and I'm thinking about the days back in the depression of '32, because I am a child of the Depression. I saw the Old South because I was a part of it. I smelt and felt and was part of the poverty of that particular era. I hardly know what held us together except for the people of our own state and the Southern region of our country. We're the type that could not be held down. The Old South resisted encroachment the same as the New South. But our state has come from the depths of poverty in our time, in my lifetime, that none of you have ever seen before. And we had become not only the backward part of a nation that felt the War Between the States; we are now part of that great, vibrant part called the Sun Belt.

I would like to be part of the future, but during the past few days I have done much evaluation and much soul-searching, and some of our

205

younger citizens may not realize that I paid a pretty high price in 1972 for doing what the people of our state and our region and our nation wanted me to do. Our effort made us the leading candidate in the '72 primaries when an attempted assassination took place against me with five bullets shot into me in 1972.

I have never used this before. I have never used it to bring any sympathy for me in former campaigns for the simple reason that I did not feel it was proper to do so. The people of Alabama have elected me governor and I have never mentioned that matter unless harassed by someone at a press conference. Those five bullets gave me a thorn in the flesh as they did the Apostle, Paul, and I have prayed they should be removed, but they were not.

I realize in my own mind, that although I am doing very good [sic] at the present time, as I grow older the effects of my problem may become more noticeable and I may not be able to give you the fullest measure that you deserve from a governor throughout another term. That's because I grow older.

In light of this, and after much prayerful consideration, I feel that I must say that I have climbed my last political mountain. But there are still some personal hills that I must climb.

But for now, I pass the rope and pick to another climber and say, "Climb on. Climb on to higher heights. Climb on until you reach the very peak. Then look back and wave at me, for I, too, will still be climbing."

And in my melancholy moments I am tempted to think of the past service as governor and my campaign when I was shot. I may be inclined to do so, as did Peter the Great upon reflecting on the death of his mother, when he remembered what the Apostle Paul said about not too much grieving over these things. But I also recall the voice of Edras, sometimes in my melancholy days and times I say, "Call me again the day that is past."

And while I may be tempted to dwell in the past and say, "Oh, what might have been," I must realize, as Peter the Great did, that it is time to lay aside that which can never return and think about the future. And now, I conclude by telling you that my heart will always belong to Alabama. I expect to be around, the Lord willing, a few more years. But as for the governmental and political arena, my fellow Alabamians, I bid you a fond and affectionate farewell."

As he ended his speech, he became very emotional and there was not a dry eye in the House of Representatives chamber. To extended applause and a sound from the people that sounded like a mournful cheer, he blew kisses and saluted them one last time.

On our way back to the Governor's Mansion, he told the Alabama State Trooper driving to pull up in front of the capital on historic Dexter Avenue and park for a few minutes. We sat there in total silence for about fifteen minutes as he looked at the capitol and occasionally took a puff of his cigar. He kept a steady gaze on the capital, and I could only imagine what he was thinking. Was he thinking of Mother lying in state, and the outpouring of love for her, as people stood in line for hours to view her body? I think he also was reflecting on the many years he had led our state from that building, and how he never gave up the fight for the average Alabamian. He was their champion, he knew it, they knew it and that would never change. His mind might have recalled his father letting him out of the car on the steps of the Alabama State Capitol as a fifteen-year-old when he served as a page in the Alabama legislature. The memories came rushing back as he relived so many moments of those years gone by. In those quiet moments with his eyes gazing upon Alabama's Capitol, he thought of the message he had taken around the nation about the values and goodness of the people of Alabama. He thought of the look in peoples' eyes as he met them and how his relationship with them had sustained him during some difficult and dark days. I remember after we had sat in silence for that time, the only thing he said was, "I hope they will not let the rich and powerful take over at the expense of the people." That summed it all up for him—what he had stood for, what he suffered for, and why he had entered the political arena so many years before.

HIS SPIRITUAL JOURNEY—THE FAMILY OF MAN

One of the most enduring and revealing testaments to his faith came from his correspondence to Arthur Bremer, the man who had shot him and left him with such pain. In the letter my father wrote, he told Arthur Bremer that, "I love you and have forgiven you, and if you will ask Jesus Christ into your heart, then you and I will be together in Heaven." This letter had not been intended for the public domain, but I found it in our family archives tucked away among other similar letters he had written Arthur Bremer. When I asked him about this one night, he said with kindness and goodness I will always remember, "Son, if I can't forgive him, my Lord won't forgive me of my sins." It was a moment that lives in me and is the true light for our lives.

He was ready to go. His wisdom had led him to grace, and the "Peace that Passeth Understanding." I know how he longed to be with Mother, and he would be, because our Lord was now his Savior. My father had a scripture framed and hanging on his wall that said, "In quiet and confidence you shall know your strength." His strength now was the stillness he had come to know, and it would take him home.

A more genuine sense of the fragile nature of humanity was revealed to my father as he lay on his back, blood flowing from his body. This was the first step on his road to Damascus, and as his life's journey continued, he would realize profound changes in his physical, mental, emotional, and spiritual life. These brought him introspection not only about himself, but the times in which he lived and gave to him a clear picture of his past, and what his future now must be.

At this moment in time, there was a bond forged with many of those he had been accused of hating. The Civil Rights workers who had been injured and killed and had shed their blood, now had a brother in George Wallace. Their common sacrifice and their common bond was their own life blood. The time had come and the hour was here when this covenant between the two was born all because of their own unique suffering and shedding of blood. As time passed, other bonds would be formed based upon forgiveness, understanding, and brotherhood. All these bonds were genuine and real and having witnessed many of them, the feeling in the room as he met with Black leaders over the years left an indelible mark on me. The love that was shared and the affection that was given and received, was truly a spiritual moment for all who were standing beside his bed. He told them of his suffering, and how he believed the Lord had kept him here for a purpose, and that was to do the Lord's work, and seek understanding among all people.

Among the Black preachers from across Alabama who met with him as well as Black leaders from across the nation, such as Jesse Jackson, Joseph Lowery and John Lewis, I will always remember the tears that were shed and the emotions that were expressed as their coming together became a virtual revival. They knew he had been in the 'shadow of death' and had suffered as many of them had. Again, it took him back to his own roots and his own love and respect for the Family of Man.

Thus begins the two lives of my father. Because of the traumatic injury he sustained and the subsequent pain he endured until his death, he was given a gift, although an expensive one, that allowed him to know as, Dr. Martin Luther King Jr. said, "He had been to the mountain top." As my father looked over his own personal mountain top and as he said in his political retirement speech, "I still have some personal hills I must climb," it reminded me of all his efforts over the years to work for change and to I believe, in his heart and mind, try and rid himself of a certain guilt he held about some of his actions and words during the early part of his career. Some of his actions were a source of regret to him.

A thought I have had over the years in thinking about the Shakespearean drama of my father's life, was how after his injury he became a quieter and more introspective man. The transition of his personality seemed to me to be a gradual one where he realized how much his life had changed, and how much he had in the past relied on being strong for the people. A large part of his personality was the strength he showed as he would walk across the stage saluting his troops, and how his overall physical movements inspired almost as much as his words.

So, here he was and would be until the day he died, a paraplegic who would suffer constant chronic pain and a man who would make an odyssey of his life seeking to nurture our common humanity. His constant faith in his knowledge of the saving grace of Jesus Christ became his clarion call. His first calling was to rally the people and seek to make a better life for them in his beloved Alabama. All of his initiatives to enhance the quality of life for his people were consistent with his empathy for them and devotion to them. His later calling because of all that had happened to him and how his life had been altered, was to be an example of how faith can strengthen and allow us to endure with hope. He did this with a grace and courage that could only come from the divine, and he was an inspiration to all who came into his presence.

His entire life had been dedicated to ministering to the people, speaking for the people and standing up for them. His place in time and his political style were meant for each other, and he was masterful in every phase of the political game. It seemed to me that the manner in which he carried himself as a defiant, bold, and confident leader was to a large extent based on how he walked and moved among the people. Now all of that was gone and he would be wheeled to every place he would visit for the rest of his life. He would have to reach deep down and find the courage to persevere and come to terms with not only his physical fate, but his own mental, emotional, and spiritual fate. In Jesus Christ, he found the "Peace that Passeth Understanding."

To spend an evening with him in his later years was always something I looked forward to. I would sit by his bed, and we would watch television together, or I would type scripture for him on the computer screen we had placed on a hospital table at his bedside. He especially enjoyed the History Channel and programs about nature and the animal kingdom. He had lost his desire to watch boxing and I found that of interest so I asked him about it one night. He said, "Son, I don't like to watch people hurting each other." This was such a contrast to the years I had spent watching boxing matches with him and remembering how much he enjoyed watching combat. The fragile nature of life had penetrated him deeply, and his heart was full of warmth for humanity, and his disdain for violence filled him with indignation.

HE WAS READY TO GO

He was ready to go. His wisdom had led him to grace and peace and I know how he longed to be with Mother, and he would be soon. He had fought the good fight and lived a life that had been full and robust. He reached great heights and had fallen to great depths. He had experienced it all in full view of the world and had done it with dignity and grace.

I struggled with something I had wanted to convey to my father for a long time, and I wanted to do it in a way that would hopefully not make him sad and melancholy. I wanted him to know before he died that he would lie in state at the Alabama State Capitol. In Alabama's history, only two people have ever had this honor: Jefferson Davis, the President of the Confederacy and Mother. I think he knew in his mind that given all he had accomplished being elected Governor of Alabama four times, and his presidential campaigns that there would be an official state funeral. Nevertheless, I wanted him to rest in the knowledge that the people of Alabama would be honoring him in a manner that would be historic and lasting. His reaction found him looking at me and then looking away with a peaceful smile.

My mother, father and son rest together at Greenwood cemetery in Montgomery, Alabama. I often think of how they whisper their love to each other in the early mornings and will do so all through eternity. They are sailing across the universe together, with their souls giving them flight. Bobbie, Peggy, Lee, and I are those arrows as Kahlil Gibran describes us in the, "Prophet," when he called the children, "The living arrows seeking the mark of the infinite." Our faith reveals to us that we will all be together again one day, whispering to each other in the early mornings.

HIS LAST DAY—I WANT TO GO HOME

He had been admitted to Jackson Hospital's Intensive Care unit in September of 1998 due to an extraordinarily high temperature. It had fluctuated between 104 and 105 degrees and was cause for great concern among his doctors and family. He was treated with heavy antibiotics and fluids to fight whatever was causing the infection and would be treated as such until the infection was gone. The infection would never be gone and would ultimately take his life. These last few days I noticed a certain resignation when I looked into his eyes. He would look at you for the longest time as though he was trying to take everything in. I had seen that look in my mother's eyes during her last days. The look in her eyes then, and my father's eyes now, was the same. They both had the look of someone seeing beyond themselves, a look of someone looking into eternity.

I had been to visit him in the hospital during that Sunday afternoon and sitting by his side we talked occasionally, but mostly he just lay there quiet and peaceful. There seemed to be a certain peace about him and an aura of tranquility. During the afternoon hours, into the twilight and into the night, he would hold the hand of the Alabama State Trooper who had been assigned to him, and he would say, "I want to go home, I want to go home." He would look at the State Trooper with hope in his eyes and the trooper would respond in a soft voice, "We'll be going home soon, Governor, we'll be going home soon."

On that September afternoon after these words were spoken, and as he continued to hold the hand of the State Trooper during the day, only fate knew this would be the last hand he would ever hold. He would gaze with affection at his friend sitting by his bedside, as though he knew this would be the last person he would spend time with in this life.

What makes these last few hours special and unique was that the Alabama State Trooper my father had fellowship with and held hands with as his life was ebbing away, was a Black man. As my father looked in the face of this Black Alabama State Trooper who was so kind and caring to him, what was he thinking? Here was George Wallace who to a large extent would always be thought of by many as a racist, holding the hand of a Black man who gave comfort and solace to him on the last day of his life. As he comforted my father, I will always remember his tenderness as he stroked my father's hand and spoke softly to him saying, "We'll be going home soon, Governor, we'll be going home soon."

CHAPTER EIGHT

The Legacy of His Journey

What is the real legacy of this journey we have taken that has had such a dramatic impact on the political landscape of our country? How do I separate the personal imprints on my life into categories of personal and political? As closely linked as they were to my life, they each became one and the same. Born from the womb of political ambition, these two forces would mold and shape my family. The pressures brought to bear on us were much more severe than most people will ever realize. The personal struggles we all had to confront were unique in their own way, but again the same in so many others. The man in the eye of the hurricane was my father of course, and the whirlwind he had caused was now consuming all around him.

From a political and public policy standpoint, my father's vision from the beginning was to uplift people and make their lives better. Regional pride mixed with a combative spirit and an excellent mind, he possessed all the tools necessary to make a mark on history, as he fought the good fight. He fought for them and suffered for them, and their affection for him ran deep. There are only a few times in our history when a man and a people have such an intimate relationship with each other, but this is one, and it reached far beyond the borders of Alabama. Millions of people ultimately in all parts of our country, came to have the same affection and loyalty for this man from Alabama, George Wallace.

He worked to double education appropriations, which included providing free textbooks to all students in grades one through twelve and increasing teachers' salaries by more than 40 percent.

The Wallace-Cater Act providing tax breaks and incentives for industries locating in Alabama was the genesis of the incentive packages Alabama has used to attract automakers Mercedes, Hyundai and Honda to Alabama.

He established the Alabama Trust Fund from oil and gas revenues to serve future Alabamians.

He worked to open 14 junior colleges and technical schools and adding 15 new trade schools to the 5 that he had worked to establish as a State Representative two decades earlier.

He worked to expand the University of Alabama Medical Center at UAB in Birmingham, and established the University of South Alabama at Mobile, the state's first new university in nearly a century. His dedication to establishing another medical school at the University of South Alabama was realized and has been of great benefit in educating new doctors.

He worked tirelessly to attract nearly $2 billion in capital investment in new and expanded industry, resulting in a hundred thousand new jobs and helping to make Alabama second in the nation in the rate of increase of per capita income.

He worked to implement the state's largest-ever highway construction and maintenance program.

He initiated programs to benefit the mentally ill and arrest water pollution; increasing support for the state's mental institutions and prison system; and increasing medical benefits to the aged and the indigent.

He worked to institute rigid ethical standards in competitive bidding for state projects while abolishing the "whiskey agent" system, through which previous governors had enriched their cronies by requiring payoffs from liquor companies for shelf space in state-controlled liquor stores.

His ever-present desire to attract new industry and expand existing industry in Alabama led him to focus much of his attention on Alabama's state docks in Mobile. Revitalizing and expanding this port of entry for the world was always a point he made to world leaders when he traveled abroad. He was in a position because of his international prominence to create interest in Alabama like no other governor before him, and that over time paid huge dividends for our state. During his last term, he expanded Alabama's state docks at the urging of the coal industry in Alabama and because of that initiative, a greater flow of goods and raw materials have been exported and imported. Alabama's state docks today are state of the art and have played a major role in the success of our Mercedes, Hyundai and Honda manufacturing plants in Alabama. As Alabama has become, as national publications call us, "The Detroit of the South," his vision and work to make our state docks first class has realized great benefits for our auto makers in Alabama.

His initiatives to assist the poor, the elderly, and our veterans made him early on a populist in the finest tradition of the word. It became apparent from the very beginning that he was a friend of the "Little Man." To fight for the less fortunate among us was a calling he felt because of his early life, and the experiences that had made such an impression on him. It was part of him, and not a position he took after some evaluation as we see so much of today. He believed what he said and said it in such a way that people were drawn to him.

His fight with the Federal Judiciary, when he reminded us that Thomas Jefferson had warned us of, "Whimsical, capricious, designing Federal Magistrates," was a fight that the people of the South warmed to because of history, and actions the Federal Judiciary were taking early in his career that would change the culture of the South. Jefferson and my father both believed that it was the duly elected legislatures who were the prosecutors of the liberties of our people, not the courts. This battle continues to rage even today and will rage as long as we are a Republic. Thomas Jefferson put it clearly when he said, "The great object of my fear is the Federal Judiciary."

His legacy in Alabama is one that follows the same pattern of populists down through history. Having taken positions and advocating policies that generally sought to focus on the needs of the "Great Middle Class," in many instances, found him in an adversarial position with the corporate establishment. As he made his decisions on matters of public policy, his heart and mind took him back to those depression days in Barbour County, Alabama. He could see the faces of a proud people in need and he felt a bond with them. He had been a poor boy who would never forget.

PRESIDENT BILL CLINTON REMEMBERS GEORGE WALLACE

There is a wonderful story President Bill Clinton relates about my father that occurred at a National Governor's Conference in Portland, Maine. This story conveys in a poignant way my father's feelings for, "The Little Guy."

President Clinton remembers:

In 1983 when I was at my first Governor's Conference in Portland Maine, Governor Wallace came all the way from Alabama. His wounds were severe and his movements labored. I was then spearheading a movement among the governors to try to reverse the actions of the Reagan administration on Social Security disability, which was basically a program for people who are disabled and can't go back to work. There was some abuse of the program and it needed to be corrected, but the

Reagan people went way overboard. They tried to kick a truck driver in Arkansas who lost his arm, who had a ninth-grade education, off Social Security disability on the theory that he really could work at a clerical job. That's the kind of thing they were doing.

So we organized a governors revolt. And, then at the last minute the congressional allies said we needed a statement from the whole conference, including the Republicans, that this isn't a good thing. So the Reagan administration sent two assistant secretaries from the Department of Health and Human Services to try to beat back our efforts. And they had to beat it back in the committee, where we were one vote short. George Wallace was on the committee. We met early in the morning, like eight o'clock, the day before. And I sat down with Wallace and told him the whole story, and I said, 'Look, I know this is a pain for you, but a lot of your people in Alabama are being really hurt, and I need your vote for this.'

I'll never forget this he said, 'It sounds to me like you are right.' Now that doesn't sound like such a big deal, except in the condition he was in, it took him much longer to get ready for work than anybody else. And he got up very early, six in the morning. He was tired from his trip and in pain all the time and he went through the difficult ritual he had to go through to get him [sic] prepared. And boy, he rolled into that committee room and made the damnedest speech you ever heard. And the guys from the Reagan administration were downcast. The governors that were trying to beat him knew they were beat. And he rolled the thing out of the committee, and rolled it through the Governor's Conference with a unanimous vote. Within a matter of months, the whole thing was reversed."

Perhaps his greatest legacy was his faith and the transformation of his life caused by tragedy and suffering. F. Scott Fitzgerald said, "Show me a hero, and I'll write you a tragedy." He was a hero to his family and the influence on us as a family that his journey brought was far reaching and deeply felt. The public spectacle that is made of virtually everything that happens to you causes a pressure and anxiety that is difficult, especially on the young. This is the case with many political families of national prominence, and I have always taken an interest in discussing this with my contemporaries and was fortunate enough to have a long discussion with John Kennedy, Jr. about our lives.

JOHN F. KENNEDY JR.

As John Jr. worked to establish *George* magazine he was determined to interview my father as the first political interview for the premier edition. He called me and we spoke about this, and he told me that he did not want our family to feel as though he was intruding on us. I assured him that we would not feel that way at all, and I told him that our fathers had known each other before he was born, and when I was a small child. My father had taken then Senator John Kennedy to visit the Alabama delegation at the 1956 National Democratic Convention.

John and I talked of what it was like to grow up in families with such historical similarities, and the reticence that it has caused in relationships with people. There are so many people who come to you and want to be close to you for a variety of reasons. Our fame was from the arena of politics and in many ways that tends to be the most intriguing to people. Dynastic political families in our nation's history, and the fame brought on by virtue of that, endure and become part of history more so than fame brought on in other professions. We discussed the sense of invasion the political arena brings and the need to separate what criticism comes your way from the personal and the political. Although, he knew as I did that emotions that emerge in this environment become in many instances, one and the same.

John's sensitivity to the desires of our family spoke of our similar experiences, and the burdens we both had to share were from the same source, political ambition.

I received a handwritten note from John where he outlined what he wanted to cover in the interview, and that his interest was purely historical and sharing all the truths about my father. I admired John Kennedy Jr. immensely and his willingness to involve himself in issues of public policy. This passion, I believe, was the same one I felt.

I will always remember where I was when I learned of the death of John Jr. His death had become one of those moments in time that we all remember, where we were and what we were doing. Such had been the case for his father, my father, and now my friend, John Kennedy Jr.

I was hunting with my sister, Bobbie, in Zimbabwe in South Africa when the news arrived of his death. His airplane was reported missing on the day we arrived in Zimbabwe for a two-week hunt. In calling my office in Montgomery, I learned that the Associated Press had called for a statement from me about his death. I remember writing at a table in one of the most remote parts of Africa about the death of a man I considered my friend and brother in ways only he and I could understand. I remember thinking that the public would never be able to understand the sense of brotherhood John and I felt for each other due to the shared burdens and tragedies of our lives. Our unique experiences gave that to us, and I recall when he and I were with other people it was as though we both knew they were spectators. The sense people have when they are with you in various situations is that they are in the presence of living breathing heirs to political legacies that shaped the political landscape of our country.

Upon our return from Africa, John's airplane with his wife and her sister had been found as the nation, we learned, had held a constant vigil trying to hope, but realizing the worst was probably the case. And so, it turned out to be, and a nation felt a blow for the Kennedy Family, such as they had felt in times before.

The following are excerpts from the inaugural edition of *George* magazine, November of 1995, from the interview of my father by John Kennedy Jr. Before the interview, John wrote of his own reflections of the man and only John would know what his final perception would be following their meeting.

John Kennedy Jr. writes:

"I'm in terrible pain, didn't sleep at all last night," George Wallace whispered as I entered his office.

I had been warned before flying to Montgomery that the former Alabama Governor, once a fire-breathing symbol of Southern autonomy, had his good days and his bad days. This apparently was not going to be one of the good ones.

Billy Graham, who knows about these things, once called Wallace the greatest speaker of his time. When he still had his health, Wallace could stir arena-sized crowds into a frenzy of anger and outrage. Today, however, wheelchair-bound since being shot by a would-be assassin in 1972 and afflicted with Parkinson's disease, Wallace can barely speak. Nor can he hear, thanks to lingering ear damage from a stint aboard a World War II B-29 bomber. To communicate with Wallace, I had to write out my questions in large block letters on sheets of construction paper.

But if it is harder for Wallace to express his passion, that doesn't mean it has disappeared. You can see the intensity in his eyes, which are clear and quick with intelligence. When he occasionally glared at me during the two days we spent together, usually in response to a question he disliked, those eyes offered glimpses of the old Wallace, the cunning politician.

JOHN KENNEDY: You and certain members of my family have had your differences over the years. I bet you'd hoped you'd seen the last of us.

GEORGE WALLACE: *Well no. I supported your father for vice-president in 1956 and for president in 1960. I voted for John Kennedy. He was a fine man—although, of course, we differed on some things. Still, some of the Kennedys came to see me in the hospital after I was shot. Your Uncle, Edward, and his wife your Aunt Ethel.*

JK: *In many respects, you and my father were so dissimilar; you spoke differently, your styles were different, you came from different backgrounds. How did all that affect your relationship?*

GW: *Well we had differences, but I don't think they had any effect on our personal or our political relationship.*

JK: *Did you ever think of yourselves as enemies?*

GW: *Political enemies sometimes, but personal enemies, no. You know, I was very fond of your father. I was at your father's funeral. I was also fond of your mother.*

JK: *Let's talk about your views on race, which had been controversial over the years.*

GW: *Well I'm honest, and I can say I'm not a racist at all.*

JK: *Still, that's a label that's been pinned on you. What were the experiences that helped shape your views on race?*

GW: *The Southern people were taught that segregation was in the best interest of all the races. I said that and I was viewed as a racist. I did a lot of things for Black people. Gave them free textbooks. And the people now understand. Black people are my best friends in Alabama.*

JK: *But isn't it ironic that the same Blacks whom you shunned thirty years ago are now willing to forgive you?*

GW: *I didn't shun them. I was for segregation because the people were for it.*

JK: *Let's look at it another way: Although you had been a segregationist earlier in your career, Blacks supported you during your final race for Governor in 1982. Even today many are willing to say nice things about you. Why?*

GW: Because I was a friend of theirs. People have always equated segregation with hatred. But that's not true. We were all taught, growing up, that segregation was in the best interest of the people.

JK: Still, today you sound like a very different man than the George Wallace of thirty years ago.

GW: I'm not a different man. I didn't hate Blacks thirty years ago, and I don't hate Blacks today. The Southern people never hated Blacks. In fact, a lot of Blacks are moving South now, because they find that it's better to live down here than it is in Chicago. Today there's more integration in Alabama than there is in Massachusetts or Chicago.

JK: It's well known that you're a born again Christian. Did your personal politics change after you were saved?

GW: No they didn't.

JK: So that wasn't when you decided segregation was wrong?

GW: Well I was taught that segregation was best for both races. But then, a few years ago, I decided it wasn't.

JK: Why?

GW: My conscience said it was wrong.

JK: And now?

GW: And now segregation is gone. Good riddance.

Later in his interview with my father, John asks him to reminisce about his career.

JK: Looking back over your career, what were you right about, and what were you wrong about?

GW: I was right about some of the issues I talked about. But, I was wrong about Civil Rights.

JK: What was your greatest political skill?

GW: Well, I've heard, and been told, that I was the best speaker who ever ran for president. There was a program on CNN recently that even said that I was the best speaker.

JK: If you could talk to anyone from the time you were Governor, living or dead who would that be?

GW: Billy Graham. Because I'm a born again Christian. It would be comforting for me to speak with him.

JK: If you could live your life over again, what would you do differently?

GW: A lot. I wouldn't have sinned as much as I did. I've sinned so much, so many times. But today, religion plays a large role in my life. I don't attend church because of being crippled, but I pray every night and I pray during the day.

JK: When did you become born again?

GW: When I was shot. It was then that I saw how fragile life was and how short it might be, so I realized you'd better be prepared to die at any time.

JK: Are you prepared to die?

GW: I'm not afraid of death like I used to be, because I'm going to heaven when I die. I'll be forgiven my sins.

JK: And you know God will forgive your sins?

GW: Of course. It says so in the Bible: God will forgive you of your sins, John.

JK: And you have faith in that?

GW: Absolutely. God hears somehow, somewhere. So no, I'm not afraid of death. I'm a saved man.

I am certain John's visit brought back memories to my father of the time he had spent with President Kennedy at the 1956 Democratic National Convention, and his visit with the president when he came to Alabama during my father's first term as governor. President Kennedy and my father were of the same generation. It has been called, and rightfully so, "The Greatest Generation," because of the sheer courage and devotion to saving the free world they demonstrated. While my father and President Kennedy had these similarities, there were also many differences in their respective backgrounds economically and socially. However,

I do believe that the men and women, who are in such positions of power to shape national public policy, feel a certain bond.

I recall a story my father told about flying from Mobile to Huntsville with President Kennedy, and how as they were flying over Birmingham, the president said to my father as he was looking down at Birmingham, "Governor, all we are saying is those businessmen down there need to hire some Negroes." My father responded, "Mr. President, the man who owns that business should be able to hire anyone he wants, because he owns the business. We shouldn't tell him who to hire." My father's respectful but forceful answer to the president did not sit well with the president, and the rest of the trip found them courteous enough to each other, but a chill was in the air. Two strong wills had confronted each other, and it was described by some who were there on Air Force One as a "standoff." I know they had great respect for each other, but clearly they were from different worlds. The ultimate destiny would find them both targets of assassins, and one would live and one would die.

Legacies, just as are our lives as I said at the beginning of this writing, can be mysterious in that they are at least two things: They are what they are and they are what others would have them to be. So much of my father's legacy is much more than a political one. The political one I came to know encompasses the entire truth, and the political one that is often the headline of a biased non-probing reporter who only "knows" my father by often-used headlines, is biased propaganda.

Because of the life he lived and the sense of connection the people felt for him, his legacy takes on more dimensions than the average political figure. The people of Alabama initially, and the rest of the nation ultimately, came to know this man and admire his sense of conviction and courage in the face of the political and personal events in his life. His legacy is one of many dramatic moments that left an indelible mark on the psyche of a nation.

The truest legacy of the Wallaces of Alabama lives within the people of Alabama. As history books and historians interpret what it all meant, the lasting and more meaningful sense of it all to me, beats within the hearts of the people. The stories they will tell of how my mother or father helped their family in a caring way at a difficult time will be passed down to their children and grandchildren.

The motto inscribed on the Wallace crest reads: "We Must Hope." In each of our lives, hope allows us to endure and to carry on, and the hope my mother and father gave to Alabama is perhaps their richest legacy.

When I reflect in my quieter moments on the journey, it is at times overwhelming. I have experienced those moments of darkness Churchill referred to as, "The Black Dog," and have been uplifted by the warmth of the embrace so freely given to us by a good and decent people. I believe for me, the understanding of, "We Must Hope," came from the Shakespearean drama, which was our lives, because through it all, the people of Alabama gave to us the Blessing of Hope. My father's example should give us hope and inspiration today relative to our responsibility to work to bridge the divide that still exists in many instances between races in our country.

TRIP DOWN HISTORY'S LANE

There I was sitting in the Clayton High School auditorium watching a play entitled, *"Wallace/The Clayton Years."* This was the auditorium where I sat as a six-year-old watching John Glenn's lift off to circle the earth in the early years of the space program. Fifty years had passed and so much life had been lived and so many lessons learned. Those years had taken me from the innocence of childhood to the hard reality of political life at the highest level and all that had meant and would continue to mean.

Here, I was watching actors portraying my mother, father, sisters, me and our friends in Clayton during those years. The time portrayed was the time my father was running for governor in 1958 while we were still living in Clayton, a small Southern town.

My good friend, Alva Lambert plays my father in the play and Alva has portrayed him on the History Channel and in other venues. His ability to capture the demeanor and voice of my father is remarkable. Also, Alva and my father were great friends so it is special for Alva to play the role.

As I watched the play with intermittent songs sung by the Pastels, a three-member group of local ladies, the memories came rushing back and took me back in time. Their rendition of songs of that period added the special touch that took the audience on the journey with me. As I watched the play, I occasionally would look to my left or right and focus on the faces of some of the people who were watching the play. One older gentleman's face gave me a glimpse of his ancestors with his chiseled features and look of many hours in the sun. There was a quiet dignity and goodness in that face, and it reminded me of so many faces I had seen over the years. In thinking about his face, I am reminded of the special look of a Norman Rockwell painting. The look in his eyes as he watched his hero, George Wallace, on stage, taking him to another time and another place, was one of pride in who he was. George Wallace had touched his heart and made him stand a little taller. In looking upon that face, I was reminded of the many homes I had been in over the years, where I would see a picture of my mother or father hanging in a prominent place. It was as though they were a part of the Wallace family, and we were part of theirs.

Over the years, I visited [sic] the State Capitol and always enjoy walking the long corridors and looking at portraits of past governors and admiring the capitol's architecture and the magnificent staircase. I often will stop at the marble bust of my mother that rests in the center of the rotunda that faces the Dexter Avenue front entrance. Her smile is one of the first sights visitors see as they enter the Capitol as their hushed tones begin to echo off the historic walls. Her smile is tranquil and soothing as visitors are drawn to her bust in silence, and then the tour guide will begin to tell them the story of Lurleen Wallace.

I have often been standing silently at her bust and then hear the sweet laughter of children behind me break the silence as they enter the capitol, and then I would hear the voice of the tour guide saying, "This is Governor Lurleen's son, George Jr." So many thoughts are going through my mind as I have stood before her and then a child will start telling me about my mother and how she loved to take my six-year-old sister, Lee, fishing. Then a little boy will start to tell me how she worked to help the mentally ill. One afternoon, a little girl told me that I had three sisters and she named them all. Most of the youngsters who tour the capital in the spring are fourth graders who study Alabama history as part of their curriculum, therefore their knowledge of my mother and father is fresh in their minds. It is at times overwhelming to reflect on how I am part of a family who had such a large impact not only on Alabama, but our nation as well.

The years slowly go by, and my mother's smile and grace continue to fill the Alabama Capitol rotunda. Her gentle smile has greeted countless thousands from all across the world for many years, and her legacy of love for Alabama will endure.

Over the years, I would visit her bust with my father and we would then go to the second floor of the capitol and view the portraits of both my parents. The famous artist, Dimitri Vale, painted both of the portraits on display in Alabama's state Capitol, and the Alabama legislature a few years ago passed a resolution stating that their portraits would never move from that location. By tradition, since Alabama became a state in 1819 the portraits of governors would be moved along the wall of the capitol as governors come and go. The Alabama legislature believed that my mother and father's legacy was so rich and embodied the best in Alabama, that a resolution was adopted to have their portraits displayed permanently in one of the most prominent places in Alabama's Capitol. Standing beside my father as he would look upon Mother, he would tell me how much she loved us all, and often he would gently weep.

As my father and I moved through the Capitol together, my shoes echoing off the marble floor, my father's feet were silent and still as he was wheeled down history's lane. As visitors would recognize my father, they looked stunned and astonished and as they approached, his smile and gesture for them to come to him made the unsuspecting visitor's encounter even more special. He would ask where they were from and invariably start telling them stories about wherever they were from. These visits to the capitol were much different from the visits so many years ago as his entourage would make its way to the House of Representatives Chamber for him to give the State of the State address. At the height of his popularity in Alabama, there would be hundreds of his supporters who would come to the Capitol for his address, and they would fill the balcony and many would wave signs in support of my father. This was always an, "In your face," reminder to the Alabama legislature of the enormous popularity and political power of George Wallace. I remember being with him as we would make our way to the chamber through the people who were lining the corridors from all across Alabama. As he moved through the people, they would actually surge toward him, try to touch him and express their full support. "You tell 'em, George. Give 'em hell, George. We are with you, Governor." As their voices would continue to rise in volume, it almost became deafening as the reverberations from the echoing marble walls seemed to make you dizzy.

These were the halcyon days for him in terms of his political strength in Alabama and his growing popularity across the country. He was young, vibrant, strong, and alive and it must have seemed to him that it would last forever. Now, as many years later, his wheelchair slowly made its way through this historic building. The excitement and virtual religious experience of those moments now must seem long ago for him as his thoughts of the past came rushing back with all their joy and sadness.

As we moved quietly and slowly through the Capitol, he would tell the trooper to stop and he would begin telling us about a particular governor. We stopped at the portrait of Chauncey Sparks who was from Barbour County and gave my father his first job in the Attorney General's office when he returned from the war. Governor Sparks had written my father a letter while he was stationed in the Philippines during the war, and in the letter the governor told my father if he could ever be of assistance to please let him know. Well, when the war was won and my father returned home, he went to Governor Spark's office with the letter in hand. He told the governor of his experience as a flight engineer on a B-29 Bomber in the Pacific theater, and that he had received his law degree prior to entering the service. He told the governor he would appreciate any help he could provide. Shortly thereafter, my father started working in the Attorney General's office as an assistant Attorney General. This was an example of one Barbour County native helping another Barbour County native and of course helping a returning veteran. My father had been a great admirer of Chauncey Sparks and I recall going with my father to visit Governor Sparks near the end of his life. As I recall, the time of this visit was just following my father winning the governor's race in 1962. We traveled to Eufaula, Alabama, which is about twenty miles from Clayton. I had been born in Eufaula and this was where Governor Sparks lived. I remember climbing a rather steep staircase with my father and we quietly entered the upstairs bedroom where Governor Sparks was. He had become totally bedridden, and I can see him now looking extremely weak. His face lit up when he saw my father and as I was introduced to him, he shook my hand and said he was glad to see me. My father sat by his bed and as they talked, you could tell how happy they were to see one another and how proud Governor Sparks was of my father being elected governor.

We would stop at Governor Jim Folsom's portrait, and he would tell us stories of how he was Governor Folsom's South Alabama coordinator and how he would introduce Governor Folsom at some of the political rallies. This was where my father experienced his first taste of statewide politics, and he had the opportunity to begin building his own base of supporters for what was to come. He always had admiration for Governor Folsom's dedication to the "Common Man." Governor Folsom's work building the farm to market roads was a lifeline for rural farmers in Alabama and helped them at a time when they needed it the most. My father and Governor Folsom did not always agree, but they had a mutual respect and admiration for each other. They had been very close at one time, but as so often happens in life, time and circumstances can cause a certain distance between people.

My good friend Randy Johnson's father, Roland Johnson, was the leader of the band that played for Governor Folsom's campaign rallies and helped make the song "Y'all Come" so popular. Roland and my father traveled together and Roland told me once that he said to my father during that time, "George C., you're going to run for governor one day." At this, my father asked him why he thought that and Roland said, "Your introduction of Folsom is longer than his speech." Roland told me how at every stop my father was shaking hands with people and making notes with names and phone numbers even then.

Roland went on to serve as the mayor of Garden City, Alabama, for over forty years and his son, Randy, and I have been close friends for years. Randy is head of the Alabama Coal Cooperative and I worked closely with him and his organization while I served on the Alabama Public Service Commission.

I am reminded of the quiet hushed tones of the people who filed by my father's casket while he was lying in state at the Capitol in September of 1998. I had already shared with him that he would lie in state, and he knew that only two people had been afforded that honor in Alabama's history. The President of the Confederacy Jefferson Davis, and Mother, were the two to have been so honored, and I wonder if he thought about that on our quiet afternoon tours.

The last few years of my father's life found him more and more confined to his bedroom. For a few years following his leaving office in January 1987, he was able to travel in the van to visit the old home place in Barbour County and to travel to other places all across the state.

There are many stories I have heard of how Governor Wallace would show up at a country restaurant in some part of Alabama for lunch and be mobbed by well-wishers and people who wanted to see him, talk to him, and touch him. He was an icon not only in Alabama, but also throughout the nation, and he was a living breathing part of Americana. He was one of their own and because of that they had deep admiration and affection for him.

In visiting with him during his last years, and as his health slowly deteriorated, my father's appearance changed. Having left office in January 1987, he lived until September 13, 1998. Following his injury in Maryland and given his condition, the doctors told us that the normal longevity span for someone of his age with his injuries was about eight years. He lived twenty-six years following the assassination attempt on his life, and while some of those additional years can be attributed to medical care, I believe his sheer will and very life force were the major reasons he lived as long as he did. Someone was quoted a few years ago as saying that, "When you were around George Wallace, he just seemed to be more alive than others." The spirit that dwelled within him was strong and steadfast, and through his sheer will, I believe, he was able to stay with us as long as he did. The last twelve years of his life as a private citizen found him on Fitzgerald Road where he, for a while, worked as a fundraiser for Troy University. He had great affection for this fine institution and his college roommate, the late Dr. Ralph Adams, was president of the university for twenty-five years. Dr. Adams took the university to new heights academically and athletically. Following the tenure of Dr. Adams many years ago, Dr. Jack Hawkins took the helm of Troy University and has taken it to even greater heights.

When my father retired from working any longer, his health had deteriorated. His hearing and speaking had diminished to the point it was difficult to communicate with him. Most people would use a yellow legal pad he kept beside his bed for visitors and family to write questions for him and express their sentiments. I have been told since he suffered from Parkinson's disease, that some of the medications he took for that affected his voice. As time passed, the once strong and confident voice of George Wallace had been relegated to a whisper. It was difficult to understand him on occasion, so it took a combination of listening and lip reading to comprehend him. We eventually got him a computer and placed it with the screen adjacent to his bed so he could read from it. I raised the font and this method of reading made it easier for him. I can see us now, me sitting by his bed typing scriptures for him, and answering any questions he had via computer. He especially enjoyed reading the scriptures and talking about them, and I will forever be glad that we had this time together. In many ways, it made up for all the time he had to be away when I was growing up. It was truly the best quality time I could have spent with him.

At this time, he was bedridden, and his face had taken on a peaceful and restful look. His face was now thin and the passing of time had made his features more prominent. His hair was now a total grey, longer and swept back to meet his pillows. What I most remember about him were his eyes, and how they had changed from the famous Wallace glare to a much softer look. He had been places and dared great things, and you could see it in his dark eyes. He had become a quieter person, a softer person, a more introspective and reflective person. I often wondered what he was thinking as he would lie there with a faraway look in his eyes. Was he thinking about Mother, and all they had been through together and how much he missed her? Was he thinking of the old records I would find him listening to at our home on Farrar Avenue in Montgomery? This was the home he had bought for Mother while she was ill and one of her last requests was that she have a home in Montgomery that was all her own. He wanted her to have everything she wanted, so she made it a home and would go rest there in between her treatments for cancer as it gave her a certain solace. I think her affection for that home was in knowing that it would be our home when she was gone. For a long time after mother's death, my father would listen to some of his and mother's favorite songs on our stereo such as Floyd Tillman's, "I Love You So Much It Hurts Me." Hank Locklin's, "Send Me the Pillow That You Dream On," Frank Sinatra's, "Time after Time," and others that would take him back to the time when they were young and in love. As I would come in the back door, he would be sitting in the living room on the sofa listening to some of their favorite songs, and I could tell he had been crying, and he would say, "Son, come sit here beside me." He would hold my hand as he was trying to hold on to himself and to Mother.

I believe he was going back in time to the time he met mother, who was working as a clerk in a dime store in Tuscaloosa, Alabama. She was sixteen and he was a twenty-three-year-old law school graduate, driving a dump truck about to enter the Army Air Corps. Mother said that my father had, "That special sparkle about himself and I was drawn to his eyes." I think he thought of her and what a wonderful wife and fine mother she had been.

He thought of how she fought so gallantly for life, and how close they had become during her last years. He thought of how they had reminisced together, never losing hope that she would recover, but both of them knowing what the inevitable would probably be. The sensitivity they showed for each other during this time was heartwarming to see, because it was so real and genuine. Life had taken its toll because of politics, but during these moments they felt the spark that had brought them together when they were young.

In his later years, he talked quite often about Faith and Forgiveness. He told me on more occasions than my memory will serve, that he used to think politics was the most important thing in his life, but he had come to realize that your Faith and relationship with Jesus Christ is what is most important. He was quoted one time as saying, "What does it matter what the world thinks of me or whether they remember? What is important is what happens to my soul when I die." He told me one night, "Son, the most important moment in my life will be when my heart stops beating, because then I will be with the Lord and your mother." His Faith was strengthened, I believe because of the suffering he had to endure for so many years. Suffering has a purifying effect on us, and in his life, I know it did. The suffering that was always there allowed him to understand the suffering of others in a way most people will never know. Whether it was physical, social, economic, mental or any other manner of suffering someone had to endure, he now felt a heightened sensitivity for their needs and he was affected deeply by their plight. He saw very clearly what most will never see, and he felt very deeply what few will ever feel. This profound empathy for the lives of others was given to him by virtue of ironically, his own pain and suffering from the assassination attempt on his life.

Would he have done it again knowing what he would have to experience? Would he have devoted his life, with all the sacrifices that were made, if he had known his personal destiny, and the destiny of his family? Certain people, I believe, are born leaders and for them not to follow this most basic instinct goes against the laws of nature. Such was the case for my father.

He would eventually rest beneath my mother's loving gaze as his casket was placed next to her bust in the Capitol rotunda as he was lying in state. I have a picture of the Dexter Avenue entrance to the Capitol being opened in the late afternoon, and as the September sun came streaming through, it rested on mother's face as she looked down on the man she had loved so much.

Now, they belonged to the ages . . .

My father meets with Dr. Joseph Lowery and others who reenacted the Selma to Montgomery Civil Rights March. "Indeed, a historic moment."

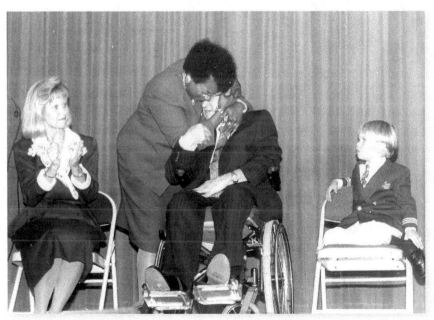

Connie Harper embraces my father, "two old friends."

Left: John F. Kennedy Jr. writes a question for my father during their interview for the first edition of "George" magazine in 1995.

My sisters and me in our old hometown of Clayton, Alabama.

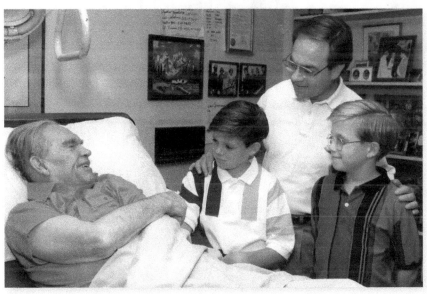

Me, Corey, and Robby visit with my father in 1995.

James Hood, one of the students wanting to register at the University of Alabama on June 11, 1963, holding George Wallace's hand when they met on July 2, 1996.

Vivian Malone meeting with George Wallace when she was the first recipient of the Lurleen B. Wallace Award of Courage, October 10, 1996.

Alabama State Troopers carry my father to his resting place next to Mother at Greenwood Cemetery in Montgomery, September of 1998.

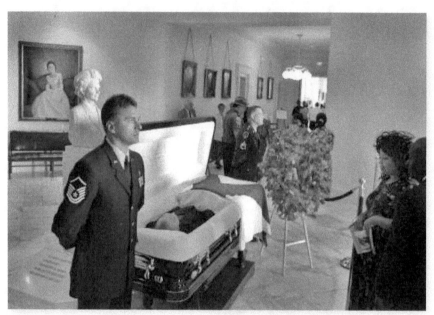

Lying-in-State

Robert Williams, a lifelong Montgomery resident salutes Gov. George Wallace's funeral cortege as it passes by on the way to Greenwood Cemetery. "This is a day of atonement and a day of unity," said Williams. "And we as Blacks and whites can be together. I am proud of what I have seen, and I am proud to have been a part of the Wallace era. I've seen a lot of changes in my lifetime."

The greatest test of George Wallace's courage was when he had to admit he was wrong. It takes a big man to say when you are wrong.

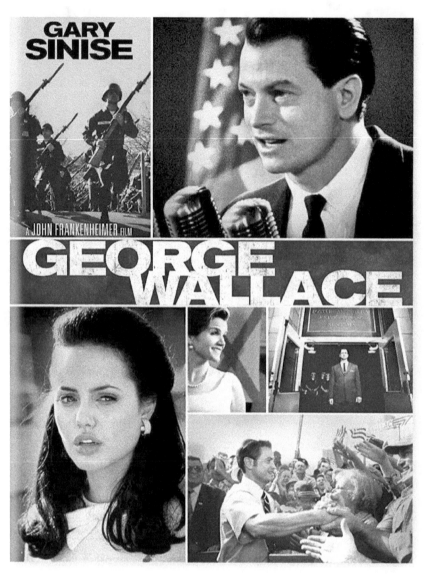

"It's a strange feeling. I really believe that George Wallace had a spiritual redemption happen to him, and it possibly took getting shot to make that happen."

Actor, Gary Sinese
Played George Wallace in Award-winning Miniseries

In a letter to me at the time of my father's death, while he was in the White House, President Bill Clinton wrote, "George Wallace was one of the most dynamic political figures of our time. Over the course of his long life, he came to symbolize reconciliation in our society and was a vital part of our national journey away from division. In this, he demonstrated great personal courage."

Wallace Family Portrait

Alabama Governor Kay Ivey had a luncheon for us during Christmas and the grandchildren got to see where I grew up.

Lower row: Grandchildren; Bo Pitman, Ella McMahon, Julia McMahon, Coles Pitman, Graeme Pitman, Jack McMahon. Second row: Courtney McMahon, daughter; Elizabeth Wallace, George Wallace, Leslie Pitman, daughter. Upper row: Robby Wallace, son; Robert Pitman, son-in-law. Inset photograph, Steven McMahon, son-in-law.

CHAPTER NINE

My Mother, Governor Lurleen B. Wallace

MOTHER

My mother was the only daughter of Henry and Estelle Burroughs Burns of Tuscaloosa. She had one sibling—an older brother, Cecil. Mother graduated from Tuscaloosa County High School at 15 by taking summer classes. Upon her graduation from high school, she was working at Kresge's Five and Dime in downtown Tuscaloosa, which is where she met my father. He would come in to buy hair oil and was struck by my mother's olive complexion and beautiful eyes. He would joke with her not knowing she had just recently turned sixteen years old. Mother talked over the years about his sense of humor and confidence and she said, "I remember liking George from the start, he had the prettiest dark eyes, and the way he'd cut up." My mother remembered of my father when he would visit her parents' home that, "He ate quite a lot."

Mother had wanted to be a nurse from her earliest recollections. To me that was consistent with her nature as a person. She has been described as pretty, bright and having a goodness about her that was easily recognized. She held empathy for people I have been told that transcended her years. It was innate, thus her desire to be a nurse was a reflection of her nature. Years later, while serving as Alabama's First Lady, she became a "Pink Lady" which was a volunteer group of ladies dressed in pink uniforms, working at various hospitals in Montgomery. I can see her now, slender and tanned in her uniform, heading to the hospital and in some ways realizing her youthful dream.

One amusing story occurred while she served as a "Pink Lady." It seems actor Burt Reynolds was in Montgomery and had come down with the flu and had been admitted to St. Margaret's hospital. As the story goes, Burt Reynolds was absolutely astonished that he was being cared for by the governor's wife. At the same time, Mother was, as were the other nurses, thrilled to be caring for a movie star.

I have heard many descriptions over the years about Mother from people who knew her in her youth. In all their descriptions of her, they tell of being drawn to her because of her goodness. When I think about that, I am struck by how that very nature captured not only her family and friends in her youth but captured the hearts of the people of Alabama in her adulthood.

An example of her effect on people was the fact that in 1966 she placed sixth in, "Most Admired Women" in the world. A survey taken by The Associated Press in surveying people in our country posed the question: "What woman that you have heard or read about living in any part of the world do you admire most? Mother was also in the top ten on two other occasions.

For the year 1966, the women named were:

1. Mrs. John F. Kennedy
2. Mrs. Lyndon Johnson
3. Indira Gandhi
4. Queen Elizabeth II
5. Senator Margaret Chase Smith
6. Mrs. George C. Wallace

7. Mrs. Dwight D. Eisenhower
8. Miss Helen Keller
9. Mme. Chiang Kai-shek
10. Pearl S. Buck

To have gone from such humble beginnings to becoming one of the most admired women in the world never affected her demeanor with her family or friends. That trait was the trait of a genuine nature, and the one that people responded to as they observed her under many extreme circumstances.

Mother's parents, Henry and Estelle Burns, were what I would call, "Salt of the Earth People." My grandfather worked on a barge, and I would sit and listen as he whittled, telling me stories about his adventures on the barges traveling up and down the Black Warrior River. The Black Warrior River was where Mother and I would go to swim and fish when I was a child. She always warned, "Be careful of the current, son." I always called my grandfather, "Mr. Henry," I don't know why, but that is what I called him. We would walk in the woods, and he would teach me things about the woods and animals. Beyond the pasture into the woods there was a good size creek where we went to swim as children.

When my father would visit my mother's home, she said that he was always talking about politics with her father. As Mother put it, "Politics, was something daddy discussed at our house with other people, not with me." How ironic to me that probably the one issue furthest from my mother's mind, was the issue that would make her a legend in Alabama.

After law school, my father was driving a dump truck for the Alabama Highway Department trying to enlist in the Army Air Corps to be a flyer. His dream was to be a pilot, but when he went to enlist, they always told him his pulse was too fast and he was turned down. He finally was accepted into the cadet pilot program by the sergeant who had turned him down several times before. The sergeant knew how much my father wanted to be an aviation cadet and told him he just had "a little nervousness." In order to make the minimum weight, he had to eat bananas and drink an enormous amount of water. The sergeant knew this, and told him while he was weighing him, "Son, you look pregnant." He passed his induction physical and was sworn into the Army Air Corps and now would await his orders. All he could think about was my mother. He had found the woman who would be the love of his life, and now he would have to go fight a war and maybe never see her again. They were so young and in love, with so much to look forward to, and there were many uncertainties in front of them.

His orders came, and he was sent to Arkadelphia, Arkansas, for months of pilot training. During this time, he contracted spinal meningitis and was close to death on several occasions. It took weeks for him to recover, and following his convalescence he made his way to Tuscaloosa, where he and mother would be married. My father used to tell me that mother was all he could think about, and how much he missed her.

Upon his arrival, he and mother were married in Judge Adolph Forester's office above the H & W Drug Store in downtown Tuscaloosa. My mother's mother had to sign a particular form to allow her to be married since mother was underage, as she was exactly sixteen years and seven months. After a wedding meal of sandwiches and cokes, they had their honeymoon in a boarding house in Montgomery, and after a three-day honeymoon, they went to Mobile where my father would leave for duty and eventually be sent overseas. Their good-bye was a tearful one because of all the unknowns they now faced.

The young love my mother and father felt for each other was the love that was rekindled many years later after my father's political ambitions had taken him away from her so much. He had come to truly realize how much she had always meant to him, and their last few years together found them reliving and feeling the love that had brought them together.

MOTHER MAKES HISTORY

My mother's race for governor in 1966 was a culmination of a sense that the governor's office was the place from which my father could continue to speak out on issues of national significance.

I can recall my mother beginning to humorously broach the subject of her running for governor with me, and inherent in her conversation would be an inquisitive tone that was searching and probing while she considered the idea. She obviously had had long conversations with my father by this time, and she understood fully the impact he was having on the national political scene. She understood why her platform as Governor of Alabama would still allow him a strong forum from which to run for president.

Mother initially had mixed and torn feelings about running for governor, I believe. She wondered if she could do what needed to be done as a campaigner and if elected, serve as governor. Her feelings about how this would delay the normal family life she had always wanted was, I know, an ever-present question in her mind. Although, I believe by this time she knew that my father was not the normal state politician who would serve and then go practice law. She knew he would always be involved in politics one way or the other until his death, because that was the nature of the man she married.

I think it is important to say that while my mother and father had struggled in their marriage because of politics, and the sacrifices that were made, her running for governor brought them back together in conversation and his being fully attuned to her. Politics was interestingly giving her what she had longed for in their marriage, a closeness they had felt when they were starting out. She, for too long, felt as though there was a mistress in their marriage, named politics. Now he would talk with her at length about issues and philosophy and political strategy. She came to fully understand his depth and breadth of knowledge that set him apart from many other politicians. She came to understand that this man she had married had become a national political leader who was making history. Mother had a tremendous admiration for my father and his intelligence and reason. She knew how in many respects he was magnificent in the career he had chosen, and now she would be the one to help him continue and he was looking to her to be there for him as never before. She would not let him down. During her campaign, she truly grew as a person and showed all the signs of greatness herself, and to this day is one of the most beloved women in Alabama history.

As a candidate, she began to explore herself in terms of her abilities and talents that had always been in the background, and in history's shadow. Once the decision was made, she became an exceptional candidate who before the campaign ended, had captured the hearts of the people of Alabama.

I would like to speak to a rumor and school of thought that has been fostered by some concerning her decision to run for governor. There has been speculation over the years that my father coerced my mother into running, and that is simply not true. All during the process of thinking it through, I can see them sitting at the family breakfast table in the Governor's Mansion that overlooks the pool and tennis court, in deep conversation. Sometimes, I would find them on the back patio with the beautiful view of the Mansion grounds, seriously discussing her running for governor. There was an intimacy between them now as they talked, an intimacy I had never seen, as they sometimes would hold hands again, as they had done long ago. Those endearing moments for them have become the enduring memories for me of that time leading up to her announcement.

The fact of the matter is that the decision to run for governor was ultimately made by her, contrary to what many of my father's critics have put forward. I recall a time when he came in from the office one day and said he had been thinking about it, and thought it best they go back to Clayton, and he could run again in four years. As the story goes, my sister, Bobbie, and Mother's best friend, Mary Jo Ventress, were sitting in the dining room with Mother when my father walked in and said, "We have decided it best that you not run for governor and I can run again in four years." At this, my mother looked at my father and said, "George, I am running for governor." You see, I believe she had come to a deep understanding of what he represented and the importance of her involvement at this time. So, to those who over the years have put forth the proposition that he coerced her into running, you are in error.

She made a good candidate who learned quickly and became adept at making a good stump speech and the people of Alabama fell in love with her. She developed the confidence necessary to allow her own warmth and personality to emerge, and I believe the people saw the best within themselves reflected in her.

It was a special time for my mother and father, as my sisters and I have joked over the years that he even seemed to have become more romantic. All of a sudden, they were inseparable and he helped her not only as a political counsel, but helped her relax from what he knew a campaign could and would do to you. They dined out more often, attended ball games and he for the first time spent more time at our lake house.

MY FATHER WAS THE GOVERNOR 'TIL MOTHER MOVED IN

One of her first political rallies for governor was in Robertsdale, Alabama. At that point, she would basically give her ten-minute speech, and then turn the microphone over to my father and he would give the fire and brimstone speech. It seemed to my father that Mother had reached what he thought should be the conclusion of her talk and he was becoming impatient. Seated beside her he tried to as inconspicuously as possible delicately pull on her skirt to signal that he was ready to speak. The first attempt did not get her attention, or she was simply ignoring him, which is what I believe she was doing. Well, it seems he did it once more and received the same reaction as before which was none. And, on the third attempt, he tugged a bit harder and that did it. Mother turned to my father from her speech and told him, "George, when I am finished; I will let you know." At that, the crowd of several thousand died laughing. From that point forward, they put that in many of her speeches, and it was a crowd pleaser. It became part of the endearing sense of humor the people felt between them and was a dimension in Alabama politics that will never be seen again.

One of my fondest memories is of her asking me to listen to her practice her speeches. The magic of Mother was that her sincerity and humility were obvious for all to see. She was one of their own as she grew up in Tuscaloosa and Greene County, and her family was of such modest means that she came to understand at an early age the hardships of life and thus the hardships of our people.

She grew as a person because of this campaign experience, and she realized a potential within herself that I am not certain she knew existed. It was a wonderful site to behold, as she and the people of Alabama developed a bond and sacred covenant between themselves, as she captured their hearts simply by being herself.

Mother was a gallant and gracious lady who touched so many lives. I have often thought that one of the quotes on her bust in the rotunda of Alabama's State Capitol from her 1967 inaugural address captures the fundamental nature of how she viewed the people she now would lead. She wanted to tell them what their spirit, courage and goodness meant to the rest of our nation for now and for posterity. She spoke with emotion and command when she told them: "Be proud to be called an Alabamian, for your courage has nurtured the flame of freedom."

Mother loved her God, family, friends, nature and all the things that bring joy to this life. An avid lover of fishing and the outdoors, her childhood tom boy ways were alive and well while she served as first lady and governor. I can recall stories of her coming home from a banquet or some rather formal function and changing from an evening gown to hunting or fishing clothes and off to the woods or the lake in a matter of minutes. The contrast while profound was natural and normal for her, and she felt just as comfortable in either situation. Her grace and dignity were present at all times, so it seemed to matter little what she happened to wear and where she happened to be.

An amusing story occurs to me which surrounds one of her hunting expeditions. A famous picture of her holding a turkey she bagged during spring turkey season has hung in my office for years and has become a favorite picture to many Alabamians across our state. It is a glowing picture of her, which genuinely personifies her love of life and the outdoors as shown by the look on her face. It never ceases to amaze me how many people happened to be with her when she bagged that turkey. If my calculations are correct, based on the number of people who have thus indicated their presence with her during the hunt, I would estimate several hundred people were quiet enough and completely still in the woods long enough to give her the opportunity to bag the turkey.

Turkey hunting is difficult enough with one person remaining motionless for hours; therefore, the multitudes who accompanied her that day accomplished a feat of astounding magnitude.

LOTS OF LAUGHTER, TOO, IN MOTHER'S LIFE

When it became apparent that mother was going to take my father's place as governor, the stage was set for many a tale. The following are just a few:

WHO SITS WHERE?

A funny interaction between Mother and my father happened on Mother's first workday as governor after she had been inaugurated the day before in January 1967. Let me remind you that for years, my father had a habit of riding in the back seat on the right side of the car driven by Alabama State Troopers. Perhaps it was, I believe, because he was right-handed and there was an ashtray attached to the door and he needed a resting place for his ever-present cigar. At any rate, mother knew where he preferred to ride and the reason for it, so she came down a few minutes early and sat in his cherished seat in the car. Well, my father came down a few minutes later moving at a good Barbour County, country clip with his cigar smoke blowing in the breeze, arrived at the car, saw mother sitting in his seat and with complete surprise said, "Oh!" At which time, my mother replied, "That's right, George, the governor sits here, and you sit over there." The state troopers were amused although they kept it to themselves as my father went around to the other side of the car and said, "Okay, honey." Mother let him have his cherished seat the next day and from then on but they continued to laugh about it.

TWO ALABAMA GOVERNORS AT THE GOVERNORS' CONFERENCE

Another amusing story occurred in Washington, DC during the term of President Lyndon Johnson. There was a national Governors' Conference in Washington, DC and there were several functions at the White House for the governors and their wives. I would remind you that at this time, Mother was the only woman governor in the nation and by virtue of her election, the third woman governor in our nation's history. The story goes like this: It seems there was to be a large banquet one evening for the governors and their wives and families in one of the beautiful dining rooms in the White House. However, prior to this, there were to be briefings for the governors on economic, domestic and foreign policy presented by members of the president's cabinet. There also was to be at the same time activities for the spouses which would have been all women with the exception of my father. The briefings for the ladies included lectures about the artwork and aesthetic integrity of the White House. As the governors and their spouses were about to separate for their assigned briefings, you can understand my father's dilemma as he looked at mother and said, "Lurleen honey, why don't you go in with the wives and I will go in with the governors." At this, mother looked at my father in that tranquil way she could and said, "George, I am going in with the governors; I didn't care where you go." As the story goes, he was last seen following her in with the governors.

My father spoke fondly over the years about President Lyndon Johnson. He talked about that Governors' Conference and how gracious the president was to Mother. He talked about how President Johnson took mother by the arm, escorted her through the White House introducing her to the elite in Washington, DC. She was truly the "Belle of the Ball."

OSCAR HARPER STORIES

There was a trip my mother made to be with my father while he campaigned in California. This trip was during the time she served as Governor of Alabama. As Oscar told the story: *She took a few days off and joined us in California. It was her only chance to see George. We were all talking up a storm when George remembered he didn't have any clean socks. "Lurleen honey, would you mind washing me out a pair of socks?" George asked her. She headed to the bathroom to wash his socks, but I said, "Wait a minute. You're the governor. You shouldn't be washing socks. He should be washing your hose. I wouldn't be washing his socks. Let him buy some or send them to the laundry." Oscar tells how my father was taken back and afraid for a minute mother was going to give him one of those stares, and hand him her hose. But she just stood there a second and then broke out laughing and washed his socks. "Oscar, don't you go setting Lurleen off, my father told him. We've got enough to do running for president without you getting her mad."*

Another example of the fun my mother had with my father after it was clear she would be governor happened when they were flying to Florence one Sunday afternoon in the state plane. Oscar was flying with them and he relates how they were all in their seats and mother was quiet and in deep thought. Then mother said, *"George it appears I will be the next governor so what you need to do is go to the Capitol and clean out your desk. I might as well take over, so you go ahead and get everything out so I can move in." My father looked at Oscar and Oscar looked at my father and they both looked to my mother to make certain she was kidding. But she just stared back, not smiling a bit. My father uneasily made like she was kidding and gave her deference in his laugh. When they were leaving the plane my father immediately let mother walk ahead of him and he said to Oscar, "Oscar let me tell you something. You know women change their minds a lot. I don't know if it is such a good idea her being elected. You know, Oscar, she fixes you with that stare, and I don't know how to take that sometimes."*

MOTHER'S BATTLE WITH CANCER

As a parent, I often reflect upon the loneliness she felt as she began to comprehend the seriousness of her illness. I recall one night entering her room and finding her sitting on the floor of her bedroom at the Governor's Mansion watching the *Dean Martin Show*. She was a big fan of his talent and singing ability and he happened to be singing, "Born to Lose," and she was crying. As she looked up at me, the hurt and anguish etched so deep within her were flowing forth and she attempted to mask this very private moment. In my state of not knowing what to do or say, and with her understanding of this, she called me to her side and embraced me with an embrace only a mother knows.

Her love of music was natural and an important part of her life. As she enjoyed the rhythms of nature, she also derived much pleasure from beautiful melodies. One of her favorite past times during our trips to Lake Martin was listening to Nat King Cole, Dean Martin, and Frank Sinatra albums in the late afternoon on our porch overlooking the lake. I am thankful my sisters and I acquired the same appreciation and understanding of music and the joy it brings to our lives.

At my age today, I realize even more clearly how young mother was when she died. I often remember thinking as a sixteen-year-old, which was my age when mother passed away, how I considered anyone in their forties as old, and only now understand the error of my thinking. As a forty-one-year-old, who had been ill for some time, she truly was entering the prime of her life ready to enjoy her family, friends and future. What a tragedy that after raising four children and enduring the hardships brought to bear on the wife of a national political figure, she was unable to enjoy the fruits of their labor together and was stricken down in the prime of life. People often remember Mother to me and invariably speak of her youth and enthusiasm. Her quiet charm, sincerity, humility, compassion, and wit endeared her to all who met her, and she left her imprint on the hearts and souls of the people of Alabama.

When I recall Mother's love for life, I am reminded of a wonderful story related by Mother's dear friend, Anita Smith Lunsford, in her book, *Lurleen Wallace the Intimate Story*. Anita tells of a time Mother was at the Governor's Beach Mansion that she so enjoyed with Lee. This was a time when she had grave doubts about whether she would win her battle with cancer. At such a time she was taking everything in and understanding the wonder of life that only someone in her position could feel. Anita writes beautifully of this beach trip:

On a few nights Lee went down to the beach with Mama and Catherine. Lurleen sat crossed legged Indian style, and drew Lee into her lap so she could cuddle her. On one night, Lurleen talked a long time with Lee about the ocean. "See the waves Lee? Aren't they pretty? But there's a little current just below the top of the water that you can't see. It's called an undertow, and it goes a different way from the water on the top. You have to be real careful or it'll pull you into the ocean." She pulled Lee closer and kissed her blonde head. Lurleen had a way with youngsters, not just her own, but everybody's. She liked to do things with them, and possessed the ability to make them feel at ease.

As Lurleen stared dreamily out on the Gulf, her eyes outlined the jigsaw pattern of the waves as they fashioned their foamy peaks atop the blue-green waters. Mother sighed deeply. At that moment, every particle of life seemed to be painted for her. Then a youthful giggle turned her head, and her picture of happiness was complete as she saw blonde Lee Wallace bouncing toward her. Reaching out to hug her energetic little daughter, mother said, "Hi there. What'cha up to? How bout helping me build a sand castle [sic]?"

Gleefully nodding yes, Lee was down on her hands and knees scooping up sand for the Wallace Sand castle [sic] Construction Project barely before the suggestion had escaped her mother's lips. Unmindful that her legs and knees were getting all gritty, mother joined daughter.

Mother busily used her long slender fingers to make the sand castle [sic] sturdy, so the wind wouldn't blow it down.

The harshest winds were on the horizon and Mother sensed as Lee could not, that this likely would be the last time sand would sift through the fingers of mother and daughter.

I can see mother now walking on the beach, graceful and athletic, her brown skin in such contrast to the white sand. She had the most beautiful skin that took on a bronze hue when touched by the sun. At this point in her life, during her initial days as governor, I have often considered what she must be thinking. She had come to know self-assurance and had realized talents within herself she hoped to use for the benefit of the people of Alabama. I believe she was developing her vision for Alabama. What a dramatic change in her life from being first lady to being governor and leading her state with her heart as well as her mind.

She understood those who would always look upon her as simply a surrogate for my father. But the truth is that what her most severe critics failed to see early on was how she would touch the hearts of a people. This transcended politics and made her special to the people of Alabama.

As she looked at the waves and took in the sounds, I believe she was content with the love she held for her family and state. And, I believe she was aware of the love given to her by so many. I think often of Mother on the beach with us, and all the joy we shared together on those sunny, summer Alabama days we thought would last forever.

The cancer that took my mother's life and the bullets that caused my father such pain and agony over the years, took them to a level of heightened awareness about the frailty of the human condition. Their suffering led them both to a faith that allowed them to persevere and reach an understanding of the strength that comes from prayer and faith. This was their rod and staff that truly did comfort them during the most trying times. I recall how my mother and father seemed to look at you with more intensity that spoke of their understanding that their time with us was limited. It is those who journey through, "The valley of the shadow of death," who are anointed with sensitivity for life brought on by that nearness to death.

I recall moving into the home my father had bought for mother during the time she was undergoing treatments for cancer. She furnished it, decorated it and at times while she was ill would have the state troopers take her to the home, and simply sit and enjoy the quiet atmosphere of this home where she knew her family would live when she died.

Out of her suffering and her example of such courage in the face of adversity, came forth from her people a love and willingness to give so as to help alleviate the suffering of others in the future.

MOTHER'S DEATH ON A STARRY NIGHT

I will never forget my father entering my upstairs bedroom in the Governor's Mansion the night of mother's death, to tell me she would not live through the night. Until that time, I suppose it was youthful optimism which turned away the obvious from my mind and heart concerning Mother's condition and the prognosis, but youth has a way of shielding us from the imminence and finality of death. My father told me she had fought long and hard but her body would simply take no more. Until that time, my hope for her recovery never wavered, so to be confronted with the stark reality of her dying was more than I could embrace. The emotions of despair, sadness, helplessness coupled with uncontrollable weeping swept over me and took my breath away. I stumbled around my room unable to focus or think, feeling faint and in a bewildered state of mind. At that moment, my father took me in his arms and held me while I wept. That moment was the one moment for which I was unprepared, which I did not expect, which I was certain would never come. Here it was with all its monstrous pain stalking me, confronting me, robbing me of that most dear to me, most dear to so many. From that moment forward, I did not cry again until many years later. I pulled myself together aware that my help would be needed even though I was only sixteen. I adopted a stoicism which helped see me through her lying in state, the eulogy, and the procession to the cemetery.

The thousands of people who traveled from miles away to pay their respects, view her body, and say good-bye did so in silence and respect. Tearfully and solemnly, they waited and wept and when speaking with each other did so in hushed tones.

My mother's death at age forty-one was a traumatic event for our family made even more so because her illness and very personal battle with cancer had been on the front pages of the paper for months. For our family, it became difficult if not impossible to endure this extremely difficult time without the glare of the press, and the curiosity of the public. The absolute luxury of anonymity and privacy were lost to our family many years before.

I can vividly recall my father saying to me as the funeral procession carried Mother's body to the cemetery, that the pain and sorrow we felt that day were shared by countless thousands of Alabamians who held her in such esteem. She was truly loved and admired by the people of Alabama and their love and concern sustained us during the most difficult days. During mother's illness, and up until the time she became totally bedridden, her valiant attempt to maintain a normal routine with her family was a true profile in courage. Her ever-present concern for her family and lack of complaint about her own pain and suffering was a testament to her courage and love for all of us.

Her fight with cancer ended on a starry night, May 7, 1968, with her family gathered around her at the Governor's Mansion. My father held her hand and gently wept as he told her to squeeze his hand if she could hear him. As her frail body moved delicately and her breathing became labored and difficult, my father told her we were all with her and that we loved her very much. Her hand tightened on my father's hand and the doctor indicated to us that the embrace of her fingers was voluntary and not reflex. As my father continued to hold her hand, her caress told us more than words could ever say. Through her hand she expressed her love and devotion for all of us. That embrace was her final gesture of affection for those with whom she desperately longed to share life and love. Just a few hours earlier, in the midst of severe abdominal pains, she had professed her never-ending faith by saying she did not want to die, but it was the Lord's will she sought not her own.

MOTHER'S FUNERAL

Reverend John Vickers in his eulogy read two poems mother had requested as her last words to us. The following poem, author unknown, was read to our family:

"I love you for not only what you are, but what I am when I am with you. I love you, not only for what you have made of yourself, but for what you are making of me. I love you for the part of me you bring out; I love you for putting your hand into my heaped-up heart and passing over all the foolish, weak things that you can't help dimly seeing there, and for drawing out into the light all the beautiful belongings that no one else had looked quite far enough to find. I love you because you are helping to make of the lumber of my life not a tavern but a temple. Out of the works of my every day not a reproach but a song."

Reverend Vickers explaining that mother had asked him to "Say to you and to the nation some very deep, very sincere, and meaningful words and wishes these words expressed to her husband, children and family." He then read those immortal words from Elizabeth Barrett Browning's "Sonnets to the Portuguese."

"How do I love thee? Let me count the ways. I love thee to the depth and breadth and height my soul can reach when feeling out of sight for the ends of being and ideal Grace. I love thee to the level of every day's quiet need, by sun and candlelight. I love thee freely, as men strive for right. I love thee purely as men turn from praise. I love thee with the passion put to use in my old griefs, and with my childhood's faith. I love thee with a love I seem to lose with my lost saints. I love thee with the breath, smile, and tears of all my life and if God choose I shall love thee better after death."

Reverend Vickers shared time with mother over the months when she would visit St. James and they would kneel at the altar in prayer. They had deep conversations about faith and her love for the Lord. She knew the inevitable in her heart and mind, as she also knew, as the scriptures told her, "To be absent from the body is to be in the presence of God." Her faith was strong, and she believed without doubt she would be waiting for us, "Just around the corner."

In his eulogy, Reverend Vickers spoke of the three essential qualities of greatness when he said:

We come to express our love for one who was anxious at all times to express her love to others. In my own mind, I am convinced beyond a shadow of a doubt that this great lady of our State embraced the three essential qualities that are necessary for greatness. These being—sincerity, compassion and humility. Certainly, she embraced these as few people in high stations ever embraced them. Someone has said, "That a truly great person is known by three particular signs: Generosity in design, humility in execution, and moderation in success," and certainly these signs were a part of her every day conduct within the State and Nation. The greatest person is the one who chooses the right with invincible resolution, who resists any sordid temptation from within and without, and who bears the heaviest of burdens cheerfully, one who is calmest in the storms and most fearless under menace and frown and whose reliance on truth, on virtue, and on God, is the most unfaltering.

Reverend Vickers spoke of her faith when he said: *Humility and love are the very essence of true religion, the humble form to adore, the loving to associate with God's eternal love. This lady embraced these essential and basic aspects of true religion. She was one, who in humility, could pray in the passing hours of life, "God, I am not worthy, but I would ask of thee, that I might live; yet, God, if this cannot be so, grant that I may be able to accept thy will as thy will is surely to be done." Kneeling at the altar of this church, our governor, conscious it seemed, that the inevitable progression of one of the most serious maladies of the human race confessed that, "My malady may be arrested, but I doubt that it will ever be cured." Needless to say, this gracious and great lady desired very much to live, yet she also was committed to the truth that whatever proved to be the will of the Father, she would seek the power to accept. A very deep and abiding faith and love and a loyalty to God became the sure strength of the life of this our beloved governor."*

Upon her death, the people of Alabama reflected on how she was forced to leave Alabama for her treatment. William R. Ireland, Sr., a dear friend of our family, and past President of the Lurleen B. Wallace Memorial Foundation wrote of this period. "The people watched with genuine concern as she left home, friends, and especially her children, to go to M.D. Anderson Cancer Hospital either for surgery or to receive follow-up radiation treatments. During one of those trips, she lamented to a newspaper reporter that it would be wonderful if the people of Alabama had such a facility so that they wouldn't have to suffer the inconvenience of traveling a great distance for cancer care." Out of this concern came the *Courage Crusade,* which was an effort to raise five million dollars for the Lurleen B. Wallace Memorial Foundation fund. This love offering from the people of Alabama was the real beginning of building a research, development, academic, and treatment institution for the fight against cancer that is now ranked as one of the finest in the nation. This campaign had initially forty thousand contributors and was the largest public drive in Alabama history. Among those who gave so freely were Alabama's school children who after being told about mother's journey, were moved to help. I occasionally meet someone who was a participant in that effort as a student, and they relate the feelings they had about her. She was to lose her battle with cancer but in winning an everlasting love from her people, her "Legacy of Love," will continue in the heart and mind of Alabama.

With my son, Robby, standing by a portrait of my mother, his grandmother, at the Governor's Mansion, Christmas 2022.

CHAPTER TEN

Early Years of My Life, 1950s – 1960s

GROWING UP IN CLAYTON, ALABAMA

Growing up in Clayton, Alabama, a small Southern town in Southeast Alabama was a life of summer afternoons which seemed to last forever. Also, of high school football games between Louisville and Clio that caused the entire town, it seemed, to gather in unity the night before the game at the Confederate monument for a pep rally. We would cheer our team to victory and, following that, drive around town in a procession of cars and blow our horns until we were assured the Clayton Tigers would win. My sister, Bobbie, was a cheerleader and I can see her now, young, strong, and athletic, leading the cheers.

Our life in Clayton was like that in any small Southern town in the 1950s. The people were your friends and there was always a sense of community and connection with everyone and everything. I can recall walking to kindergarten with my mother and father, my father carrying my little chair balanced on the top of his head as we walked to my first day. The kindergarten was in an old antebellum home just a few houses down the street from our home on Eufaula Avenue.

I can see my mother now, hanging clothes on the clothesline in our back yard before we had a clothes dryer. The clothesline was in a field of clover where I used to lie, and to this day fresh clover takes me back in time to those summer days. I remember looking up at her face and as she would smile at me, I remember thinking how beautiful she was.

Our backyard held beyond it the National Guard armory where a large celebration was held following my father's election as Governor of Alabama in 1962, but that was to be a later time and for a five-year-old, light years away. Often, I would walk with my mother to the Home Economics building of the Clayton High School where she would sit and talk with her close friend, Mary Jo Ventress. Mary Jo is a Southern lady with a genteel nature and an intelligence and sense of goodness that reaches out and touches you.

As a youngster, time crawled by on those lazy summer days and the feel of the good earth underneath your feet in the spring was always greeted with great anticipation. Walking to the community swimming pool took me down by a lily pond where that oasis of summer awaited the gleeful laughs of the children of Clayton. The walk to the pool was always an adventure for me, as it took me several blocks from our home through a field and down a moderately steep earthen incline which had been worn by the footsteps of young toes dancing toward the lure of water and fun.

Our home was a comfortable one-story house with large front and backyard, my tree house, a basketball goal, and a fig tree where my mother and Bobbie would pick figs from which Mother made fig preserves. Large pecan trees producing a good crop of pecans from year to year stoically resided there, and occasionally found my father climbing one of them to shake pecans from their outstretched limbs. I remember watching him as he seemed to climb to the very top of a tree, and violently shake the limbs releasing the pecans from their lofty roost. Mother was somewhat alarmed and amused at the same time and she told him, "George, you're going to fall and break your neck!"

Our home was located on beautiful Eufaula Avenue where many large, old, Southern homes were located with long walkways leading to them. All the homes possessed large trees and spacious lawns that added to their grace and charm. Ours was comfortable and roomy with two large bedrooms and a smaller bedroom where my parents slept. Off the front entrance to the right was our living room with a fireplace and a piano. From there toward the rear of the house was a formal dining room which we only used on special occasions. Beyond the dining room was a breakfast room which was separated from the kitchen by a long counter. All these rooms were large and spacious. The den was separated from the hallway by two French doors. Toward the rear of the house from the den was an area that held the washer and dryer. This location was where I worried my mother silly about the logistics of Santa Claus delivering presents all over the world in one night. She explained to me that Santa had helpers. "Helpers," I exclaimed, "If he had helpers then he would need a million or more helpers," I suggested to her. The progression of our conversation was that the child was trying to use logic and reason and the parent was holding fast to the magic of Santa Claus.

Beyond our home was Clayton High School and beyond the school was the cotton gin where I found myself when the trucks would bring the cotton to be weighed and graded. I always found pleasure in going down to the cotton gin and watching the men as they pulled the suction tubes over the trucks to sift the cotton. The noise was deafening, and I always wondered what it would be like to stick my head into one of the suction tubes to see what would happen. Thank goodness I never did!

I remember taking dancing lessons from a lady who came to Clayton, making her rounds in rural Alabama and the small towns. My mother, Bobbie, Peggy, and I took lessons in the auditorium of Clayton High School. We worked to become proficient in the

Fox Trot, Waltz, and other dances whose names thankfully slip my mind. We took lessons two nights a week and I can recall having time to watch *The Many Loves of Dobie Gillis* on one of the lesson nights. Following the lessons that lasted a few weeks, the dance contest was held with some of the other towns surrounding Clayton. Clio, Louisville, and Blue Springs, to name a few, were some of the communities represented at the contest. My dance partner was my sister, Peggy, and we danced with enthusiasm and energy and were awarded a trophy, of which we were very proud.

My recollections of the years in Clayton are mostly filled with a sense of tranquility and peacefulness. This was a time when a six-year-old could walk a few blocks from his home to the downtown area of Clayton without concern on the part of his parents. It was a simple time when the promise of the '50s included trust among people especially in a small town in South Alabama. When I watch reruns of *The Andy Griffith Show,* Mayberry reminds me of Clayton. I remember walking the few blocks to the Jitney Jungle grocery store and charging a piece of bubble gum. It occurred to me years later that I should have charged more than one piece of bubble gum so as to have one for later. Perhaps, this is the mindset of a child to think only of the moment. Knowing what was awaiting my family, those youthful moments would in time, and seem far away. On my walk to the grocery store and my other adventures, I would pass beautiful old homes which have that character and bearing that has been lost in most of the homes built today in our newer neighborhoods.

The Napiers lived next door, an elderly couple who had been missionaries in Africa, China, and other exotic places. As you entered their home, a large staircase met you which wound to the second floor. The entire downstairs area was filled with furniture and artifacts from their travels across the world. There was always a sense of darkness and mystery in the Napier home, but coupled with this there was a profound sensation of other worlds of which I could only dream. Mrs. Napier would often invite me to eat with her on her screened-in back porch. Her porch provided a clear view of our house and our backyard so we could eat and I could still be in touch with my own world. Mrs. Napier was a very pleasant woman who listened intently and patiently as I related to her the adventures of my world. Thinking back, I realize how insignificant my goings and comings were, but her interest in what I was saying and how I felt about things will be forever etched in my memory. I believe Mrs. Napier retained her sense of curiosity and wonder as the years progressed. I have some difficulty remembering Mr. Napier, and believe I saw him only on a couple of occasions as I believe he was ill most of the time. I think about Mrs. Napier when I go back to Clayton and while her home is still standing, Mrs. Napier and her husband died many years ago.

Our home was a few steps from Clayton High School, which included grades 1 through 12, and I can recall walking with my mother to school on my first day in the first grade. The sense of anticipation and anxiety which were a part of that day no doubt was experienced by the parents as well as the children. As parents, we all experienced and revisited those moments in our mind when our own children reached school age, so we were taken back in time.

My first-grade teacher's name was Mrs. Dominy and in her room, we sat at tables which circled the room leaving the center open for our coming together as a class for stories which were read to us, and for naps taken after lunch.

The children with whom I attended school were by and large from the rural areas of Barbour County and many were from poor families. This was evident by the clothes they wore and, in many instances, the overall look of a child. I will always remember how I felt and how I went out of my way to befriend them because of their economic deprivation. There were two boys I can recall wearing overalls to class and sometimes wearing no shoes. These two boys lived on farms in the country and once I visited one of the farms with my father who helped the parents fill out their taxes. He did this for many of the rural families in Barbour County, both Black and white, and never considered being paid and would not have accepted anything for helping. While he was inside with the parents, I played with the youngster in the yard. I asked my father about this some years later and he told me that he had done this for many families in the county and never took any money for helping. Because of my father's understanding of the plight of the rural Southerner for the years especially following the Great Depression, he endeavored to help because the needs were so great and it was his way of showing his deep respect and appreciation for the Southern people.

One of my fondest experiences as a child was visiting my grandparents, Estelle and Henry Burns, who lived at the time in Greene County, Alabama. Their home was in the country where my grandfather farmed and raised cows and chickens. There was a well, an outhouse, two dogs (Trixie and Princess), a mule, and a creek beyond the pasture, a barn and lots of fun for a small boy with boundless energy. What a place! You could feed the cows, swim in the creek beyond the pasture, play in the barn, eat watermelons under the China berry trees, and best of all enjoy my grandmother's homemade biscuits in the morning. Often, there were cake walks at the community center just up the road where we would circle the room while the music played and when it stopped, jostle one another to land on the chalk mark on the wooden floor that would win you a cake. Farther up the road was a small country store with delicacies such as cokes and candy and a few of the necessities the grownups needed such as bread and milk.

It has always fascinated me how a house can seem so large when you are a child, and so small when the same house is viewed from adulthood. My grandparents' home was a small, shingled house with two small bedrooms, a den, kitchen and a bathroom with indoor plumbing, a gift from my father to my grandparents, which thankfully meant no more trips for me to the outhouse which was beyond the garden and the snakes in the dark. My sister, Peggy, visited my grandparents' home a few years ago and I recall her relating to me the trauma she felt in seeing it again. It is true that we cannot go home again and this trip for my sister proved that to her. The home place was in great disrepair, and she became emotional as the memories of years gone by washed over her.

I recall as a very young boy, my father coming through our front door at our home in Clayton, Alabama, and telling us that he would be a candidate for Governor of Alabama in 1958. My youth was such that I did not understand the significance of the moment, but I recall vividly our family gathering in the middle of our den and my mother, father, Bobbie, Peggy, and me embracing as he told us of his decision. That was a moment when we were embracing a life that would have an impact on our state and country, but also as a family embracing those twins of joy and pain that would become our constant companions to this day.

TENSION THAT POLITICS BROUGHT TO MY PARENTS' MARRIAGE

Let me take you back in time to the period after my father lost his first gubernatorial bid in 1958, and during his preparation to run again in 1962, and how that affected our family. At that time in Alabama, if you had been the runner-up in the Democratic primary for governor, then you were the odds-on favorite to be nominated during the next election cycle. Because of this, my father had to be away from Clayton for extended periods of time as he continued to organize the state in preparation for the 1962 race for governor.

Mother was in Clayton with Bobbie, Peggy, and me, basically raising us by herself, and there was a considerable amount of pressure on her financially. It seems my father would go out of town many times and not leave Mother with enough money for groceries and living expenses while he was traveling the state. I have heard from Mother's dearest friend, Mary Jo Ventress, that during those days, my father really did not remember to send Mother grocery money, so she would borrow money from Mary Jo and other friends until my father came home from one of his campaign trips. It certainly was not intentional; it was simply an example of his absent-mindedness when it came to family matters.

My father was a man of many talents that set him apart from others. Totally driven by a cause he saw as larger than himself, he tended to be distracted and not as attuned to his family as he should have been. He reminisced about this a good bit in his later years and sought our understanding of what he was trying to do, why he had to be gone so much, and how he regretted the sacrifices Mother had to make during that time. The stress was real and inevitably there were even rumors by some that they talked of divorce. My father's brother, Gerald, who was like a surrogate father to me during my younger years, often would be dispatched to visit Mother at her mother and father's home in Greene County. The visit was a simple enough one in that Gerald was to talk Mother into coming back home. I can remember as a little boy leaving Clayton late at night after Mother and my father had a heated argument. We climbed into the car headed for our grandparents' home and as Mother drove late into the night, we would help her stay awake as we sang, "The Old Rugged Cross," "In the Garden," and "He Lives." Mother often would try to drive behind an eighteen-wheeler because she believed, on the winding highway known as 82 West, that it was safer, especially at night with her children in the car. It was late many times when we left Clayton headed for Greene County at a time when my mother and father's volatile encounters tested their love.

The most strain between my mother and father occurred I believe during this time between 1958 and 1962. Mother had three young children to care for, and our father for all practical purposes was an absentee father. His absences were not something he particularly enjoyed, but the very nature of politics is that you must move among the people. As time passed and my father became a national political figure, she was very proud of him and came to understand more and more the reason for the absences early on.

THE TRAVELING CARNIVAL COMES TO CLAYTON

There are times in our young lives when our parents make those first impressions on us. So it was for Bobbie, Peggy, and me during our younger years.

I can recall the traveling carnival coming to Clayton every now and then, and how my father would move among the carnival operators making certain they knew he would not tolerate any dishonest behavior toward the people of Barbour County. He was speaking not only as a concerned citizen, but during the time I was walking with him, he was the circuit judge and he made it clear to them that as the circuit judge he could and would put them in jail if they were dishonest with the people.

There was a game at the carnival that the barker would suggest was a game of strength where you hit a target on the ground with a large rubber hammer that would send a projectile up the pole to ring the bell. The whole ploy was to make those watching believe it had to do with strength so the barker would challenge the men watching to ring the bell. While he was challenging them, he would often use one hand to ring the bell and then challenge them to do it with two hands.

After watching for a while my father realized that it was not how hard you hit it, but rather where you hit it. He paid for a chance, rang it the first time, and then circulated among the men and told them where to hit it, and so a certain country justice was extracted from a dishonest carnival operator.

BLESSED ARE THE PEACEMAKERS

I remember as a young boy, about six years of age, going with my father to one of Clayton's high school football games one Friday night. The high school was located just a block from our home and it was to be the place where the play about our family, *Wallace/The Clayton Years*, was to be performed, but that would be many years later.

On this particular Friday night, a group of men had gathered down by the field house just out of the light and view of the crowd. It appears two of the men had determined to settle some differences between themselves the old-fashioned way. They would engage in a pugilist contest as their friends gathered around them and urged them on. My father heard about this and I happened to be with him at the time, so he took me by the hand and we headed for the field house. I remember him putting me off to the side, and then stepping right in the middle of the conflict and getting everyone's attention immediately. He put his finger in the chest of each man and told them to stop and stop they did. He spoke to them about conducting themselves as men of honor and to consider what they were doing in the face of their community. He told them he expected more from them, and they should never forget to conduct themselves with dignity for themselves and their families. He talked of being a community and how the brotherhood among its citizens was the life blood of their community. It was a Sunday school lesson and he touched them in a way that took them to another level of reflection about themselves and their conduct. I recall how the men thanked my father, and we all walked back together to watch the ballgame. "Blessed are the peacemakers for they shall be called children of God." Matthew 5:9

NOT ALL POLITICS

My father, at one time in his life, was an excellent poker player. There were a few men in Clayton who dealt the cards occasionally, and my father enjoyed sitting in. He had earned a reputation as one of the best poker players in Barbour County, and rumor is he stopped playing because he was a circuit judge and that was not the kind of reputation he wanted to foster in the Bible Belt, Barbour County, Alabama. The skill he possessed that made him a superior poker player was his famous memory. He had the most remarkable ability to remember people and their names. In all my travels, I continue to hear story after story of his remembering peoples' names. I did ask him about this one time and whether he had a method or system he used to help him remember people and he simply said, "No son, I just meet people and remember them." Recently, I have heard of people who can remember everything that has ever happened to them. I'm not sure if my father had a memory to that degree, but his was extraordinary.

It seems that during one of his poker games, Mother's patience had run thin because for the short length of time he was home, rather than being with her and the children, he was playing poker with his buddies. She drove up to the location of the poker game which was being held in the back of an old grocery store, and she marched Bobbie, Peggy and me to the table and told Dad, "Here are the children, George; you take care of them for a while."

I remember a time when we had a hole in the floor in our den that needed repair, and I can remember Mother asking my father on several occasions to fix it. I suppose after he had heard it enough, he brought in a board, nails, and a hammer, nailed the board to the floor, looked at Mother and said, "Lurleen that hole is fixed," and of course it was only covered. None of this distraction was intentional on the part of my father, as he loved us dearly; it was just a manifestation of being consumed with politics. Politics will captivate you if you allow it to. In my father's case, I think he captivated it. I can see my father arriving at my grandparent's home to spend some time with us, but he never seemed to relax. Being on a farm in rural Alabama on those slow summer days was not my father's idea of living and never would be. He had to be among the people, so consequently the traditional role of a father was not really present in our home. It has been written by some of his critics, who lower their standards by speculating on someone's family life, that he neglected his family. They write as if they were there and I have always found that interesting. There is no question that he was gone much of the time leaving Mother alone with children, and her dream of a normal life in Barbour County, Alabama. That was what she wanted the most and would never have. But to suggest that we had been abandoned in the literal sense is absurd. In studying the history of those men from *The Greatest Generation* I've noted this was not unusual behavior for men upon returning from the war. They got on with life, made up for lost time in beginning a career and their wives were able to stay home and raise the children. This wasn't neglect or mistreatment, they thought they were doing the best for their families and in most instances they were. One too often judges history after applying today's customs and standards to that time long ago, which is a mistake.

Our years in Clayton were typical for those of any Southern family living in a small town. The family atmosphere that pervades small town U.S.A. was at its richest in the middle and late fifties.

These were the years prior to the assassinations of President John Kennedy, Martin Luther King, Jr., and Robert Kennedy. The turmoil of the sixties was a far cry from the innocence of the fifties, as it was a time when we were content with who we were and where we were. This was a time when we felt a connection with one another and sensitivity for our sense of community. Your neighbors were your neighbors and your friends in times of happiness and in times of sadness.

MONTGOMERY—OUR NEW HOME

The journey I made through the political world was made with my three sisters, Bobbie, Peggy, and Lee. Bobbie and Peggy are older than me and Lee is ten years younger. Lee, being born in 1961, was not with us during many of the days I have noted in this book. Bobbie, Peggy, and I were close growing up and found ourselves in many instances witnesses and victims to the consequences of political ambition. The Wallace children are unique in Alabama history, in the sense that our mother and father both served as Governor of Alabama, and our father sought the Presidency of the United States.

The 1958 governor's race found me most of the time standing on a chair to reach a microphone asking people to, "Vote for my daddy." After memorizing a two-page speech as a six-year-old, it seemed only natural that I should travel the state and solicit votes and support for my father while he was traveling and speaking in another part of Alabama. Of course, it was cute to have a six-year-old, who in many instances fell asleep on stage in the lap of some County Commission candidate, who then woke me when it was time to speak. It was novel, got the attention of the voters and helped them remember the name Wallace. I suppose it also gave me the ease to give a speech as I grew. The fear of giving a speech is something difficult for me to understand. The governor's race was a tough contest with my father losing a runoff to John Patterson. Following this race, we moved to Montgomery so my father could be closer to the political pulse and where he could launch his campaign for the governor's office in 1962.

I recall moving to Montgomery while in the fourth grade and the disruption this caused as it meant leaving all the familiar people and places that had been my life. My experience with Montgomery up until this point had been basking in the Christmas lights at Normandale Shopping Center on our Christmas trips to Montgomery. It is a sign of the times that the lights at Normandale today could not hold a candle to the lights and decorations which adorn the modern malls, but in many ways the lights at Normandale seemed to shine a little brighter and the colors possessed more magic due to my youth and the anticipation of Christmas, which can only be felt by a child. My other memories of Montgomery had, until this point, included shopping for school clothes with my mother and occasional trips with my father while he was preparing to run for governor in 1958.

Our move to Montgomery found us in a two-bedroom apartment on Fairview Avenue, quite a contrast from our spacious home in Barbour County, Alabama. After living in this apartment for a year, we rented a house in the neighborhood close to Huntingdon College where, many years later, I received my Bachelor of Arts Degree. This felt more like a home for our family, and this is where we lived while my father continued organizing and preparing for his next race for governor in 1962.

The 1962 governor's race found me once again making speeches for the campaign and traveling across the state. This race found my father and Senator Ryan de Graffenried in a runoff which my father won, and at that point in Alabama's history as I have mentioned before, the Democratic nomination was tantamount to victory as the Republican Party in Alabama was not very strong at that time. The Democratic Party in the South was strong primarily due to two reasons: There was still a memory of the hope Franklin Roosevelt gave the people of the South and the rest of the nation during the height of the Great Depression, and the second reason was the historical recollection of the pain the Radical Republicans under the leadership of Thaddeus Stevens during Reconstruction had brought to the South. These two factors played a major role in the people of Alabama and the South having deep affection and affinity for the Democrat Party. Of course, this has changed, and now the South has a strong Republican Party structure with many Republican elected officials from the statehouse to the courthouse.

The night of his victory in 1962 was a much different one from his loss in 1958. In 1958, I remember going back to Clayton late that night, but before we left, a dear friend, Dave Silverman, wanted us to come by his jewelry store in downtown Montgomery. Dave was an interesting man who had been very successful in several businesses and was totally devoted to my parents. Dave actually traveled later with my father during the presidential days. Anyway, we stopped by his jewelry store, and he wanted each of us to choose any item in the store we wanted as his gift to us. I remember my father and mother protesting, but they soon realized it meant so much to Dave that they relinquished. I remember choosing a gold I.D. bracelet and I believe he had watches he wanted my mother and father to see. I remember even as a six-year-old, thinking how quiet it was in the car as we made our way home to Clayton. Following the 1958 race, my father went through a period of depression that concerned his friends, but after a period of time he turned his thoughts to the next governor's race in four years. He hit the road again and did not stop until he had won in 1962.

His victory in 1962 was the culmination of all the sacrifices that had been made by many, and his total dedication and focus on being elected governor was successful. He had worked so hard for so long and I can only imagine how he must have felt to have his lifelong dream realized. I remember him giving his speech and how radiant Mother looked and thinking back I know she was relieved. I don't know what would have happened to my father had he lost the second time. Knowing what he had gone through for some time after the 1958 loss, a second loss I believe would have been worse not only for him, but for Mother. The crowd was large and many held posters with the name of their county as he delivered a gracious, warm, and inspiring victory speech. I remember his friend, Oscar Harper, telling me that there was a particular time during the 1962 campaign when you noticed the crowds had become much larger, and there was just magic in the air. His reputation was growing and as word got out the people responded. Politically speaking, today that would be referred to as, "Big Momentum." He had captured the imagination of the people of Alabama, and yes, to a large extent it, was his position on segregation that had captured them.

THAT COLD INAUGURATION DAY IN 1963

The inauguration in January 1963 was an extremely cold day. I recall wearing long underwear and having hand warmers to help keep my hands warm. I wondered how the band members were able to march and play their instruments in such extreme weather. Over the years, I have met people who were in their high school bands, and when I asked them about the parade, they talked about how cold it was, but told me they would have marched regardless of the weather.

The impact of inauguration day and what had happened to my family was beginning to register with my sisters and me, and it was though we had been thrust into a dream world. The parade and the overall pageantry seemed to be endless as bands and floats drifted by the reviewing stand. Following the parade, the time had arrived for my father to speak to the people of Alabama. He spoke with energy and command, being interrupted many times with applause and cheers. I listened as he seemed to pierce the cold air with his energy and volume. My father was always one of the most charismatic speakers I have ever heard and his ability to move people was legendary and without equal. My mother, sisters and I listened and unknowingly, our lives changed forever at that moment in time.

In my father's later years, he often said, "I was wrong about segregation, but I was right about the government in Washington, DC, attempting to control every aspect of our lives." I find it interesting yet understandable, why the other sections of this controversial speech have never been discussed. The segregation phrase was the most controversial one in the speech, and the one that thrust him onto the national stage. Yet beyond that phrase, if you follow his thoughts concerning his disdain and defiance of an all-powerful omnipotent central government, you see that his words were clearly prophetic relative to the battle that rages today on the political landscape.

Read carefully this excerpt from the speech and you will see that the same sentiments are being expressed today:

To realize our ambitions, and to bring to fruition our dreams, we as Alabamians must take cognizance of the world around us. We must refine our heritage, re-school our thoughts in the lessons our forefathers knew so well, in order to function, to grow and to prosper. We can no longer hide our heads in the sand and tell ourselves that the ideology of our free fathers is not under attack, and is not being threatened by another idea . . . for it is. We are faced with an idea that if centralized government assumes enough authority, enough power over its people, that it can provide a utopian life . . . That if given the power to dictate to require, to demand to distribute to edict and to judge what is best and to enforce, that will produce only 'good' then it shall be our father . . .

and our god. It is an idea of government that encourages our fears and destroys our faith, and where there is faith there is no fear, and where there is fear there is no faith. In encouraging our fear of economic insecurity, it demands we place the economic management and control with government; in encouraging our fear of educational development, it demands we place that education and the minds of our children under management and control of government, and even in feeding our fears of physical infirmities and declining years, it offers and demands to father us through it all even unto the grave. It is a government that claims to us that it is bountiful as it buys its power from us with the fruits of its rapaciousness of the wealth that free men before it have produced and builds on crumbling credit without responsibilities to the debtors . . . our children. It is an ideology of government erected on the encouragement of fear and fails to recognize the basic law of our fathers that government does not create wealth . . . people produce wealth . . . free people; and those people become less free as they learn there is little reward for ambition . . . that it requires faith to risk . . . and they have none . . . as the government must restrict, penalize and increase its expenditures of bounties . . . then this government must assume more and more police powers and we find we have become government fearing people . . . not God fearing people. We find we have replaced faith with fear . . . and though we may give lip service to the Almighty, in reality government has become our god. It is therefore basically an ungodly government and its appeal to the pseudo-intellectual and the politician is to change their status from servant of the people to master of the people . . . to play at being God . . . without faith in God . . . and without the wisdom of God. It is a system that is the very opposite of Christ for it feeds and encourages what is degenerate and base in our people as it assumes the responsibilities that we ourselves should assume. Its pseudo-liberal spokesmen have never examined the substitution of what it calls 'human rights' for what it calls individual rights, for its propaganda play on words has appeal for the unthinking. Its logic is totally irresponsible as it runs the full gamut of human desires.

The strong simple faith and sane reasoning of our Founding Fathers has long since been forgotten as the so called, 'Progressives' tell us that our Constitution was written for "horse and buggy days."

These thoughts conveyed years ago are just as meaningful today as they were then. The same battle rages regarding a usurpation of our freedoms outlined in the *Constitution*. Individual Freedom, Human Liberty, and the Rights of Man are the cornerstones of that sacred document forged after our founders threw off the yoke from Great Britain. My father talks in this speech about the effort by government to become our god, as it creates an expectation in the minds of many that government's role is to be a caretaker. He knew that as the left seeks to move us to a secular and humanist culture, we would begin to see an erosion of the principle of less government our founders worked so hard to give us. Because of the departure from this principle, we see a clash of cultures battling today for the very heart and soul of a nation.

It is interesting to note that the "Segregation Forever" phrase was not a phrase he actually wanted to use. He wanted to say, "Freedom Today, Freedom Tomorrow, and Freedom Forever." His fight was with the Federal Government and the issue of segregation became inextricably linked with the "States Rights" issue that was the cornerstone of his philosophy. As you will see, the issue of segregation became his ball and chain, and try as he might in making his arguments about the importance of the states outlining their own timetable relative to segregation, to many he would always be looked upon as a racist. To him the 10th Amendment was alive and well, but under assault by the Federal Government and this was the essence of his resistance, thus his initial desire to use the word freedom.

One of my father's ghost speech writers was Asa Carter. Asa authored, *The Rebel Outlaw Josey Wales* that became an extremely successful movie starring Clint Eastwood. Asa used the name,

Forrest Carter, and it was after the publication of *Josey Wales* that the *New York Times* revealed that he was Southerner, Asa Earl Carter. In 1991, what many believe to be his memoir, *The Education of Little Tree*, was re-issued and became a best seller on the *New York Times* best seller list. Asa Carter was clearly a brilliant writer but a racist of the first order. His background in broadcasting early on and his association with racist groups and his founding of other racist groups was problematic for my father. It is suggested that some of the political operatives around my father utilized Asa's writing genius, while making certain he was kept at a distance. However, there was one instance when I met Asa Carter and I remember it vividly. The day after the 1970 Democratic primary for governor, when my father was 30,000 votes behind Albert Brewer, there was a knock on our back door and as my father opened the door, Asa Carter walked in. I was introduced and recall how dark his hair and eyes were. He had a look of intensity and an aura of mystery about him that struck me. Asa had run for governor in 1970 and received 1.5% of the vote. What I remember most about the moment was how my father seemed impatient and immediately walked Asa toward the living room for them to talk. As they were walking my father asked, "What's on your mind, Asa?" The ring of the question had a hurry up get to the point feel to it that was consistent with my father's dilemma at that time. From a pragmatic standpoint, whatever political following Asa Carter had would naturally gravitate to Wallace and not Brewer and my father knew this. He also knew he was behind and the runoff would be very close. So, here he was meeting with perhaps the leader of the most ardent segregationists in Alabama, when he had moved on to another place in his heart and mind. Who knows what they talked about, but one thing is certain—it was about getting votes.

Some of the harder core segregationists around my father clearly wanted the "Segregation Forever" phrase in his inaugural speech because it was the paramount issue in the 1962 race for governor, and people felt very strongly about it. I believe the reason he ultimately used the segregation phrase was because that was the issue that was on the hearts and minds of the voters at that time. It was a political decision. That was the issue he had decided to rise to political power on, and as he tossed the gauntlet, he had to know there would be a reckoning.

Following the official inauguration, there was a reception held at the Governor's Mansion at 1142 South Perry Street where we met thousands of people from all across Alabama. It had a modern-day Jacksonian feel as this administration would be for the folks. I recall standing by my mother and father and as people entered the Governor's Mansion my father seemed to call every name of the person entering and ask about their family members, many of whom he would name. It was a masterful performance, and his famous memory became one of his most significant political tools over time. "People like to be remembered," he told me once and he had the capacity like no one I have ever known to remember them all. We smiled and shook hands until we were exhausted and had shaken the last hand.

LIFE IN THE GOVERNOR'S MANSION

My sisters and I attended public schools in Montgomery County. Peggy and I attended Bellingrath Junior High School and Bobbie Jo attended Sidney Lanier High School. My father was asked one time where his children attended school and he responded that his children attended the public schools in Montgomery which were integrated. Our lives were as normal as possible given the fact that our father was Governor of Alabama. However, as his profile became more pronounced nationally, it became more difficult for us as our family received threats and the mansion itself was fired upon from passing automobiles. You could see the holes where the bullets had struck the front of the mansion. The first instance of this happening found my father coming out the front door of the Mansion and raising the anxiety of the security personnel on duty. These developments found my sisters and me escorted to school by security men. I often come in contact with those I went to junior high school and high school with, and they invariably will mention how they remember the security men who followed us around. My fellow classmates understood and while they were concerned about me, they also found it to be exciting.

Growing up in the Governor's Mansion was unique and exciting except for the gunshots that were fired. The Governor's Mansion is a beautiful Greek revival Southern antebellum home with spacious grounds, a tennis court, a swimming pool, servant's quarters, and a guest house for visitors.

My father and mother thought it important to keep the mansion open seven days a week for tours, and it became difficult to walk from room to room on the second floor without a tourist looking around the corner to see you, and whisper they had seen a member of the governor's family.

I remember very clearly waking up one Saturday morning and running downstairs headed to the kitchen for breakfast. I was about eleven years old, half asleep, and still had my pajamas on and as I got to the bottom of the stairs, I realized I was in the midst of about fifty girl scouts. I was shocked and it was made worse by my being at that awkward age that all I could say was, "Good morning," turned and set a land speed record headed back up the stairs to the sound of girls giggling behind me. From then on, I looked before going down the front stairs.

I loved to slide down the banister when we first moved into the Governor's Mansion. Thinking back, it was certainly dangerous, but not for an eleven-year-old or so I thought. With my pajamas on and after the banisters had received a good polishing as they so often did, I could zip right down and hop to the floor at the end of the ride. One day I slid down and unbeknownst to me Mother had placed a Tiffany lamp on the desk where visitors signed in for their mansion tour. Well, as I got to that point on my ride down, my foot hit the top of the lamp and I can see it now falling to the floor, it seemed in slow motion. That scene will forever be etched in my mind and, needless to say, Mother was none too happy about the matter. As I have told friends over the years, "The lamp hit the floor and Mother hit the ceiling."

I had a habit of practicing my golf swing in front of the large mirrors in the parlor of the mansion. They were called the infinity mirrors as they faced each other and when you looked into them the reflections seemed to be endless. The foundations for the mirrors were beautiful ornate marble with leaves of gold protruding from the base itself. Well, in practicing my golf swing and working on the preferred inside out swing, I came too close to one of the beautiful gold leaves and smacked it good and across the floor it flew. To this day when I visit the mansion, I can show you where they have painted over the place I hit with my golf club many years ago.

CHAPTER ELEVEN

My Music

MOTHER NURTURED MY LOVE FOR MUSIC

It was always the music that beckoned me the most. It was a world that existed parallel to the world of politics and a family amid some of the most controversial events of the day. And because we were at the center of such contentious times and historic events, it was the music that was a comfort and solace to me when I needed it most.

My earliest recollections find me sitting on the piano bench beside my mother at our home in Clayton. I was so young that she would pick me up and place me close to her. She would play and sing and I would bask in the wonder of it all. One of her favorites was, "Carolina Moon," and I can hear her today singing it. I remember vividly the impression songs and melodies on the radio had on me. Sitting up late at night after everyone else had gone to sleep, I would then turn on my wooden case radio with the tube in the back that had to heat to an orange glow before it would play. The radio dial itself had the same orange glow, and years later I thought of people listening to Franklin Roosevelt's fireside chats and gazing at a similar dial. I would lay my head on the table beside the radio and listen to Elvis Presley, Fats Domino, Buddy Holly, Jerry Lee Lewis, Del Shannon, Brenda Lee, and others. Interestingly enough, many years later I received a call from Brenda Lee while I was serving as Alabama State Treasurer. Her son was stationed at Maxwell Air Force Base in Montgomery and she was calling to ask for my assistance with a matter concerning her son. I will always recall my secretary coming into my office and telling me Brenda Lee was on the phone, and my asking her, "The Brenda Lee," and she said, yes, "The Brenda Lee." I could also find the Grand Ole Opry on WSM radio out of Nashville, Tennessee, playing country and bluegrass music. I realized years later when I became fairly proficient with the guitar, how much these songs had influenced my own music.

Traveling with my band from the time I was fourteen playing concerts across Alabama was fascinating because at that time our records were being played on radio stations in Alabama and parts of the Southeast. The young people had heard us on the radio and we were celebrities to them. Consequently, there was much anticipation and excitement when we held a concert.

ROBERT WOODS SINGS THE BLUES

I was also drawn to the blues in an interesting way. The Governor's Mansion at the time had several work release inmates who lived on the mansion grounds with us. One of the inmates was a man named Robert Woods. Robert was a Black man from Barbour County, our home, and had been sentenced to prison by my uncle, Judge Jack Wallace, my father's brother. Robert was the perfect example of impetuous youth and making a mistake, but he was one of the kindest and most gentle man I have ever known. Robert played the guitar in the evening in his quarters, and I would hear this fascinating sound through the wall of his bedroom, I now know was the blues. I remember that it struck me like a bolt of lightning. Why I do not know, but I do know it had a dramatic impact on me. I told Robert one day I had heard him play and how much I enjoyed listening, and he thanked me and responded that he had heard I had gotten a guitar and if I ever wanted to "Strum some," to just let him know. I was ready to go, and the next evening I went to his room to listen and learn. His room was comfortable, and he had a small record player where he listened to Muddy Waters, Howlin' Wolf, John Lee Hooker, Ray Charles, and Lightning Hopkins.

A prison inmate and a Black man in the Deep South seemed to come out in his music and it was very moving. As his fingers gracefully and effortlessly brought the blues from the strings, there was a peaceful and joyful expression on his face. To have been born a Black man in the 1920s in the Deep South brought with it all the heartache he and his people had suffered. In those moments in time, he seemed to find genuine freedom from all he had endured and continued to endure. He would help me make the chords by placing his fingers over mine, showing me where to touch the strings and on which fret. Robert did not know the names of the chords, but he knew where to place his fingers. You could say he was literally a feel player. We would talk, and he told me of the time he got his first guitar and about learning to play. He told me to be patient and work at it, which I did night and day. I spent many nights with Robert and as I became more proficient as a guitarist, we had some wonderful times together playing the blues. Robert made a statement to me one night I will never forget: He said, "You know, it's hard to sing the blues when you're doin' alright." The music that brought us together was a bridge between different generations and races. When I consider the turmoil going on outside Robert's bedroom between the races in the sixties, I find the bond of brotherhood, understanding, affection we forged through music to be one of the treasures in my life, and I believe there is a lesson here for us all. Thank you, Robert . . .

I recorded at famed Muscle Shoals studios in Alabama with the legendary producer Rick Hall and that is where we recorded, "How Lonesome Can It Be." An interesting bit of rock and roll trivia is that I recorded in the same spot using the same microphone Percy

Sledge used when he recorded the classic, "When a Man Loves a Woman." I also had the honor of being asked to be a voting member of the Alabama Music Hall of Fame in its first year. I remember how proud I was to vote for W.C. Handy, Father of the Blues from Florence, Alabama, and Rick Hall in the Producer category from Fame studios in Muscle Shoals, Alabama.

I also recorded in Atlanta with Buddy Buie who hails from Dothan, Alabama. Buddy Buie's legend is long and will endure.

Buzz Cason has become a good friend of mine and you will know him from some of the hit songs he has written, produced and published. He co-wrote "Everlasting Love" a song that was a huge hit by several artists. Of the many gold records and awards he has received he has a plaque citing "Seven million plays" on the air for "Everlasting Love." In addition, he has written hits for Martina McBride such as "Love's the Only House," songs for Pearl Jam, U2 and the Beatles recorded his song "Soldier of Love" in 1964. He wrote and published songs along with Bobby Russell such as "Little Green Apples," "Honey," and "The Joker Went Wild." He also published "She Believes in Me," by Kenny Rogers, and has recorded such artists as Olivia Newton John, The Doobie Brothers, Emmylou Harris, Merle Haggard, and The Gatlin Brothers. His list of published hits is long and impressive.

I have become good friends with one of Buzz's guitar players, Randy Layne, who is a fine musician and producer. Randy and I are presently working on some songs about the South.

In recent years, I have gone back into the studio to record and write music again. My friend, Del Couch, who is an old family friend of Elizabeth's family in Palmetto, Florida, is a gifted musician who has a great recording studio named Howling Dog Studio. He has the latest Pro-Tools digital equipment and holds a master's degree from Berklee School of Music in Boston. Del's wife, Diane, is one of the finest singers in Florida and a charismatic entertainer.

CONTRACT WITH MGM RECORDS IN LOS ANGELES

As a twenty-one-year-old, I signed in 1972 with MGM Records in Los Angeles, California. The president of the company at the time was Mike Curb, who in his mid-twenties became President of MGM Records. He was a record industry phenomenon and after meeting with him at the offices of Buddy Lee who was my booking agent at the time in Nashville, I signed with MGM as a writer and an artist. Mike Curb's genius was that he had an understanding of music and an acute anticipation of what the public's taste would be in music. To give you an example of Mike Curb's genius, he took the Osmond Brothers from their barbershop quartet days on the Andy Williams Show to one of the most successful and exciting rock bands in the world. "Why Don't They Understand," was the song Mike picked for our first session in Los Angeles and with famous engineer, Ed Green, and Frank Sinatra's arranger and conductor, Don Costa, the session was a great success and the song was a pick hit in Billboard magazine. About this time, I was asked to be part of the Hank Williams Jr. road show and I eventually did two tours with Hank, before returning to college.

TRAVELING WITH MY FRIEND, HANK WILLIAMS JR.

Hank and I immediately felt a kinship and bond that was forged from being the sons of legendary fathers. Hank and I would often, late at night, sit in the back of his tour bus as it traveled the country; play our guitars, especially the blues, and talk of being the namesakes of famous men. I remember one night, Hank making the statement that it was hard standing in the shadow of a very famous man. I remember thinking about that for a minute and saying that I rather liked to think of it as standing in their light also. Later Hank wrote and recorded, "Standing in the Shadows," that related in song what he had told me late that night. As he and

I sought to express ourselves, there would always be the inevitable comparisons from others we would have to endure. For Hank as a musician, and for me as I entered politics, because our fathers had made such a huge impact and lasting impression on the minds and hearts of the people, our work for many would always fall short. It was the inevitable comparison that would become ever present, but out of it was born a resolve that only he and I can understand. I know we have both spoken of this in our music. During the late night as the tour bus was traveling down the highway to our next show, Hank would talk of wanting to play his own music and express himself musically. He was of course under constant pressure to play only his father's songs because he was told that was only what the people wanted to hear. He was very proud of his father and the music he had written, but as musicians we each have within us our own music we seek to share with others. It is part of the artistic nature to want people to hear your own creations to be fulfilled as an artist. He had a struggle on his hands, and I could see it clearly as we became friends. As we talked of these things, it became apparent to me that we were feeling much of the same pain born from our shared experience.

Traveling on the tour bus with Hank Jr. was an exciting experience for a twenty-two-year-old. We would go from town to town, working mostly the Southeastern part of the country. I would open the show with about three songs and would thank the audience for their prayers and concern for my father following the assassination attempt on his life the year before, in 1972. The response from the crowd would be deafening, and so these country music lovers were also supporters and admirers of my father. Hank had a great band that included Jerry Rivers, who was the original fiddle player with Hank Sr., and he and I became great friends as he would tell me of the genius of Hank Sr. Jerry was also the one designated to pay me after every show. Lamar Morris was the leader of the band and he hails from down around Georgiana, Alabama. He is one of Alabama's many talented musicians and recorded a song about my father many years ago.

The similarities between the country music tours and the political campaigns became evident to me immediately as we traveled from town to town. The large crowds would gather and there was the buildup of the night until Hank Jr. finally came on to close the show. This always reminded me of the political rallies where the buildup was for my father's speech. Following the show, the people would gather around Hank to shake his hand and get an autograph, and I would have many people come to me expressing their support and admiration for my father, and that they also enjoyed my songs.

I remember one night in the spring of 1973 when Hank called me at the Governor's Mansion and asked me to come over to Cornelia's mother's home to visit because he wanted to talk to me about something. Cornelia's mother, Ruby, and Audrey Williams, Hank Jr.'s mother, were close friends, and when Audrey would come to Montgomery she would stay with Ruby. When I arrived at Ruby's home on historic Hull Street in Montgomery, I could tell that she and Audrey had been drinking a bit too much, and that Hank and his mother had been in an argument. I spoke to Ruby and Audrey, and they told me Hank was in the shower. I went back to his bedroom where he was in the bathroom with a towel around him shaving. He was glad to see me and wanted to talk about his career. He had grown weary of only playing his father's music and he was also frustrated with some of the business aspects of his career. He told me that he was tired of paying so many people percentages of his earnings from his record sales and concert appearances. He wrote of that in one of his compositions when he said, "You bring fifty thousand home and they say you're overdrawn, it'll just about get you down." He was alluding to the conversation he was having with me about having to pay so many people around him for the work he was doing. Hank is three years older than I am, so in 1973 he would have been twenty-five years old. He was a young man now and not a little boy anymore pleasing the crowds with a Hank Williams Sr. imitation. I remember telling Hank that there was only one Hank Williams Jr. and without you they have nothing. You can book yourself and take control of your career and the others will have no choice but to accept it. He was struggling and shortly after that he fell down a mountain in Montana and received devastating head injuries that nearly killed him. He had complete face reconstruction, and it was always fascinating when I spent time with him following his recovery that his eyes were the only part of him I recognized. They were the same eyes I had known and remembered as we spent time together all those nights on his tour bus. Following this, Hank started playing his own music and it was accepted in a way that probably far exceeded his wildest expectations. I am very proud of him and the self-actualization he has realized. His father would also be proud.

Hank wrote several songs about his father including, "Living Proof," "Standing in the Shadows," "Family Tradition," and others that included lyrics that spoke of his feelings about his father's journey and legacy, and how that legacy had impacted his life.

I also wrote and recorded a tribute song to my father that speaks of his journey entitled, "Singer of His Song." The lyrics are:

> *A man must live and learn,*
> *And do his best and be concerned,*
> *And when his time is here, for the world*
> *Its vision clear*

(CHORUS)
He stood all alone,
I'm a singer of his song,
His life was spared, his faith was shared
For all the world to see,
(VERSE)
He stood among the crowds,
And spoke their truth and oh so proud,
Then one day his voice was stilled,
But not his soul or his spirit's will
(CHORUS)
When he reaches for my hand,
My eyes look to this man
He dared to take their stand for right,
And fight the endless fight (VERSE)
The South flowed in his veins,
Bob Dylan talked about the rain,
He prayed to make things right,
And through his pain he saw the light
(CHORUS)
When he reaches for my hand,
My eyes look to this man,
He dared to take their stand for right,
And fight the endless fight . . .

These lyrics for me were my attempt to put down in music what I believe my father represented to the country and to me. These words convey the faith, spirit, and courage he demonstrated through the devastating period of his life when he was shot.

I have often thought that rather than focus on the inevitable comparisons that are made between fathers and sons, to concentrate more on what our family represents and the people we seek to serve. Certainly, the experiences Hank Jr. and I have had brought us sadness at times, but they also brought great joy to us in being members of families that have brought something historic and lasting to our culture. I guess you could say, for everything won there is something lost.

The early influence on me from my mother in exposing me to music, that solstice for the soul, was one of the great awakenings in my life. Music and politics would move within me in a parallel dimension causing a dichotomy in thought, action, and reflection that at times caused the strongest of struggles.

NATIONAL TELEVISION PROGRAMS FOR ME

During this period, I was invited to appear on several of the national talk programs to perform, and as I traveled later in my father's presidential campaigns, people from across the country would mention that they had seen me on some of those programs. I appeared on the Virginia Graham program twice and twice on the Mike Douglas Show. On one of my appearances on the Virginia Graham Show, Ms. Graham tried to match me up with Lucy Arnez, who is a fine actress and the daughter of Lucille Ball. It made for an interesting program and was innocent fun that the audience enjoyed. I also appeared on the Dick Cavett Show, The David Frost Show, The Today show, The Regis Philbin Show from Los Angeles, Good Morning America, The Merv Griffin Show, The Ralph Emery Show in Nashville, and many other programs.

The life I experienced as a young man because of music was like a dream come true. I remember playing what was called at the time, "The Big Bam Concert." This was a rock and roll show sponsored by WBAM Radio in Montgomery and they booked some of the biggest rock acts of the day for a Saturday night concert at Garrett Coliseum, and thousands of teenagers would attend. I was invited to play because "Missing You," was number one on WBAM's top forty at the time, and when I was introduced, and started playing the song the screams from the audience were deafening and I was overwhelmed. The song had touched a nerve with young people, and now I knew how my father must have felt on many occasions when he was speaking. An interesting bit of rock and roll trivia is that Tommy Shaw, who is from Montgomery and became famous as a member of the very successful group Styx, was with the local band that backed me up. I am very proud of Tommy as we all are in Alabama.

In the summer of 1970 following the governor's race, "Missing You" was released, and it became a very popular song across the South, and in other parts of the nation. At the height of the popularity of "Missing You," a department store in Normandale shopping center arranged for an autograph party where they would sell my records and I would autograph them for the teenagers. My father rode with me to the shopping center and all the way there he kept telling me that people did not turn out much for these kinds of things. As he was telling me that, I realized he was preparing me for a disappointment. The look on his face when the state trooper rounded the corner, and we saw at least four hundred teenagers waiting to get in, was a look of shock and disbelief. Although he knew the record was successful, I don't believe he was prepared to see that kind of response to my music. It was a world of which he knew very little, but he did know that in some sense I had captured the attention of my generation as he had his. I can see him now telling the teenagers "Tell your mama and daddy hello for me." He was always campaigning but I could tell how proud he was.

I played a show in Columbus, Georgia, with Sam the Sham and the Pharaohs during the time of their big hit "Wooly Bully." I met with Sam in a hotel room before the show and had a great time hearing about his life as a performer. For all his antics on stage and during his performances as a wild man, he was a very astute businessman who had full control of his career.

Another group I played with was The Bobby Fuller Four of "I Fought the Law and the Law Won," fame. About a year after this concert, Bobby was found dead in an automobile, and to this day his death remains a mystery. Bobby and I were standing together backstage before he went on, and he was showing me some of his famous guitar licks that gave his songs that riveting and driving feel. His death at such an early age is reminiscent of other great musicians who have left us way too soon.

Tanya Tucker and I played a concert together in Montgomery in 1976, and she had previously played at some of my father's political rallies when he ran for president and she also performed for the 1974 governor's race. She was a great admirer of my father and I ran into her several years ago in Gulf Shores, Alabama. I was in a souvenir shop and I spotted her even though she was wearing a baseball cap. When I walked up to her, she recognized me and we took a trip down memory lane and had a wonderful visit.

While recording at MGM in Los Angeles in 1973, we had taken a break from the session and Mike Curb told me there was someone he wanted me to meet. He took me to the next studio and introduced me to Lou Rawls, who had his own session that day. We visited and he could not have been nicer to me as he wished me well with my music. Lou Rawls is a legend and had one of the most distinctive voices of our era.

An interesting story about Sammy Davis Jr. is that he was recording with MGM during the time I was with them. Sammy was a great entertainer and a fixture in Las Vegas for many years not only as a solo act, but as a member of the famous "Rat Pack," that included Frank Sinatra, Dean Martin, Joey Bishop, and Peter Lawford. For all his success as an entertainer and artist Sammy had never had a #1 record. Mike Curb, who was President of MGM at the time and had signed me, approached Sammy with a song he wanted him to record called "Candyman." As Mike told the story, Sammy resisted the idea as he just didn't think the song was right for him. Well, the rest is history, and it was the only #1 song Sammy Davis Jr. ever had even with all his other success. My Uncle Gerald and I were on our way to Los Angeles for a recording session in 1973 and we stopped over in Las Vegas for a couple of days and saw Sammy Davis Jr. in concert and we were asked to come to the after-performance-party backstage. Sammy was so very kind and introduced me to everyone there that included several movie stars and famous musicians. What a unique experience for me as such a young man.

It was my pleasure to play with many other famous artists over the years that included Tony Joe White, Willie Nelson, Bobby Bare, Billy Grammer, Hank Locklin, Hank Thompson, Hank Snow, Mel Tillis, Roy Clark, Ferlin Husky, Marshall Tucker Band, Jeanne C. Riley, Grand Pa Jones, Penny DeHaven, The Newbeats, Herman's Hermits, and Lou Christie.

CHAPTER TWELVE

The Arena Awaits Me

WATCHING THE MASTER IN ACTION

Making the decision whether to be a candidate in 1986 for State Treasurer was in my mind predicated on what my father's decision was relative to seeking a fifth term as governor. He did not enter that race, which I'll speak more about later, so I began my own political career.

My first political lesson from my father concerning my race for State Treasurer occurred one Sunday afternoon in December of 1985. My friend, Frank Wilson, and I met with my father in his therapy room at the Governor's Mansion to go over strategy. My father was reclined on his therapy bed with a cigar fired up ready to talk about political strategy, and Frank and I were about to see a political genius in action. First, he started naming counties and the county co-coordinators. He had various positions for the campaign in each of our 67 counties and he knew each one of these people by name with no notes in front of him. He told us of the uniqueness of the various counties and the idiosyncrasies the counties possessed. His wisdom and understanding of human nature were alive and well when he started talking about the individuals within the counties. He knew their backgrounds, what their ambitions were, what their weaknesses were and in essence, I believe he knew more about his key people around the state than they knew about themselves. It was a masterful performance and one I will never forget. As he started, he told us to get something to write on, so Frank pulled his check book from his pocket and commenced to writing these words of wisdom about the famous Wallace organization. I see Frank often in Montgomery and he has kept the check book that got us started on my first statewide campaign as a candidate in 1986.

What I found over time, especially when I entered politics, was that the stark difference in my nature and my father's was a surprise to people, although I did find that given the times in which I served in public life, the lower key businesslike approach was better suited for the times.

MY FIRST VICTORY

We won the race for Alabama State Treasurer in a tough run-off campaign against Jim Zeigler, who was serving as a member of the Alabama Public Service Commission at the time and had developed quite a reputation around the state as a strong consumer advocate. A statewide televised debate was held on Alabama Public Television during the three-week runoff, and I believe the debate, along with several of the large daily newspaper endorsements helped our effort in winning.

We visited every county and worked the courthouses and went to all the places people gather, the restaurants, parks, shift changes and when we had time, I would walk through neighborhoods knocking on doors and talking to whoever came to the door and leave them a brochure. As I would work a particular neighborhood in a town, I remember how surprised people were that I was at their front door. You see a statewide race does not find many candidates working neighborhoods, but I believed doing this some in each town would have a positive impact as word spread that we had been canvassing a neighborhood. I had reports later that it did have the intended effect and that helped us. Knowing the advantage we had with name identification, it must be remembered that name identification cuts both ways. Given this, I always tried to work a bit harder and a bit longer and be more innovative because there would always be the question in the minds of some as to whether I was just running on my name. This attitude, I believe, served me well when I ran for office and while I served in public office.

INITIATIVES IMPLEMENTED WHILE STATE TREASURER

We advocated and implemented initiatives I believed would help Alabamians, and in implementing these, thousands of Alabamians lives have been enhanced.

The first program we introduced to the Alabama Legislature was the Linked Deposit Program designed to provide loans for small business start-ups or expansion. There was also a dimension of the program that provided low interest loans to family farmers across Alabama. This program lives on today and continues to help small businesses and farmers in Alabama.

The second program we started was the Prepaid Affordable College Tuition Program or as it has come to be known in Alabama, P.A.C.T. We were the third state in the nation to implement the concept that provides real financial savings to parents hoping to send their children to college. Having worked in higher education for eight years prior to seeking the office of State Treasurer, I saw on a daily basis how many middle-income parents did not qualify for financial assistance for their children in terms of the federal grants and the need-based programs. Loans were available for the working middle class while the poorest among us received the grants. I certainly am in favor of helping the least among us, but at the same time, the very people who did not quite meet the formula criteria to qualify for a grant because they made a few hundred dollars a year too much, were the people whose tax dollars made all the financial assistance programs possible for which they did not qualify. To me that was patently unfair, and I believe this experience became the genesis in my mind to find a way to help these people as well.

Alabama's P.A.C.T. Program became a model for the nation and my staff assisted many states around the country in establishing similar programs. I will always be proud of the work Brenda Emfinger and our staff did in establishing one of the soundest programs, from an actuarial standpoint, in the nation as cited by *U.S.A. Today* and *Money Magazine*.

We also established a first-time homeowner's program to assist people in purchasing their first home. As I travel today, people still mention to me how they were helped by one of these programs and that is very gratifying. That for me helps make up for all of the negative dimensions that can be found in the political arena. Public service is about serving others, and the Wallace family tradition of doing that affected me as a young child as it molded and shaped my view of public service.

The primary duty of the State Treasurer is to invest the state's money and make certain it is drawing interest for Alabama's General Fund. The General Fund is the fund that serves all non-educational state agencies and departments. Whether it is Mental Health, Medicaid, Department of Corrections, State Law Enforcement, assistance for the elderly, the poor and our children, the General Fund is the way in which these vital services are funded.

MOTHER'S EARLIER EXECUTIVE ORDER

A bit of family history about state deposits drawing interest is that it was my mother's administration that started the policy. Prior to her executive order mandating this, the large banks in Alabama held these funds interest free and had the time of their lives. Since her original executive order establishing the policy and the subsequent legislation making it law, the state has received well over two billion dollars to help our people. Serving as State Treasurer and officially administering the policy she created brought me a great sense of pride.

MAKING POWERFUL ENEMIES

One of the issues that concerned me while serving as State Treasurer was the high interest rates on credit cards. During the time I served as Treasurer from 1987-1995, interest rates on credit cards sometimes tripled the prime interest rate. I always thought this was unfair to the people and when it was discussed with the banks, they always talked about handling charges, and how the credit card rates they charged were essential to cover these costs. The argument the large banks used was very weak, and it was clear they were taking advantage of their credit card holders. I remember talking to my father about this and he thought I was right but told me I would in all probability not have any success in the legislature because the banking lobby was so strong. This is one example of many things I have seen while serving in public life of how people are so often treated by those with power, money and influence. Largely, my public life has been driven by attempting to make certain the voice of the average citizen is heard. In doing this, I have made some powerful political enemies, but if I had it to do over again, I would not change a thing.

The Alabama State Treasurer serves as a member of the Alabama Board of Adjustment, a board that financially compensates individuals or other entities that have a legitimate claim against the state of Alabama. I was presented with a claim for $250,000 to be paid to a "shell" agency that called itself Technology Plus, located on a University campus in north Alabama. Clearly, there must be reasonable justification before the state of Alabama can legally make fair compensation to anyone making a claim to the board of adjustment, and in this case, the justification was sorely lacking. The result of our investigation found that this was an agency set up to funnel taxpayer money to some powerful politicians, their family and friends for doing no work whatsoever. After a thorough investigation people were indicted and convicted, including a powerful Alabama state senator, and thus I made some powerful enemies once again.

I will always remember some advice my father gave me as our campaign was getting started that spoke to his understanding of human nature. He told me, "Son, you inherit all my enemies and not all my friends." That has been the case, and I believe some of the intensity toward me by some of his enemies is only accentuated by a philosophical approach to public life that threatens their control and power. It is interesting that over time you develop an understanding of who will help you and who will not. There are some who say all the right things to you about supporting you, but you know in your mind and heart they will not be there. Human nature is interesting, and you develop a sixth sense about people, their motives, and the level of their sincerity. Politics can be a fast-track lesson in life.

I always enjoyed dropping by my father's office when he served as governor just to say hello and to visit some of his staff. I knew all his staff and we had been through so much together that we always felt like family. On many occasions when I would visit the governor's office, I would simply walk around his office and look at the portrait of Robert E. Lee hanging majestically over the beautiful gold fireplace or gaze out the window facing Dexter Avenue where so much history had taken place. I would simply be there and he was comfortable with that, and I believe he frankly liked me being present for some of these private meetings as part of my education.

I recall a meeting one time with a group of the CEOs of the major banks in Alabama who were lobbying him about a bill pending in the Alabama Legislature that would place some additional charges on their customers. My father looked at them with his cigar in his mouth and as he took a puff and blew the smoke toward the chandelier he said. "Let me ask you fellas this. Do you still have that penthouse on the top floor of your beautiful building in Birmingham, the one where I have eaten and the food was served by butlers in white coats? Why we had a view of Birmingham that was the most beautiful I have ever seen. Do you still have lunch there every day?"

The bankers began to stammer and cleared their throats knowing where he was taking them. He continued, "I'll tell you what my suggestion is to you. Close that private dining room down and save money by eating at the Krystal every day. You know they have good hamburgers there and that is where most of your depositors eat anyway, and it would give you an opportunity to know them better." They tried to respond but he would hammer them again by citing information from their annual reports that spoke of his knowledge of their banks' performance. His argument to them as big business executives seemed primitive and elementary, as they did not see or feel what he was talking about. It was foreign to them in the world in which they lived.

He closed the meeting by telling them he appreciated them but could not support the bill because in his judgment it would hurt the average Alabamian. For my father to look at a public policy issue in this light, reveals how he was affected by his childhood and those ever-ringing words in his mind from his father and grandfather. When he considered the two different worlds of the business executives and the average working family, and how when a piece of legislation that was just another attempt to nickel and dime the customers of these banks came before him, it was inevitable where his sentiment would be.

Politics is over for me as a political candidate and I feel a sense of relief. I had wondered how it would feel when it finally ended and now I feel rested about my years in public service, along with a feeling of accomplishment. Inherently from the beginning, my desire was to be as sensitive as possible to the needs of the average Alabamian. Having that sensitivity was one of the most vivid memories of my childhood, and it was instilled in me from my earliest recollections. Fighting for the folks was the essence of the Wallace movement, and I am proud that we never wavered from that duty.

I have often told this story in my speeches as I have traveled the state of Alabama over the years and I see a modest home along one of our rural highways, I like to imagine who lives there, and I imagine a husband, wife and two children reside there. The father has an auto repair shop he started with his brother fifteen years ago, a business that was their dream growing up. The mother is a public school teacher and they are the proud parents of two children. The daughter is a cheerleader at the high school and their son is on his second tour of duty in Iraq. These people are the heart and soul of Alabama and our nation, and they are the ones whose goodness and patriotism will save us.

The "Great Middle Class," as they have been called, are those of our people who hold everything together, they are everything; they are the spirit and essence of what we are as a people. These are the people who provide the civility and sense of order in our culture, and they have long adhered to a moral compass that teaches moral absolutes in human behavior. Seeking to appeal to the brighter side of our nature, these moral absolutes seek the best within us and bring it forth in order to nurture the goodness upon which this country was founded.

Perhaps my entering politics was a destiny predetermined because of the family history, and it is interesting to consider that what caused such alienation was now the very thing that would ultimately bring us together. He took a keen interest in my race for Alabama State Treasurer in 1986 and was generally surprised at how we handled the campaign and the kind of candidate I became. I remember him calling me the morning after a statewide televised debate with my opponent, and I will always recall the sound of his voice and how different it was from anything I had ever heard in my life. He was ecstatic and upbeat and talked about the debate and how well I had done. Was he thinking that I had entered his environment and had handled myself well? Was he seeing someone for the first time, someone who had always been there?

I have often wondered if I had not been born into the Wallace family if I would have entered politics. I believe the answer is probably no. My indoctrination into the political world, being the only son of George Wallace, had a profound impact on me as his populist message stirred something within me. From the time I was a small child during my father's first race for governor in 1958, people would come up to me and say, "Little George, you're going to run for governor one day yourself." The fact of the matter is that George Wallace's son will never be Governor of Alabama.

"He knew both victory and defeat; he displayed courage; he endured pain. He experienced the roar of men's applause and the shattering gun blast of despair," said the Rev. Franklin Graham, son of the late Rev. Billy Graham, in his eulogy.

"He accepted God's forgiveness when he confessed and repented of his sins. The result was that he was changed and became a man redeemed," Graham said. "He received forgiveness from communities that once saw him as their enemy. The result was that he became a trusted friend."

Printed in the USA
CPSIA information can be obtained
at www.ICGtesting.com
LVHW020807121123
763661LV00100B/4739